G R A P H I S    D I A G R A M    2

# GRAPHIS DIAGRAM 2

. . . . . . . . . . . . . . . . . . . . . . . . . . . . . . .

THE INTERNATIONAL SHOWCASE OF DIAGRAM DESIGN AND TECHNICAL ILLUSTRATION

EINE INTERNATIONALE SAMMLUNG HERVORRAGENDER DIAGRAMME UND TECHNISCHER ILLUSTRATIONEN

LA VITRINE INTERNATIONALE EN MATIÈRE DE DESIGN DE DIAGRAMMES ET D'ILLUSTRATION TECHNIQUE

EDITED BY • HERAUSGEGEBEN VON • EDITÉ PAR:

B. MARTIN PEDERSEN

PUBLISHER AND CREATIVE DIRECTOR: B. MARTIN PEDERSEN

EDITORS: CLARE HAYDEN, HEINKE JENSSEN

ASSOCIATE EDITOR: PEGGY CHAPMAN

PRODUCTION DIRECTOR: JOHN JEHEBER

DESIGNER: JENNY FRANCIS

PHOTOGRAPHER: ALFREDO PARRAGA

GRAPHIS INC.

FRONT AND BACK COVER ILLUSTRATIONS: PETER KRÄMER

(OPPOSITE) PETER KRÄMER / FRANKFURTER ALLGEMEINE GMBH

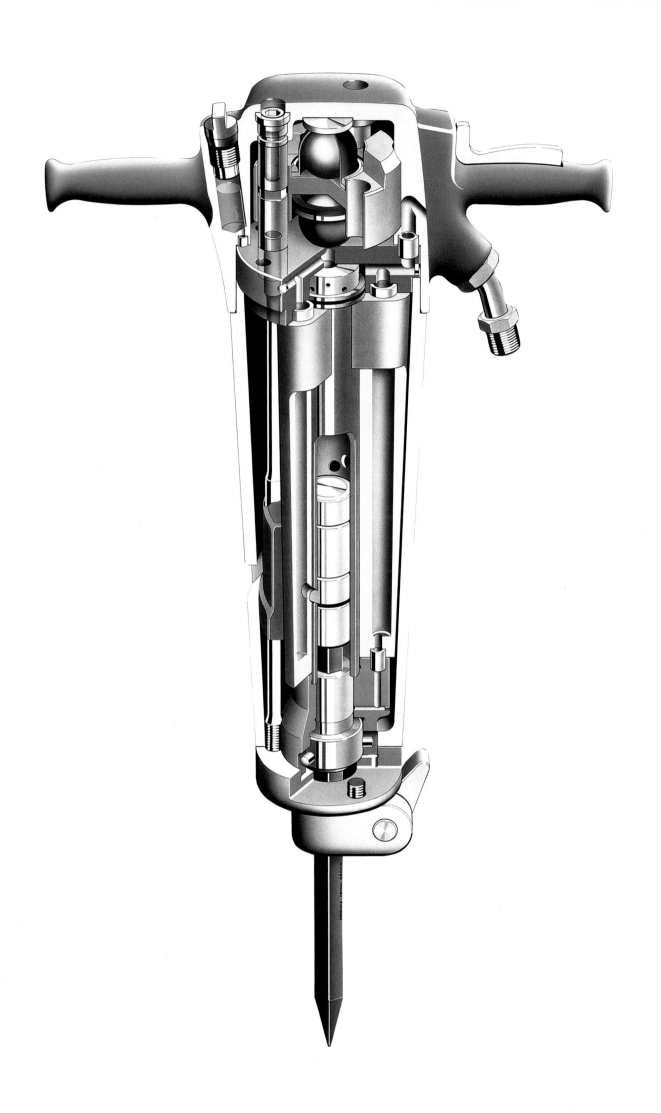

# CONTENTS

# INHALT

# SOMMAIRE

## REMARKS

WE EXTEND OUR HEARTFELT THANKS TO CONTRIBUTORS THROUGHOUT THE WORLD WHO HAVE MADE IT POSSIBLE TO PUBLISH A WIDE AND INTERNATIONAL SPECTRUM OF THE BEST WORK IN THIS FIELD.

ENTRY INSTRUCTIONS FOR ALL GRAPHIS BOOKS MAY BE REQUESTED FROM:
GRAPHIS INC.
141 LEXINGTON AVENUE
NEW YORK, NY 10016-8193

## ANMERKUNGEN

UNSER DANK GILT DEN EINSENDERN AUS ALLER WELT, DIE ES UNS DURCH IHRE BEITRÄGE ERMÖGLICHT HABEN, EIN BREITES, INTERNATIONALES SPEKTRUM DER BESTEN ARBEITEN ZU VERÖFFENTLICHEN.

TEILNAHMEBEDINGUNGEN FÜR DIE GRAPHIS-BÜCHER SIND ERHÄLTLICH BEIM:
GRAPHIS INC.
141 LEXINGTON AVENUE
NEW YORK, NY 10016-8193

## ANNOTATIONS

TOUTE NOTRE RECONNAISSANCE VA AUX DESIGNERS DU MONDE ENTIER DONT LES ENVOIS NOUS ONT PERMIS DE CONSTITUER UN VASTE PANORAMA INTERNATIONAL DES MEILLEURES CRÉATIONS.

LES MODALITÉS D'INSCRIPTION PEUVENT ÊTRE OBTENUES AUPRÈS DE:
GRAPHIS INC.
141 LEXINGTON AVENUE
NEW YORK, NY 10016-8193

ISBN 1-888001-13-5 © COPYRIGHT UNDER UNIVERSAL COPYRIGHT CONVENTION • COPYRIGHT © 1996 BY GRAPHIS INC., 141 LEXINGTON AVENUE, NEW YORK, NY 10016 • JACKET AND BOOK DESIGN COPYRIGHT © 1996 BY PEDERSEN DESIGN • 141 LEXINGTON AVENUE, NEW YORK, NY 10016 USA • NO PART OF THIS BOOK MAY BE REPRODUCED IN ANY FORM WITHOUT WRITTEN PERMISSION OF THE PUBLISHER • PRINTED IN SINGAPORE BY CS GRAPHICS.

(OPPOSITE) FRANKE TECHN. GRAFIK / SIG
(FOLLOWING PAGE) MARTY SMITH TECHNICAL ILLUSTRATION / SELF-PROMOTION
(PAGE 20) RONNIE PETERS / SIEMONS NIXDORF

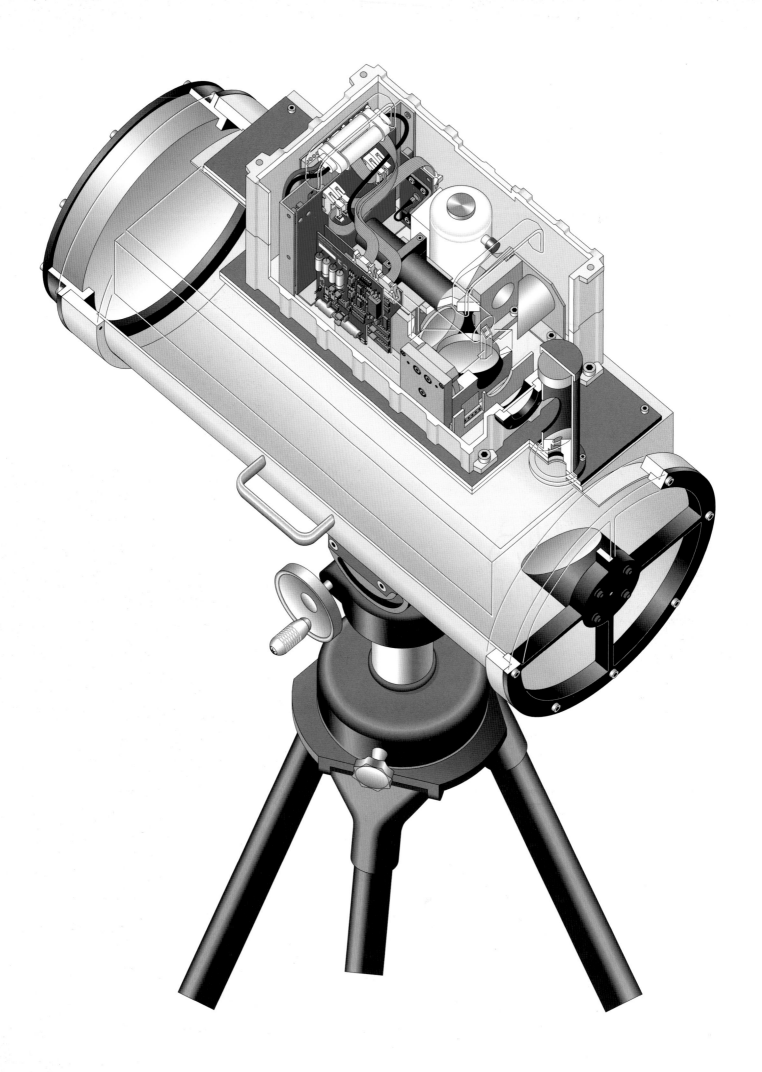

# COMMENTARIES

# KOMMENTARE

# COMMENTAIRES

*Roger Cook*

There are 166,540 references to diagrams on the Internet and not one totally defines diagrammatic principles. This is daunting for a designer who graduated from Pratt Institute in 1949, and is now unable to wean himself off the pad and pencil in the age of electronic graphic communication. But it is not defeating. We can co-exist with the computer without venturing into cyberspace. I often huddle with my staff designers, all of whom have mastered the machine, sketching out my thoughts on how to simplify and diagram information. We collaborate. They keypunch and shepherd the mouse. Our mission remains the same: to inform with impact. The hurdles remain the same, too. If the diagram gets in the way of our client's message, we have failed. If the reader cannot grasp in a split second precisely what we are trying to communicate, we have stumbled. No matter how visually enticing the chart, the graph, the map, the table, or the icon, there must be a shortcut connection between eye and brain that does not short-circuit understanding. Diagrams are an alternative language which translates complexity into clarity at a time when people are

**ROGER COOK** IS PRESIDENT OF COOK AND SHANOSKY ASSOCIATES, INC., AN INTERNATIONALLY RECOGNIZED GRAPHIC DESIGN FIRM LOCATED IN NEWTOWN, PENNSYLVANIA. CLIENTS INCLUDE BRISTOL-MYERS SQUIBB COMPANY, IBM, VOLVO, BLACK & DECKER, AND BASF CORPORATION. COOK AND SHANOSKY HAS BEEN PROFILED IN MANY PUBLICATIONS, INCLUDING *PRINT*, *GRAPHIS*, *COMMUNICATION ARTS*, AND *NOVUM GEBRAUCHSGRAPHIK*, AND HAS ACHIEVED INTERNATIONAL RECOGNITION IN MAJOR DESIGN EXHIBITIONS INCLUDING THE WHITNEY MUSEUM AND THE GRAND PALAIS IN PARIS. IN 1985, COOK AND SHANOSKY RECEIVED ONE OF THE FIRST 13 PRESIDENTIAL DESIGN AWARDS FOR THE DESIGN OF THE US DEPARTMENT OF TRANSPORTATION SYMBOL SIGNS. COOK IS A GRADUATE OF THE PRATT INSTITUTE AND A MEMBER OF THE AIGA AND ART DIRECTORS CLUBS OF NEW JERSEY AND PHILADELPHIA.

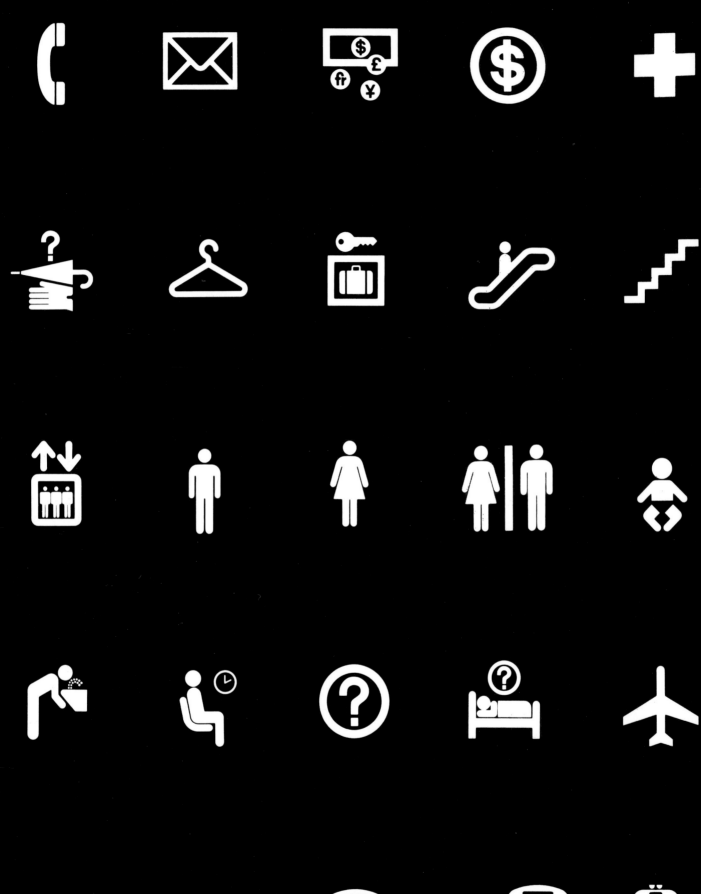

skimming more and reading less. ■ Indeed, as much as one may resist it, we are gradually moving from a text-based to a visually oriented society. As James Miho, director of the design department of Art Center College in Los Angeles, explains: "From the crude diagrams of cave dwellers to the oral traditions of societies in China, Africa and the Amazon, to the visual design of words in the Chin Dynasty, to today's computer networking and three-dimensional modeling software, we have come full circle." ■ The challenge in diagramming today—whether in electronic or print media—is to make the work creative and compelling. Communication follows. Our firm faced that challenge in the early 1970s, prior to the United States Bicentennial, when we were commissioned by the Department of Transportation, through the AIGA, to design a uniform set of fifty pedestrian-oriented symbols, now in use throughout the world. ■ Our clients—whether they be the chief executive officer, a consumer or a corporate stockholder—continue to challenge us to produce more creative solutions. Daniel Goldberg, president and CEO of Medical Inter-Insurance Exchange, claims "creative graphs are absolutely crucial. If our annual report went only to financial analysts, it would have no graphs, diagrams or pictures because Wall Street would take the time to dig through it." But, he adds, "our shareholders are doctors who give me three seconds to communicate sophisticated financial information." ■ With the explosion of new public companies on Wall Street today and the pressure on securities analysts to ferret out firms with the best potential for long term earnings, one analyst says the solo diagram needs help. "A chart or graph is better than a list of numbers," says Kim Ritrievi, chemicals and photographic analyst for First Boston Company in New York City. "But the combination of a graphic and a few words which deliver a conclusion is the most effective communication." Ironically, in the real world, simpler is better when the precious commodity of an analyst's time is involved. Ritrievi insists pie charts can hardly be improved for illustrating market share or distribution of sales: "Your eye is drawn right to the biggest slice of the pie and the rest is ancillary." ■ Echoing Ms. Ritrievi's notion of "less is more" in diagramming corporate results, Barbara Lucas, Black & Decker's vice president and corporate secretary, says "we want to eliminate clutter and concentrate on only a few important 'takeaways.' Unless you have something to say or show that is integral to your overall message, do not chart it. If it's extraneous, it dilutes the message." The "why" of diagramming still collides with the "how". The harmony of function and form is elusive to all but a few gifted designers, particularly today when unfortunately the computer seems to have assumed the role of creative director. But is this a problem worth pondering? "When it comes to storing pure information for retrieval, there are two problems," says Kenneth Hine, head of communications design at Syracuse University and a principal of MKH Design in Syracuse: "First, we are moving at the speed of light with electronic mail, interactive media, and custom-designed Web sites. Second, we are so overwhelmed by the sheer quantity of the information, it is impossible to retrieve that which is useful to us." ■ Hine says graphic de-

signers must become the library scientists of the electronic information age. "Only we can, through diagrams, access the information without trivializing it and provide the links with the rest of the world. We select and edit so as to make information accessible and understandable." Hine frets, however, that current and future generations of graphic designers, mesmerized by the awesome capabilities of mushrooming computer power "will become much more interested in making the chart or diagram seductive or sexy and that the aesthetic considerations will swamp functional considerations." That only fuels his biggest fear: "people feeling overwhelmed and tuning out to vital information." ■ Diagrams may be visual shorthand but they must not be shortcuts for the designer with a demanding client and a looming deadline. I think of diagrams as architectural blueprints whose structural integrity is at stake with each keystroke or mouse click. "Diagrams must be semantically sound and pragmatically efficient," insists Massimo Vignelli, president of Vignelli Associates in New York. "They should not be cartoons or exercises in abstract art." ■ Vignelli shares Hine's view that the computer-literate designer does not ensure greatness or visual lucidity. "The visual, electronic vocabulary is in so many hands of people who cannot master the language; communications are terrible," says Vignelli. He credits The New York Times and Gannett's USA Today—two newspapers with vastly different journalistic standards and presentation—for their expert use in diagrams to quickly communicate news content without wasting words or minutes. "Never before have we had the possibilities that we have since the computer for doing great things." However, laments Vignelli, "speed is the parameter today rather than quality." ■ Other influential designers have seen the future in diagrams and are convinced it is electronic. Krzysztof Lenk, who teaches information graphics at the Rhode Island School of Design and is president of Dynamic Diagrams of Providence, Rhode Island, insists "diagramming methods have not changed but the cognitive aspects of the human brain reach overload and anything but the most basic diagrams are confusing." Lenk agrees that the fundamental pie chart is the most easily understood, but designers have discovered new ways to implement a message without it bouncing off the brain. ■ Clement Mok, creative director for Apple Computers throughout most of the 1980s, contends that graphic simplicity is no longer the goal as we race toward the new millennium. "When you have 'black box' hybrids like the telephone, the computer and the Internet, you need diagrams which are much more than just visual vocabulary," maintains Mok who heads Studio Archetype in San Francisco. "Diagrams are no longer a snapshot but more of a narrative, a summary, which show cause and effect. Otherwise, you have abstractions on top of abstractions and nothing is understood." ■ Still, even the most enduring form of diagramming could not exist without a verbal explanation. Even football "chalk talk" has moved from the hand-drawn, one-dimensional plane—the blackboard—to the electronic playing field. Next stop? Three-dimensional, lifelike scrimmaging in the cyberstadium.

(OPPOSITE PAGE AND FOLLOWING SPREAD) DURING THE UNITED STATES BICENTENNIAL, THE US DEPARTMENT OF TRANSPORTATION ASKED AN AIGA COMMITTEE TO CONDUCT A STUDY OF INTERNATIONAL SYMBOL SYSTEMS (23 IN EXISTENCE AT THE TIME) AND TO DEVELOP A UNIFORM SYSTEM FOR USE IN THE UNITED STATES. THE SYSTEM, DESIGNED BY COOK AND SHANOSKY ASSOCIATES, INC. CONSISTS OF FIFTY DIFFERENT SYMBOLS THAT WERE ORIGINALLY CREATED BY HAND. THE SYSTEM IS NOW USED INTERNATIONALLY.

Im Internet findet man 166'540 Verweise auf Diagramme, aber nicht einer definiert die Prinzipien eines Diagramms. Ziemlich entmutigend für einen Designer, der bereits 1949 sein Studium am Pratt Institute abgeschlossen hat und es im Zeitalter der elektronischen graphischen Kommunikation nicht fertig bringt, sich von Papier und Bleistift zu trennen. Deshalb muss man sich aber keinesfalls geschlagen geben. ■ Wir können mit dem Computer koexistieren, ohne uns in den Cyber Space hinauszuwagen. Ich sitze oft mit meinen Mitarbeitern zusammen, die alle den Computer beherrschen, und erkläre ihnen anhand von Skizzen, wie sich Information vereinfachen und in einem Diagramm darstellen lässt. Sie geben die Befehle ein und führen die Maus. Unser Anliegen ist dasselbe: wirksam zu informieren. ■ Auch die Hürden sind dieselben. Wenn das Diagramm mit der Botschaft des Auftraggebers kollidiert, haben wir versagt. Wenn der Leser nicht in Sekundenschnelle begreifen kann, was wir herüberbringen möchten, sind wir gestrauchelt. Wie ansprechend das Diagramm, die Karte, der Plan oder die bildliche Darstellung optisch auch sein mögen, zwischen Auge und Verstand sollte eine blitzschnelle, direkte Verbindung hergestellt werden, ohne dass es zu einem Kurzschluss kommt. Diagramme sind in einer Zeit, in der die Leute die Dinge eher überfliegen als lesen, eine alternative Sprache, die Komplexität in Transparenz übersetzt. ■ Ob es uns gefällt oder nicht, wir entwickeln uns Schritt für Schritt von einer Text- zu einer visuell orientierten Gesellschaft. James Miho, Leiter der Design-Klasse am Art Center College in Los Angeles, erklärt das so: «Mit der heutigen Computervernetzung und der Software für die Herstellung dreidimensionaler Modelle schliesst sich der Kreis, der bei den elementaren Diagrammen der Höhlenbewohner begann und sich über die verbalen Traditionen der Gesellschaften in China, Afrika und den Amazonasgebieten und die visuelle Darstellung von Worten in der Chin-Dynastie fortsetzte.» ■ Die Herausforderung bei der Erstellung von Diagrammen – ob in elektronischen oder Print Medien – liegt darin, sie originell und packend zu machen. Dann folgt die Kommunikation. Unsere Firma hatte in den frühen 70er Jahren eine solche Herausforderung zu bewältigen, und zwar noch vor der Zweihundertjahresfeier der USA. Es handelte sich um einen durch das AIGA vermittelten Auftrag des Verkehrsministeriums, fünfzig für Fussgänger bestimmte Symbole zu entwerfen. Heute werden sie in der ganzen Welt eingesetzt. ■ Unsere Auftraggeber, ob es sich nun um Geschäftsführer, private oder institutionelle Anleger handelt, stellen uns immer anspruchsvollere Aufgaben, die kreative Lösungen verlangen. Daniel Goldberg, Präsident und CEO des Medical Inter-Insurance Exchange, behauptet, dass «kreative Diagramme ungeheuer wichtig sind.» «Wenn unser Jahresbericht nur an Finanzanalysten verschickt werden würde, hätte er keine Graphiken, Diagramme oder Bilder, weil die Leute von der Wall Street sich die Zeit nehmen, sich durchzubeissen.» «Aber», so fügt er hinzu, «unsere Aktionäre sind Doktoren, die mir drei Sekunden geben, um ihnen komplizierte wirtschaftliche Informationen zu vermitteln.» ■ Angesichts der explodierenden Anzahl von Firmen, die an die Börse gegangen sind, und angesichts des Drucks auf Finanzanalysten, die Firmen herauszupicken, die das beste Potential für langfristige Gewinne haben, braucht das Solo-Diagramm nach Meinung eines Analysten Hilfe. «Eine Graphik oder ein Diagramm ist besser als eine Aufstellung von Zahlen», sagt Kim Ritrievi, Analystin für die Bereiche Chemie und Photographie für die First Boston Company in New York. «Aber die Kombination eines Diagramms mit einer in wenige Worte gefassten Schlussfolgerung ist die effektivste Form der Kommunikation.» Ironischerweise sieht es in der Realität so aus, dass einfacher besser bedeutet, wenn es sich um die so wertvolle Zeit eines Analysten handelt. Ritrievi vertritt die Ansicht, dass sich Tortendiagramme für die Darstellung von Marktanteilen oder von der Aufsplitterung der Verkäufe am besten eignen: «Das Auge wird direkt auf das grösste Stück des Kuchens gelenkt, und der Rest ist Nebensache.» ■ Barbara Lucas, Vize-Präsidentin und Corporate Secretary von Black & Decker, teilt Ms. Ritrievis Überzeugung, dass weniger mehr ist: «Wir wollen alles Beiwerk beseitigen und uns auf ein paar wenige wichtige Dinge ‚zum Mitnehmen' beschränken. Wenn man nicht etwas zu sagen hat, das Bestand der Hauptbotschaft ist, sollte man es nicht darstellen. Wenn es irrelevant ist, verwässert es die Botschaft.» ■ Das ‚Warum' eines Diagramms kollidiert noch immer mit dem ‚Wie'. Die Harmonie von Funktion und Form ist für alle, mit Ausnahme einiger sehr begabter Designer, schwer definierbar, besonders heute, wo der Computer anscheinend die Rolle des Creative Directors übernommen hat. Aber ist das ein Problem, über das sich nachzudenken lohnt? «Wenn es sich darum handelt, reine Information zum Abruf bereitzuhalten, gibt es zwei Probleme», sagt Kenneth Hine, Leiter des Studienganges Communication Design an der Syracuse University und einer der Direktoren von MKH Design in Syracuse, N.Y. «Erstens: Wir bewegen uns dank E-mail, der interaktiven Medien und persönlich zugeschnittenen Web Sites mit Lichtgeschwindigkeit. Zweitens: Wir sind schon von der reinen Menge an Information so überwältigt, dass es unmöglich ist, das für uns Nützliche herauszupicken. ■ Hine sagt, Graphik-Designer müssten die Bibliothekare des elektronischen Informationszeitalters werden. «Nur wir können, ohne sie zu trivialisieren, durch Diagramme Information zugänglich machen und die Verbindungen zum Rest der Welt herstellen. Wir selektionieren und redigieren, um die Information zugänglich und verständlich zu machen.» Hine befürchtet jedoch, dass gegenwärtige und zukünftige Generationen von Graphik-Designern, fasziniert von den beeindruckenden, ständig wachsenden Möglichkeiten des Computers, sich mehr dafür interessieren werden, ein Diagramm verführerisch oder sexy zu machen, so dass funktionale Überlegungen gegenüber ästhetischen Gesichtspunkten in den Hintergrund rücken. Und das nährt seine grösste Befürchtung: «Die Leute fühlen sich überfordert und schalten ab, auch wenn es um lebenswichtige Information geht.» ■ Diagramme mögen die visuelle Kurzschrift sein, aber sie dürfen für den Graphiker keine Abkürzung sein, die ihm angesichts eines anspruchsvollen Kunden und eines nahenden Abliefertermins gelegen kommt. Ich betrachte Diagramme als architektonische Blaupausen, deren strukturelle Integrität mit jedem

**ROGER COOK** IST PRÄSIDENT VON COOK AND SHANOSKY ASSOCIATES, INC. COOK AND SHANOSKY WURDEN IN VIELEN ZEITSCHRIFTEN VORGESTELLT, DARUNTER IN *PRINT*, *COMMUNICATION ARTS* UND *NOVUM GEBRAUCHSGRAPHIK*, UND AUSSTELLUNGEN WIE Z.B. IM WHITNEY MUSEUM UND IM GRAND PALAIS. TRUGEN ZU IHREM INTERNATIONALEN RUF BEI. 1985 ERHIELTEN COOK AND SHANOSKY EINE DER ERSTEN 13 PRESIDENTIAL DESIGN AWARDS FÜR DIE PIKTOGRAMME, DIE SIE FÜR DAS US DEPARTMENT OF TRANSPORTATION ENTWARFEN.

Tastendruck oder Maus-Klick auf dem Spiel steht. «Diagramme müssen inhaltlich solide und in pragmatischer Hinsicht effizient sein», fordert Massimo Vignelli, Päsident von Vignelli Associates in New York. «Sie sollten weder Cartoons noch Experimente in abstrakter Kunst sein.» ■ Vignelli teilt Hines Ansicht, dass die Beherrschung des Computers durch einen Graphiker keinesfalls Grossartigkeit oder optische Anschaulichkeit garantiert. «Das visuelle, elektronische Vokabular ist in den Händen von so vielen Leuten, die diese Sprache nicht beherrschen; die Resultate im Bereich der Kommunikation sind fürchterlich», sagt Vignelli. Er lobt die New York Times und Gannetts USA Today – zwei Zeitungen, die hinsichtlich des journalistischen Niveaus und der Aufmachung sehr verschieden sind – wegen ihres ausgezeichneten Einsatzes von Diagrammen, die den Inhalt von Nachrichten schnell vermitteln, ohne Worte oder Zeit zu verlieren. «Noch nie hatten wir so viele Möglichkeiten, grossartige Sachen zu machen, wie heute mit dem Computer.» Jedoch, so bedauert Vignelli, «heute geht es in erster Linie um Schnelligkeit statt um Qualität». ■ Für andere einflussreiche Designer liegt die Zukunft des Diagramms in der Elektronik. Krzystof Lenk, der Informationsgraphik an der Rhode Island School of Design unterrichtet und Präsident von Dynamic Diagrams, Providence, Rhode Island, ist, behauptet, dass sich «die Methoden der diagrammatischen Darstellung nicht verändert haben, sondern dass die kognitiven Fähigkeiten des menschlichen Gehirns an der Grenze zur Überbelastung angelangt sind, so dass alles ausser ganz elementaren Diagrammen verwirrend wirkt.» Lenk ist ebenfalls der Ansicht, dass das Tortendiagramm die am leichtesten verständliche Darstellungsweise sei, wobei er aber einräumt, dass Graphiker neue Wege zur Übermittlung der Botschaft gefunden haben, die den Verstand des Betrachters nicht überfordern. ■ Clement Mok, fast während der gesamten 80er Jahre Creative Director für Apple Computer, ist seinerseits überzeugt, dass es heute, wo wir uns rapide auf das neue Jahrtausend hinbewegen, nicht mehr um graphische Schlichtheit geht. «Wenn man Black-box-Hybriden wie Telephon, Computer und Internet vor sich hat, braucht man Diagramme, die mehr sind als nur visuelles Vokabular», argumentiert Mok, der das Studio Archetype in San Francisco leitet. «Diagramme sind keine Momentaufnahmen mehr, sondern eher Erzählungen, Zusammenfassungen, die Ursache und Wirkung zeigen. Sonst bekommt man Abstraktionen über Abstraktionen, und nichts wird verstanden.» ■ Allerdings kommt auch die solideste Form der diagrammatischen Darstellung nicht ohne verbale Erklärung aus. Selbst beim Fussball hat das elektronische Spielfeld die von Hand beschriebene Tafel, die den Spielstand anzeigte, ersetzt. Nächste Station? Dreidimensionales, lebensnahes Rugby-Gerangel im Cyber-Stadion.

ROGER COOK LES DIAGRAMMES À L'ÈRE DE L'ÉLECTRONIQUE

Sur Internet, on trouve 166 540 références à des diagrammes, mais aucune n'en définit les principes schématiques de manière précise. Décourageant pour un designer sorti frais émoulu du Pratt Institute en 1949 et qui, aujourd'hui, à l'ère de la communication électronique, a de la peine à se séparer de son bloc et de son crayon. Mais nous aurions tort de nous avouer vaincus pour autant. ■ Nous pouvons coexister avec l'ordinateur sans nous aventurer dans le cyberespace. Je réunis souvent les graphistes de mon équipe qui eux maîtrisent parfaitement leur machine, et leur explique comment simplifier l'information et la représenter schématiquement. Nous collaborons. Ils prennent les commandes et guide la souris. Nous poursuivons le même objectif: informer avec le maximum d'impact. ■ Les obstacles restent les mêmes également. Si le diagramme va à l'encontre du message du client, nous avons échoué. Si le lecteur ne comprend pas en une fraction de seconde ce que nous essayons de communiquer, idem. Peu importe l'esthétique d'un diagramme, d'un graphique, d'une carte ou d'un plan, il doit se produire une connexion instantanée entre l'œil et le cerveau sans que la compréhension ne soit court-circuitée. A une époque où les gens ont tendance à survoler un texte plutôt qu'à le lire, les diagrammes constituent un langage de substitution à même de traduire la complexité en clarté. ■ En effet, que nous le voulions ou non, nous nous orientons vers une société où le visuel prend le pas sur l'écrit. James Miho, directeur du département de design à l'Art Center College de Los Angeles, l'explique en ces termes: «Avec les réseaux informatiques et les logiciels permettant de réaliser des modèles à effet tridimensionnel, la boucle est bouclée, des diagrammes primitifs des hommes des cavernes aux traditions orales de sociétés en Chine, en Afrique et en Amazonie en passant par la représentation visuelle de mots pour la dynastie Chin.» ■ Le défi à relever dans la réalisation de diagrammes – que le support soit électronique ou imprimé – consiste à faire preuve de créativité pour que le résultat soit séduisant. Puis vient la communication. Notre société a relevé un tel défi au début des années soixante-dix, juste avant la célébration du bicentenaire des Etats-Unis. L'AIGA nous avait chargés à l'époque de créer une cinquantaine de pictogrammes destinés aux piétons pour le compte du ministère des transports américain. Aujourd'hui, on peut encore les voir dans le monde entier. ■ Nos clients – chefs d'entreprises, investisseurs privés ou institutionnels – continuent à nous mettre au défi de trouver des solutions toujours plus créatives. Daniel Goldberg, président et directeur général de Medical Inter-Insurance Exchange, est convaincu que «les diagrammes créatifs sont d'une importance cruciale». «Si notre rapport annuel s'adressait aux seuls analystes financiers, il n'y aurait pas de graphiques, ni de diagrammes ni d'images, parce que les gens de Wall Street prennent le temps de le décortiquer. Et, ajoute-t-il, nos actionnaires sont des docteurs qui me donnent trois secondes pour communiquer des données financières complexes!» ■ Au vu de la multiplication des sociétés cotées en bourse et de la pression exercée sur les analystes financiers chargés de ferrer les sociétés présentant les meilleures perspectives de bénéfices à long terme, un diagramme seul, selon l'opinion d'un analyste, a besoin d'aide. «Un graphique ou un diagramme vaut mieux qu'un alignement de chiffres», estime Kim Ritrievi, analyste des secteurs Chimie et Photographie pour la First Boston Company à New York. «Mais la combinaison d'un graphique et d'une conclusion en quelques mots constitue le type de communication la plus efficace.» Pourtant, ironie du sort, dans la réalité, plus c'est simple mieux c'est, surtout lorsque le temps – si précieux – d'un analyste est en jeu. Kim Ritrievi pense qu'il est difficile de trouver mieux que les fameux camemberts pour représenter des parts de marché ou illustrer la répartition des ventes: «L'œil est automatiquement attiré par la plus grande part du camembert, et le reste ne compte pas.» ■ Barbara Lucas, vice-présidente et secrétaire générale de Black & Decker partage sur ce point l'opinion de Kim Retrievi: «Nous cherchons à éliminer le superflu et nous nous concentrons sur un petit nombre d'éléments importants 'à emporter'. Si l'on n'a rien à dire ou à montrer en rapport avec le message global, mieux vaut renoncer aux diagrammes. Un diagramme hors de propos ne fait que diluer le message.» ■ Le «pourquoi» d'un diagramme continue à se heurter au «comment». Hormis pour quelques designers particulièrement doués, l'harmonie de la fonction et de la forme reste pour tous difficile à définir, surtout aujourd'hui, à l'heure où l'ordinateur semble se substituer au directeur de la création. Mais ce problème vaut-il la peine d'être débattu? «Lorsqu'il s'agit de stocker de l'information pure, nous nous trouvons confrontés à deux problèmes», explique Kenneth Hine, directeur du département communication design à la Syracuse University et recteur de MHK Design à Syracuse, New York: «D'une part, le courrier électronique, les médias interactifs et les sites du Web taillés sur mesure pour les besoins personnels de chacun nous permettent de nous déplacer à la vitesse de la lumière. De l'autre, nous sommes à ce point submergés par les informations qu'il nous est impossible de trier ce qui nous serait utile.» ■ Selon Hine, les designers graphiques sont appelés à devenir les bibliothécaires de l'ère de l'information électronique. «Nous seuls sommes capables de rendre l'information accessible par le biais de diagrammes sans la banaliser et de créer des liens avec le reste du monde. Nous sélectionnons et remanions l'information de façon à la rendre accessible et compréhensible.» Hine craint toutefois que les générations actuelles et futures de designers graphiques, fascinés par les possibilités infinies de la CAO, cherchent avant tout à réaliser de beaux graphiques ou diagrammes, occultant ainsi la fonctionnalité au profit de considérations purement esthétiques. Cette crainte nourrit ce qu'il redoute le plus: «Les gens se sentent dépassés et déconnectent, même s'il s'agit d'informations vitales.» ■ Si les diagrammes s'apparentent à une forme de sténographie visuelle, ils ne doivent pas se limiter à un raccourci tombant à point nommé pour un client exigeant ou un délai qui se rapproche. Je considère les diagrammes comme des plans d'architecture, dont l'intégrité structurelle peut être menacée par une simple pression sur une touche ou un clic de trop sur la souris. «Les diagrammes doivent être cohérents du point de vue sémantique et efficaces sur le plan pragmatique», insiste Massimo Vignelli, président de Vignelli Associates à

New York. «Ils n'ont pas besoin d'être animés ou de faire dans l'art abstrait.» ■ Comme Hine, Vignelli ne pense pas que le fait qu'un graphiste maîtrise parfaitement l'ordinateur garantisse un résultat génial ou la clarté visuelle. «Le vocabulaire visuel, électronique, est entre les mains de trop de gens qui ne maîtrisent pas du tout ce langage. Les résultats dans le domaine de la communication sont consternants.» Par contre, il ne tarit pas d'éloges à l'égard du New York Times et de USA Today – deux quotidiens très différents au niveau de l'approche journalistique et de la présentation – pour la qualité et l'impact de leurs diagrammes qui communiquent rapidement et à bon escient le contenu d'informations sans mots ni perte de temps inutiles. «Jamais nous n'avons eu de telles possibilités de réaliser des choses aussi fantastiques depuis que nous avons l'ordinateur.» Et ce même si, comme le déplore Vignelli, «la vitesse est le paramètre-clé, plus que la qualité». ■ D'autres designers influents sont convaincus que l'avenir du diagramme est dans l'électronique. Selon Krzysztof Lenk, professeur de la section information graphics à la Rhode Island School of Design et président de Dynamic Diagrams, Providence, Rhode Island, «les méthodes de la représentation graphique n'ont pas changé, mais les capacités cognitives du cerveau humain sont arrivées à saturation, de sorte que tout ce qui s'écarte des diagrammes simples prête à confusion.» Il convient que les diagrammes semi-circulaires sont les plus faciles à comprendre, mais affirme que les graphistes ont trouvé d'autres moyens de communiquer un message sans mettre le cerveau à trop rude épreuve. ■ Clement Mok, directeur de la création chez Apple Computers durant les années quatre-vingts, pense pour sa part que la simplicité graphique n'est plus aujourd'hui l'objectif premier alors que nous nous dirigeons à grand pas vers le troisième millénaire. «Lorsqu'on a devant soi des hybrides de boîte noire comme le téléphone, l'ordinateur et Internet, on a besoin de diagrammes qui soient plus qu'un simple vocabulaire visuel», poursuit Mok, aujourd'hui directeur du studio Archetype à San Francisco. «Les diagrammes ne sont plus des snap-shots; ils s'apparentent davantage à une histoire, à un résumé, qui met en lumière les causes et les effets. Autrement, on va d'abstraction en abstraction et on ne comprend plus rien.» ■ Toutefois, même le meilleur diagramme ne peut se passer d'une explication verbale. Même dans le monde du football, le terrain de jeu électronique a remplacé le bon vieux tableau noir sur lequel figuraient les scores inscrits à la main. Prochaine étape? Une mêlée de rugby virtuelle dans un cyberstade.

**ROGER COOK** EST PRÉSIDENT DE COOK AND SHANOSKY ASSOCIATES, INC., UNE SOCIÉTÉ DE DESIGN MONDIALEMENT RÉPUTÉE ÉTABLIE À NEWTOWN, PENNSYLVANIE. SA CLIENTÈLE INCLUT DES NOMS PRESTIGIEUX, TELS QUE BRISTOL-MYERS SQUIBB COMPANY, IBM, VOLVO, BLACK & DECKER ET BASF CORPORATION. COOK AND SHANOSKY A ÉTÉ PRÉSENTÉE DANS PLUSIEURS PUBLICATIONS, DONT *PRINT*, *GRAPHIS*, *COMMUNICATION ARTS* ET *NOVUM GEBRAUCHSGRAPHIK*, ET LES EXPOSITIONS QUI LUI ONT NOTAMMENT ÉTÉ CONSACRÉES AU WHITNEY MUSEUM ET AU GRAND PALAIS À PARIS ONT CONTRIBUÉ À SA RENOMMÉE INTERNATIONALE. EN 1985, LA SOCIÉTÉ S'EST VU DÉCERNER L'UN DES TREIZE PREMIERS PRESIDENTIAL DESIGNS AWARDS POUR SES PICTOGRAMMES RÉALISÉS POUR LE COMPTE DU MINISTÈRE DES TRANSPORTS AMÉRICAIN. DIPLÔMÉ DU PRATT INSTITUTE, ROGER COOK EST MEMBRE DE L'AIGA ET DE L'ART DIRECTORS CLUB DU NEW JERSEY ET DE PHILADELPHIE.

*Richard Saul Wurman*

The kingdom of understanding is ruled by the emperor, Diagram. The kingdom, rich in fiefdoms, is filled with inherent rules and applications. The applications of the diagram run the gamut from the timeline to scientific, statistical, comparative and organizational charts. Whatever form they take or subject they address, diagrams all form the navigational, cartographic means to clarity. ■ In this land of the diagram, complexity is digested and transformed into clarity; time is made to stop so it can be observed in the timeline. Things of disparate size all decide to have the common lover of comparative analysis and spatial location imbues us all with the calmness of orientation. ■ The creation of a personal path to learning is the goal of any diagram. ■ The land of the diagram is the dreamland of the responsible graphic designer. ■ When a responsible designer arrives at that often contentious fork in the road at the intersection of performance and aesthetics, he chooses to create a diagram which *is* good rather than one which simply looks good–though ultimately these solutions look great. Responsible diagrammatic illustrations extend information and enable the viewer

RICHARD SAUL WURMAN HAS RECEIVED BOTH MASTER AND BACHELOR OF ARCHITECTURE DEGREES FROM THE UNIVERSITY OF PENNSYLVANIA, WHERE HE GRADUATED WITH HIGHEST HONORS IN 1959. SINCE THE PUBLICATION OF HIS FIRST BOOK IN 1962 AT THE AGE OF 26, HE HAS PUBLISHED OVER 60 BOOKS BASED ON THE SINGULAR PASSION OF HIS LIFE: MAKING INFORMATION UNDERSTANDABLE. HE HAS BEEN AWARDED NUMEROUS GRANTS AND AWARDS, INCLUDING SEVERAL GRANTS FROM THE NEA, A GUGGENHEIM FELLOWSHIP, AND IN 1996 THE CHRYSLER DESIGN AWARD. HE IS FOUNDER OF ACCESS PRESS LTD., AND THE TED CONFERENCES.

to see in a new way things they've always seen but never seen. ■ The diagram is the intellectual shorthand of the visual communicator, a shorthand that has exploded with sophisticated imagery facilitated by our electronic adoptions. ■ Since one only understands something relative to something else one already understands, diagrams depicting comparative information, statistics, or scientific information need to be based on a common beginning point of general understanding. ■ The nature of the idea or thought that one desires to communicate controls the choice of the organizing principle used. Thrown on the floor, 140,000 words do not make a dictionary. Their alphabetical organization creates the dictionary and the way in to understanding. There are only five such principles: location, alphabet, time, category and hierarchy. ■ A successful diagram induces memory through its organization of information. The diagram needs such a front door, a threshold of principle and a pattern made understandable. ■ One of the diseases of our society is that technology enables us to do what we can do too easily. If a personal computer enables you to not only create a pie-chart, but to also do it as a line chart or to do it in 256 or millions of colors–you do that! Then, successively, you make it three-dimensional, rotate it so it's an oval rather than a circle, shade the cylinder that you've created, explode wedges in space and fill this virtual space with shadows of floating wedges. ■ Each move made rendered the information less understandable. Each change was done because of the seduction of facility. The graphic designer almost certainly did not consider whether a pie-chart was even the correct choice in the first place, since for most statistical representation, it isn't. ■ Cartography has its dangers and seductions also. Many cartographers are under the illusion that the more you put on a map, the better the map is. But a map is a pattern made understandable. Only two patterns can be understood at one time as their relationship inevitably creates a third. ■ Remembering what you are interested in is learning. ■ A closing fable: A young man named Michelangelo stands in front of a huge granite monolith. He stands there at a time in history before the technologies that brought us the hammer and chisel have occurred. He gazes at this rock. He dreams his dream and the best that he is able to say is "What a wonderful stone you are." ■ As this fable continues: Michelangelo now stands in front of the same rock. Into one hand is thrust a hammer and into the other a chisel. He looks at his hands and at the tools that they hold, gazes at the stone and with epiphanic zeal he says "I must let Moses out." A jealous assistant grabs the hammer from his hand, hits Michelangelo on the head and kills him. ■ I love technology, I choose my assistants well, and I know creative thoughts come from me and not my tools.

. . . . . . . . . . . . . . . . . . . . . . . . . . . . . . . . . . . . . . . . . . . . . . . . . . . . . . . . . . . . . . . . . . . . . . . . . . . . . . . . . . . . . . . . . . . . . . . . . . . . . . . . . . . . . . . . . .

**R I C H A R D   S A U L   W U R M A N** DIE DIAGRAMME ODER DAS KÖNIGREICH DER VERSTEHENS

. . . . . . . . . . . . . . . . . . . . . . . . . . . . . . . . . . . . . . . . . . . . . . . . . . . . . . . . . . . . . . . . . . . . . . . . . . . . . . . . . . . . . . . . . . . . . . . . . . . . . . . . . . . . . . . . . .

Im Reich der Verständigung herrscht das Diagramm mit allen seinen ihm innewohnenden Regeln und Formen. Graphiken, Darstellungen technischer Funktionen, Kartogramme, Organigramme...ob für wissenschaftliche Zwecke, statistische oder vergleichende Erläuterungen – in welcher Form und zu welchem Zweck auch immer, Diagramme sind Navigationsmittel auf dem Weg zum Verstehen. ■ Im Reich des Diagramms werden komplexe Fakten verdaut und dann transparent gemacht: die Zeit wird angehalten, so dass sich der Zeitablauf betrachten lässt; Dinge von ganz unterschiedlicher Grösse lassen eine vergleichende Analyse zu, und wir können uns auf Hinweise verlassen, die uns eine problemlose räumliche Orientierung ermöglichen. ■ Ziel eines jeden Diagramms ist es, jedem den Weg zum Verständnis aufzuzeigen. ■ Das Land des Diagramms ist das Traumland des verantwortungsbewussten Graphikers. ■ Wenn ein verantwortungsbewusster Graphiker auf seinem Weg an die Stelle gelangt, wo sich die so oft diskutierten Wege von Form und Funktion treffen, dann gelingt ihm ein Diagramm, das nicht nur gut aussieht, sondern tatsächlich gut ist. Verantwortungsbewusste diagrammatische Darstellungen vermitteln Information und ermöglichen dem Betrachter, vertraute Dinge auf eine ganz neue Art zu sehen. ■ Das Diagramm ist die intellektuelle Kurzschrift des Graphikers, eine Kurzschrift, die mittlerweile, vor allem dank der Elektronik, mit einem enormen Bildvokabular angereichert ist. ■ Da man nur etwas im Vergleich zu etwas begreift, das man bereits versteht, müssen Diagramme mit vergleichender Information, Statistiken oder wissenschaftlicher Information auf einer Basis aufbauen, die allgemein verstanden wird. ■ Die Art der Idee oder des Gedankens, den man vermitteln möchte, bestimmt die Wahl des geeigneten organisatorischen Prinzips. Auf den Boden geworfen, versammeln sich 140'000 Worte nicht zu einem Wörterbuch. Erst ihre alphabetische Ordnung macht das Wörterbuch aus, das nur auf diese Weise Zugang bietet. Es gibt nur fünf solche Prinzipien: Ort, Alphabet, Zeit, Kategorie und Hierarchie. ■ Ein erfolgreiches Diagramm unterstützt das Gedächtnis durch die Organisation der Information. Das Diagramm braucht eine solche Eingangstür und eine Schwelle, die aus einem der Aufbauprinzipien und einem verständlichen Schema besteht. ■ Eine der Krankheiten unserer Gesellschaft ist, dass die Technologie uns unsere Aufgabe zu leicht macht. Wenn ein PC einem erlaubt, nicht nur ein Tortendiagramm herzustellen, sondern es auch als Flussdiagramm darzustellen und es in 256 oder Millionen von Farben zu machen, dann nutzt man diese Möglichkeiten. Nach und nach macht man das Diagramm dann noch dreidimensional, dreht es, so dass aus einem Kreis ein Oval wird. Der Zylinder, den man gemacht hat, bekommt einen Schatten, und man lässt keilförmige Formen im virtuellen Raum explodieren, der wiederum mit Schatten gleitender, keilförmiger Objekte angefüllt wird. ■ Und jeder dieser Schritte hat die Information weniger verständlich gemacht. Die Leichtigkeit war es, die zu jeder Änderung verführte. Der Graphiker hat ziemlich sicher nicht einmal darüber nachgedacht, ob ein Tortendiagramm überhaupt die richtige Darstellungsmöglichkeit ist – für die meisten statistischen Darstellungen eignet sich diese Form nämlich überhaupt nicht. ■ Auch kartographische Darstellungen bergen Gefahren bzw. Verführungen in sich. Viele Kartographen werden von der Illusion geleitet, je mehr man in eine Karte hineinpackt, desto besser werde sie. Aber eine Karte ist ein Muster, das verstanden werden muss. Nur zwei Muster können gleichzeitig ver-

**RICHARD SAUL WURMAN** HAT SEIN STUDIUM DER ARCHITEKTUR 1959 AN DER UNIVERSITY OF PENNSYLVANIA MIT AUSZEICHNUNG ABGESCHLOSSEN. DER HERAUSGABE SEINES ERSTEN BUCHES IM JAHRE 1962 IM ALTER VON 26 JAHREN FOLGTEN BISHER ÜBER 60 BÜCHER, DIE ALLE MIT DER PASSION SEINES LEBENS ZU TUN HABEN: INFORMATION VERSTÄNDLICH ZU MACHEN. ER HAT VERSCHIEDENE AUSZEICHNUNGEN UND SUBVENTIONEN ERHALTEN, DARUNTER ZUSCHÜSSE VOM NEA (NATIONAL ENDOWMENT FOR THE ARTS) UND EIN GUGGENHEIM FORSCHUNGSSTIPENDIUM. WURMAN IST GRÜNDER VON ACCESS PRESS LTD. UND INITIATOR DER TED-KONFERENZEN.

standen werden, weil ihre Beziehung zueinander unweigerlich ein drittes Muster schafft. ■ Man denke daran, dass das erklärte Ziel des Interesses Lernen ist. ■ Zum Schluss eine Fabel: Ein junger Mann namens Michelangelo steht vor einem grossen Monolithen aus Granit. Er steht dort zu einer Zeit, in der die Technik uns noch nicht einmal Hammer und Meissel beschert hatte. Er blickt auf den Felsen. Er träumt seinen Traum, und alles, was er sagen kann, ist: «Was für ein wunderschöner Stein du bist.» ■ Und die Fabel geht weiter: Michelangelo steht vor dem selben Felsen. In einer Hand hält er einen Hammer, in der anderen den Meissel. Er blickt auf seine Hände und auf die Werkzeuge in ihnen, blickt auf den Stein, und mit emphatischen Eifer sagt er: «Ich muss Moses herauslassen.» Ein eifersüchtiger Assistent reisst ihm den Hammer aus der Hand und erschlägt Michelangelo damit. ■ Ich liebe Technologie, ich suche mir meine Assistenten gut aus, und ich weiss, dass die Einfälle von mir kommen und nicht von meinen Werkzeugen.

................................................................................

**RICHARD SAUL WURMAN** LES DIAGRAMMES OU LE ROYAUME DE LA COMPRÉHENSION

................................................................................

Au royaume de la compréhension, le diagramme règne en maître. Graphiques, représentations de fonctions techniques, cartogrammes, organigrammes... qu'il soit utilisé à des fins scientifiques, statistiques ou comparatives, le diagramme revêt différentes formes répondant à des règles précises. Peu importe le type de représentation ou le sujet traité, les diagrammes sont autant de boussoles nous permettant de naviguer vers la clarté. ■ Au pays du diagramme, des données complexes sont digérées, puis transformées pour aboutir à la clarté. Le temps, arrêté, peut être étudié dans sa durée. Des éléments de différentes grandeurs peuvent être comparés, et nous disposons de repères fiables qui nous permettent de nous orienter aisément dans l'espace. ■ Ouvrir la voie à la compréhension, voilà l'objectif de tout diagramme. ■ Le pays du diagramme est le pays imaginaire du designer graphique responsable. ■ Lorsqu'un designer responsable arrive à la croisée des chemins tant débattus de la forme et de la fonction, il crée un diagramme qui ne se contente pas d'être esthétique, mais qui est bon. Un bon diagramme met en relief des informations et apporte un éclairage neuf sur des faits connus. ■ Pour le graphiste, le diagramme s'apparente à une forme de sténographie intellectuelle, une sténographie qui s'est enrichie d'une imagerie sophistiquée avec l'électronique. ■ Dans la mesure où l'on ne peut comprendre une chose qu'en la comparant à une autre chose déjà connue, les diagrammes illustrant des données comparatives, des statistiques ou encore des informations scientifiques doivent reposer sur une base universelle, compréhensible par tous. ■ La nature de l'idée ou de la pensée que l'on souhaite communiquer détermine le choix du principe organisateur le plus adéquat. Jetés en vrac, 140 000 mots ne font pas un dictionnaire. Seul leur classement par ordre alphabétique fait du dictionnaire un dictionnaire, soit un outil ouvrant la voie à la compréhension. On dénombre cinq principes de ce type: lieu, alphabet, temps, catégorie et hiérarchie. ■ Un diagramme réussi facilite la mémorisation de par l'organisation des informations. Le diagramme requiert une telle porte d'entrée et un seuil, reposant sur l'un de ces principes et un schéma compréhensible. ■ L'un des maux de notre société est que la technologie nous facilite par trop la tâche. Si un micro-ordinateur vous permet de créer aussi bien un graphique en demi-cercle qu'un organigramme et de les rendre en 256 ou en plusieurs millions de couleurs, et bien vous le faites! Puis, vous songez à le représenter en 3D, à lui imprimer la forme d'un ovale plutôt que celle d'un cercle, vous ombrez le cylindre ainsi créé et faites éclater des formes coniques dans l'espace virtuel, peuplé à son tour des ombres d'objets coniques flottants. ■ Or, chacune de ces étapes nuit un peu plus à la clarté de l'information. Chaque modification a été apportée pour avoir cédé à la facilité. Presque à coup sûr, le designer graphique ne se sera même pas préoccupé de savoir si un diagramme semi-circulaire convient à son propos; pour la représentation de statistiques, il s'avère justement souvent que ce n'est pas le cas. ■ La cartographie présente les mêmes dangers et séductions. Nombre de cartographes ont l'illusion que plus une carte comprend d'informations, meilleure elle est. Mais une carte est une représentation schématique qui doit être claire. On ne peut comprendre plus de deux schémas à la fois dans la mesure où leur association en crée inévitablement un troisième. ■ Il faut se souvenir qu'apprendre est ce qui nous intéresse. ■ La fable de la fin: Un jeune homme du nom de Michel-Ange se tient face à un imposant monolithe de granit. L'histoire se déroule à une époque où l'homme ne connaît ni le marteau ni le burin. Le jeune homme étudie le bloc d'un air songeur. Il rêve son rêve, puis s'exclame: «Quelle belle pierre tu es!» ■ La fable continue: Michel-Ange se trouve à nouveau devant la même pierre. Dans une main, il tient un marteau, dans l'autre un burin. Il regarde ses mains, ses outils, fixe la pierre, puis, dans un élan frénétique, s'écrie: «Il faut que je libère Moïse». C'est alors qu'un assistant jaloux lui arrache le marteau des mains, lui assène un violent coup sur la tête et le tue. ■ J'aime la technologie, je choisis mes assistants avec soin et je sais que mes idées viennent de moi et non pas de mes outils de travail.

EN 1959, **RICHARD SAUL WURMAN** TERMINE SES ÉTUDES D'ARCHITECTURE À L'UNIVERSITÉ DE PENNSYLVANIE AVEC MENTION. A LA PUBLICATION DE SON PREMIER OUVRAGE EN 1962, RÉDIGÉ À L'ÂGE DE 26 ANS, SUCCÈDENT PLUS DE 60 LIVRES, TOUS CONSACRÉS À SA GRANDE PASSION: RENDRE L'INFORMATION COMPRÉHENSIBLE. BÉNÉFICIAIRE DE LA BOURSE DE RECHERCHES GUGGENHEIM, IL S'EST VU DÉCERNER PLUSIEURS DISTINCTIONS, ET DIVERS INSTITUTS, DONT LE NEA, LUI ONT ALLOUÉ DES SUBVENTIONS POUR SES TRAVAUX. RICHARD SAUL WURMAN EST LE FONDATEUR D'ACCESS PRESS LTD. ET L'INITIATEUR DES CONFÉRENCES TED.

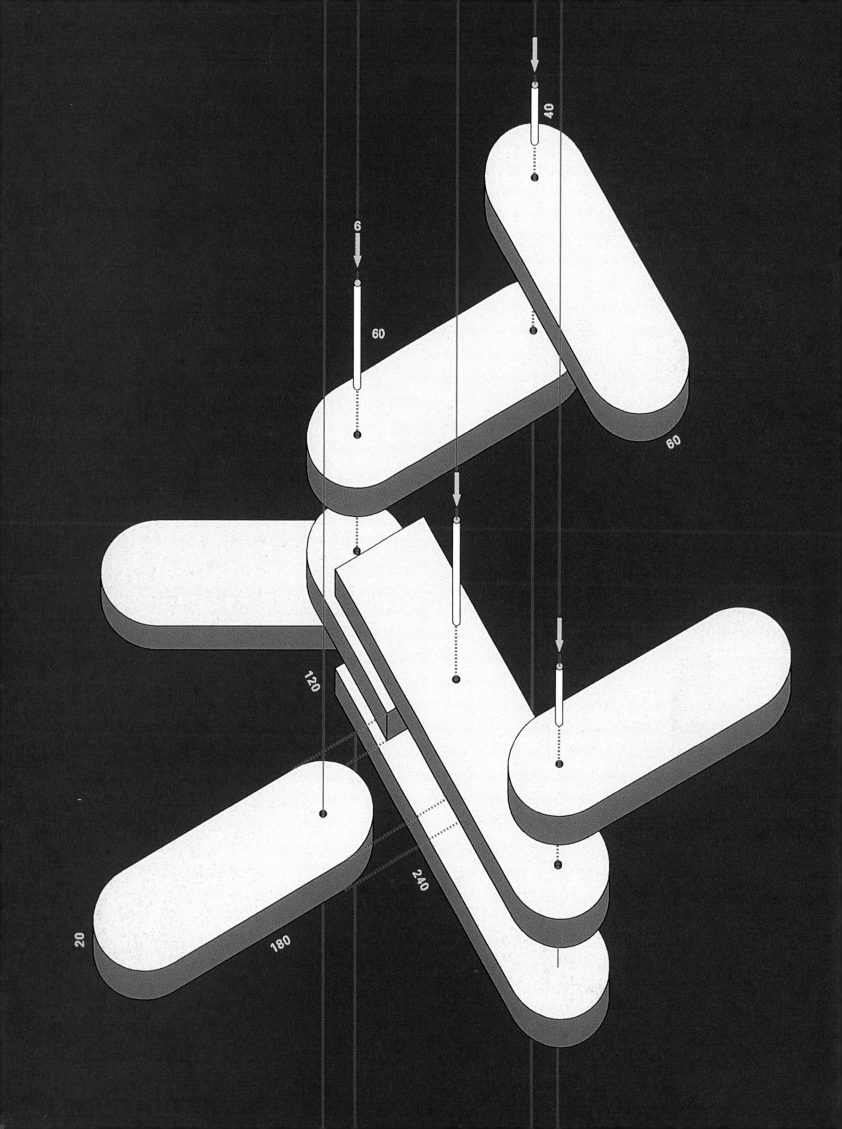

GRAPHIS

DIAGRAM

TWO

HISTORICAL

GESCHICHTE

RAPPEL HISTORIQUE

*(PRECEDING SPREAD)* ■ *Wood carvings by the Eskimos of Greenland representing the topography of the coastal fjords. Courtesy of the National Museum of Denmark, Department of Ethnography, and of the Gronlands Landsmuseum.*

● *Hölzer der Grönland-Eskimos, aus denen die Topographie der fjordenreichen Küsten ablesbar ist. Mit freundlicher Genehmigung des National Museum of Denmark, Department of Ethnography, und des Gronland Landsmuseum.*

▲ *Bois des esquimaux du Groenland indiquant la topographie des côtes riches en fjords. Aven l'aimable autorisation du National Museum of Denmark, Department of Ethnology, et du Gronlands Landsmuseum.*

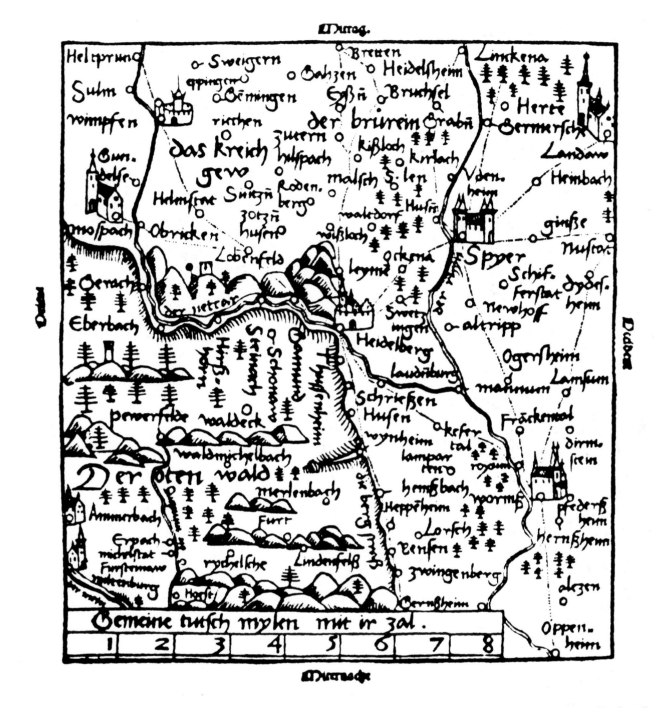

*(LEFT)* ■ *Representation of a part of life after death (grave of the Senedjem–No. 1–19. Dyn., Western Thebes) with the falcon-headed sun god in the pediment bringing momentary light to the gloominess of the underworld. Below is the deceased with his wife offering prayers to the deity and at work in the fields–being a stage of purgatory. This form of the simultaneous portrayal of events can also be found in many modern diagrams. From* ÄGYPTEN *(Egypt), Silva Verlag, Zürich, with photographs by Maximilian Bruggmann.*

● *Darstellung eines Teils des Jenseits (Grab des Sennedjem - Nr, 1- 19. Dyn., Theben-West) mit dem falkenköpfigen Sonnengott im Giebelfeld, der vorübergehend Licht in die Finsternis der Unterwelt bringt. Darunter der Verstorbene mit seiner Gemahlin beim Anbeten von Gottheiten und bei Feldarbeiten, die eine Stufe der Läuterung sind. Diese Form der gleichzeitigen Darstellung von Handlungen ist auch in vielen modernen Diagrammen zu finden. Aus* ÄGYPTEN, *Silva-Verlag, Zürich, mit Photos von Maximilian Bruggmann.*

▲ *Représentation d'une partie de l'au-delà (tombe de Sennedjem no 1, XIXe dynastie, Thèbes-Ouest) avec, au tympan, le dieu solaire à tête de faucon qui porte temporairement la lumière dans l'obscurité du «pays souterrain». En bas, le défunt et son épouse adorant les divinités et engagés dans les travaux des champs, étape de sa purification. Cette forme de représentation simultanée se retrouve dans nombre de diagrammes modernes. Extrait du livre* ÄGYPTEN, *Ed. Silva, Zurich, photos de Maximilian Bruggmann.*

*(RIGHT)* ■ *Regional map of Heidelberg and environs. Woodcut by Sebastian Münster, 1528. From* VOM ALTEN BILD DER WELT (OLD IMPRESSIONS OF THE WORLD) *by Werner Beck, courtesy of the Nationale Forschungs- und Gedenkstätten der klassichen deutschen Literatur, Weimar.*

● *Regionalkarte von Heidelberg und Umgebung. Buchholzschnitt von Sebastian Münster, 1528. Aus* VOM ALTEN BILD DER WELT *von Werner Becker, mit freundlicher Genehmigung der Nationalen Forschungs- und Gedenkstätten der klassichen deutschen Literatur in Weimar.*

▲ *Carte de la région de Heidelberg. Gravure sur hêtre par Sebastian Münster, 1528. Illustration tiréede l'ouvrage* VOM ALTEN BILD DER WELT *de Werner Becker, reproduite aven l'autorisation des Nationale Forschungs- und Gedenkstätten der klassichen deutschen Literatur à Weimar.*

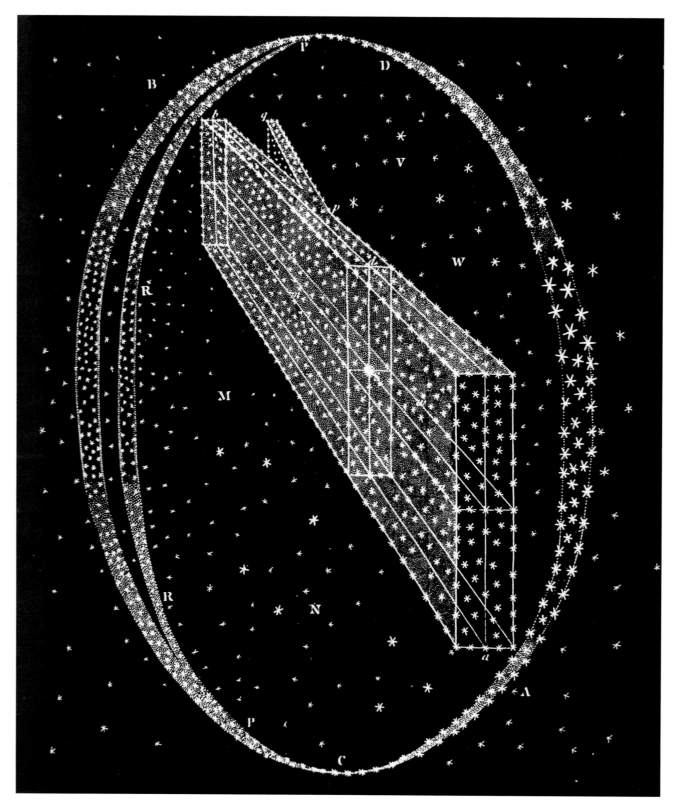

■ *Diagram by Sir William Herschel, German-born British astronomer, published in 1784 to explain the form of the galaxies. The earth is depicted with an S in the cluster of stars reaching from a to b. Herschel, through systematic oobservation of the heavens, developed the theory of stellar evolution. It was he who discovered the planet Uranus. From* Observations Tending to Investigate the Construction of the Heavens, *by Frederick William Herschel. Philosophical Transactions, London 1784.*

● *Von William Herschel im Jahre 1784 veröffentlichtes Schema, das die Form der Milchstrasse erklären soll. Die Erde ist hier mit S in der von a bis b reichenden Sternansammlung gekennzeichnet. Herschel war der erste, der dank seiner systematischen Sternzählungen die Milchstrassen- und mit ihr die Fixsternforschung auf sicheren wissenschaftlichen Boden stellte. Aus* Observations Tending to Investigate the Construction of the Heavens, *von Frederick William Herschel. Philosophical Transactions, London 1784.*

▲ *Schéma censé expliquer la form qu'a prise la Voie lactée, publié par l'astronome William Herschel en 1784. La Terre est identifiée par le sigle S parmi les étoiles groupées entre les points a et b. Grâce à ses comptages systématiques d'etoiles, Herschel a été le premier à établir sur de solides bases scientifiques l'etude de la Voie lactée et des étoiles fixes. Extrait de l'ouvrage original de Frederick William Herschel,* Observations Tending to Investigate the Construction of the Heavans, *paru dans les Philosophical Transactions, Londres 1784.*

Map of the world circa 1570-1573 by Abraham Ortelius, which depicts Australia as "a land unknown to man." The quotation by Cicero loosely translated means: "Ah, what human endeavors can be reagarded as great when compared to the eternal greatness of the whole world?" From the Ryhiner collection of the Municipal and University Library, Berne.

Erdkarte um 1570/73 von Abraham Ortelius, welche den Erdteil Australien als «dem Menschen unbekanntes Land» bezeichnet. Der Satz von Cicero lautet singemäss: «Ach, was kann in menschlichen Dingen schon Grosses gesehen werden angesichts der ewigen Grösse der ganzen Welt.» Aus der Ryhiner-Sammlung der Stadt- und Universitätsbibliothek Bern.

Planisphère terrestre d'Abraham Ortelius, vers 1570/73, où l'Australie figure comme «pays connu de personne». La citation de Cicéron signifie: «Que peut-on donc voir de grand dans les entreprises humaines si l'on considère l'immensité éternelle de tout cet univers!» Document figurant à la collection Ryhiner de la Bibliothèque municipale et universitaire de Berne.

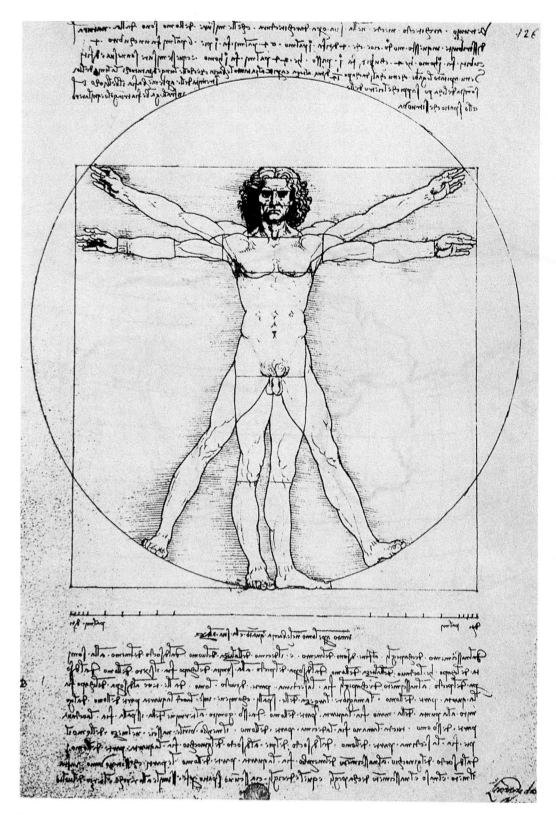

■ *Leonardo da Vinci's famous "Figure of Vitruvius" with which he explained the Vitruvius principle: "The natural center of the human body is the navel. If the man lies with outstretched arms on his back and a compass point is placed at his navel, his fingers and toes are at the circumference: the human figure can also be placed in a square, in which the height from the skull to the sole of the foot is as wide as the outstretched arms." Document held by the picture archives of the Galleria dell'Academia, Venice.*

● *Leonardo da Vincis berühmte «Figur zu Vitruv», mit der er die Prinzipien des Vitruvs über die Proportionen erläutert: «...Beim menschlichen Körper ist die natürliche Mitte der Nabel. Liegt ein Mann mit ausgestreckten Armen und Beinen auf dem Rücken, und wird auf seinem Nabel ein Zirkel angesetzt, so werden seine Finger und Zehen die Kreislinie berühren; ebenso kann man die menschliche Gestalt auch in ein Quadrat einpassen, da die Höhe vom Scheitel bis zur Fusssohle gleich der Breite der ausgestreckten Arme ist.» Galleria dell'Accademia, Venedig.*

▲ *La célèbre «Figure de Vitruve» où Léonard de Vinci explique les principes de Vitruve quant aux proportions: «Le centre naturel du corps humain, c'est le nombril. Lorsqu'un homme est couché sur le dos, bras et jambes écartés, la branche d'un compas posé sur son nombril esquissera un cercle passant par ses doigts et ses orteils; onpeut de même inscrire la figure humaine dans un carré, pusique la hauteur de l'homme, du sommet du crâne à la plante des pieds, égale sa largeur d'un bout à l'autre des bras écartés.» Galleria dell'Accademia à Venise.*

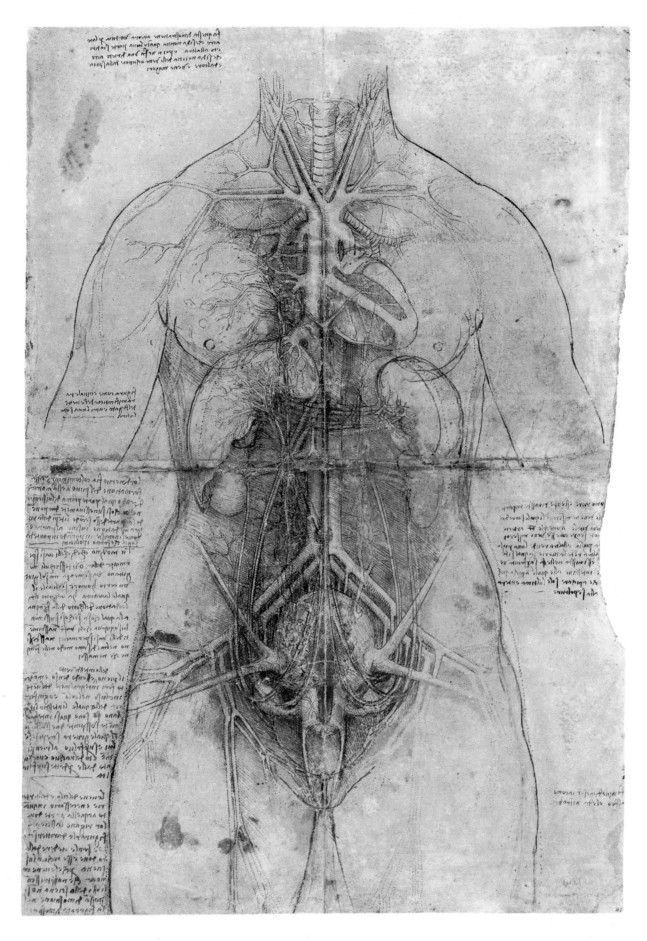

■*Study of the female organs, by Leonardo da Vinci. Pen, ink and wash over black crayon. Windsor Castle, Royal Collection. (Copyright: Her Majesty the Queen)*
●*Studie der weiblichen Organe, von Leonardo da Vinci. Feder, Tinte, laviert, über schwarzer Kreide. Windsor Castle, Royal Collection. (Copyright: Her Majesty the Queen)*
▲*Etude des organes féminins par Léonard de Vinci. Dessin à la plume passé au lavis sur craie noir. Collection Royale de Windsor. (Copyright: Sa Majesté la Reine Elisabeth)*

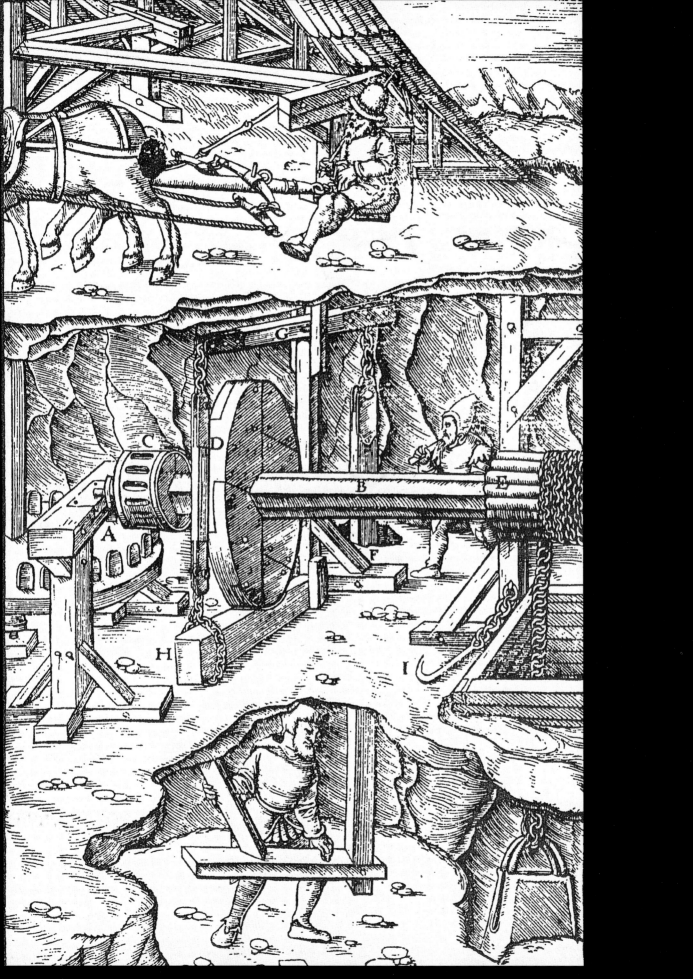

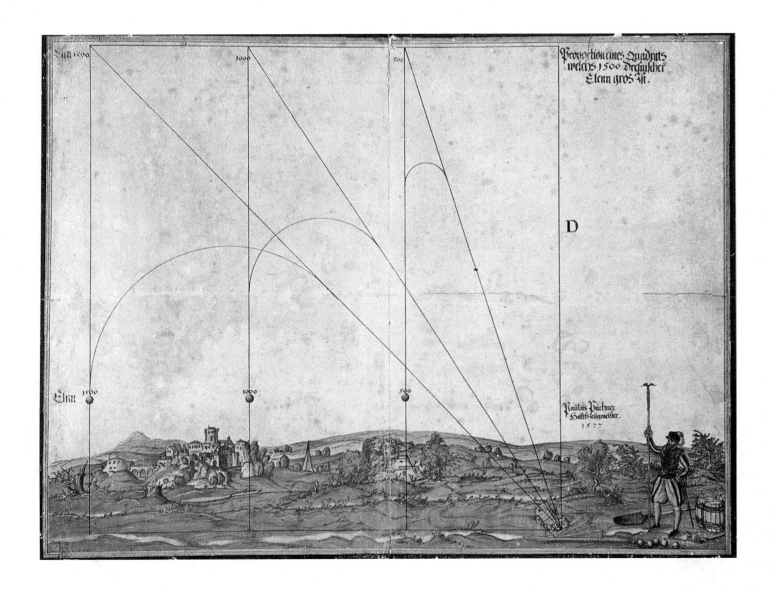

*(LEFT)* ■ *Historical rendering showing the function of various equipment in an iron mine. From the book* L'ARCHITETTURA DELLE MACCHINE - IL RINASCIMENTO, *published by Gabriele Mazzotta in cooperation with Fiat.*

● *Historische Darstellung der Funktion eines Eisenbergwerks mit den verschienden Einrichtungen zur Erleichterung der Förderung. Aus dem Buch* L'ARCHITETTURA DELLE MACCHINE - IL RINASCIMENTO, *erschienen bei Gabriele Mazzotta in Zusammenarbeit mit Fiat.*

▲ *Illustration du fonctionnement d'une mine de fer et des équipements servant à l'extraction. Image extraite de* L'ARCHITETTURA DELLE MACCHINE – IL RINASCIMENTO, *ouvrage publié par Gabriele Mazzotta en collaboration avec Fiat.*

*(RIGHT)* ■ *Flight path of cannonballs. The illustration shows that the range of fire is dependent on the angle of inclination of the mortar. Map by Paulus Puchner, Dresden 1577. Mathematics–Physical Salon, Dresden.*

● *Darstellung der Flugbahnen von Kanonenkugeln. Hier wird verdeutlicht, dass die Schussweite vom Neigugnswinkel des Mörsers abhängt. Karte von Paulus Puchner, Dresden 1577. Mathematisch-Physikalischer Salon, Dresden.*

▲ *Représentation des trajectoires de boulets de canon. On voit ici que la portée d'un mortier dépend de l'angle d'inclinaison. Carte de Paulus Puchner réalisée à Dresde en 1577. Mathematisch-Physikalischer Salon, Dresde.*

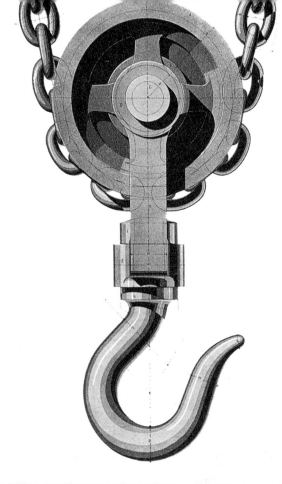

(TOP) ■ *Single part of a crane that served to load and unload barges in the 19th century. From the collection of Charles Dollfus.*
● *Einzelteile eines Krans, der im 19.Jahrhundert zur Ent-und Beladung von Frachtkähnen diente. Sammlung Charles Dollfus.*
▲ *Pièces constitutives d'une grue du XIXe siècle qui servait au chargement et déchargement des péniches. Coll. Charles Dollfus.*

(BOTTOM) ■ *Part of a 19th century steam engine developed by von Heilmann in 1890.*
● *Teil einer Dampflokomotive aus dem 19. Jahrhundert (1890 von Heilmann entwickelt).*
▲ *Partie d'une locomotive à vapeur du XIXe siècle (contruite en 1890 par Heilmann).*

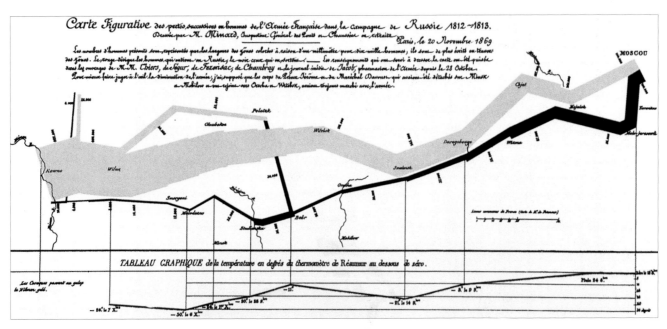

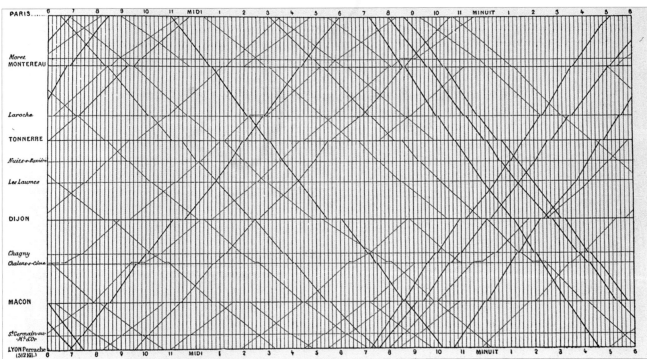

(TOP) ■ *Losses suffered by Napoleon's army in the Russian campaign, 1812-1813. The brown line illustrates the losses on the march to Moscow. The path of retreat from Moscow is depicted by the dark lower band. The temperature line (shown in Réaumur minus degrees) and corresponding dates show very clearly how extreme cold contributed to the casualties. By Charles Joseph Minard, (1869). Bibliothèque de l'Ecole Nationale des Ponts et Chaussés, Paris.*

● *Diagramm der fortgesetzten Verluste von Napoléons Armee beim Russlandfeldzug 1812-1813. Die braune Linie verdeutlicht die Verluste beim Marsch auf Moskau, die Schwarze die Verluste beim Rückzug. Sehr deutlich wird der Zusammenhang mit der Kälte, die im unteren Teil in Minus-temperaturen (Réaumur), auch mit dem jeweiligen Datum versehen, angezeigt ist. Charles Joseph Minard. Bibliothèque de l'Ecole Nationale des Ponts et Chaussées, Paris.*

▲ *Représentation graphique des pertes subies par l'armée de Napoléon durant la campagne de Russie de 1812 à1813. La ligne brune indique les pertes essuyées lors de l'avancée sur Moscou, la noire celles de la retraite. Le rapport est évident avec les chutes de température au-dessous de zéro portées au bas du graphique de Charles Joseph Minard en dégrés Réaumur, avec les dates. Bibliothèque de l'Ecole Nationale des Ponts et Chaussées, Paris.*

(BOTTOM) ■ *Train schedule from Paris to Lyon from the 1880s. Arrivals, departures, and the length of stops are depicted by horizontal lines. The stations are separated in proportion to their actual distance. The slope of the vertical lines reflects the speed of the trains–the closer to vertical the line, the faster the train. E.J. Marey. La Méthode Graphique, Paris 1885.*

● *Fahrplan für die Strecke Paris - Lyon. Ankunfts - und Abfahrts - und Abfahrtszeiten lassen sich an den horizontalen Linien ablesen, sowie auch die Aufenthaltsdauer. Der Abstand zwischen den Stationen entspricht proportional der wirklichen Distanz. Der Neigungswinkel der vertikalen Linien zeigt die Schnelligkeit der Züge (je steiler, desto schneller). Ein weniger starker Raster hätte noch zur besseren Lesbarkeit beigetragen. E.J. Marey. La Méthode graphique, Paris 1885.*

▲ *Horaire de chemin de fer, trajet Paris-Lyon. Lignes horizontales: heures d'arrivée et de départ, temps d'arrêt dans les gares. L'écart entre les gares correspond proportionnellement aux distances sur le terrain. L'angle d'inclinaison des lignes verticales indique la vitesse des trains (qui augmente avec la verticalité). Une trame moins forte aurait accru la lisibilité de l'ensemble. Extrait de l'ouvrage d'E.J. Marey, La Méthode graphique, Paris 1885.*

■ *Tantric diagram of kundalini Yoga. Yogis worship the the Hindu supreme goddess Shakti which lies dormant within the body as a coiled serpent (kundalini) and must be aroused to reach liberation. Collection of Dr. Frank R. Reiter, Berlin.*

● *Tantrishces Diagramm des Kundalini Yoga. Die hier verkörperte Schakti wird vom weiblichen Prinzip Prakriti repräsentiert das im Hindu-Tantrismus die kinetische Energie bedeutet. Sammlung Dr. Frank R. Reiter, Berlin.*

▲ *Diagramme tantrique du Kundalini Yoga. La Chakti incarnée ici est représentée par le principe féminin de la Prakriti qui signifie l'énergie cinétique dans le tantrisme hindou. Collection du Dr Frank R. Reiter, Berlin.*

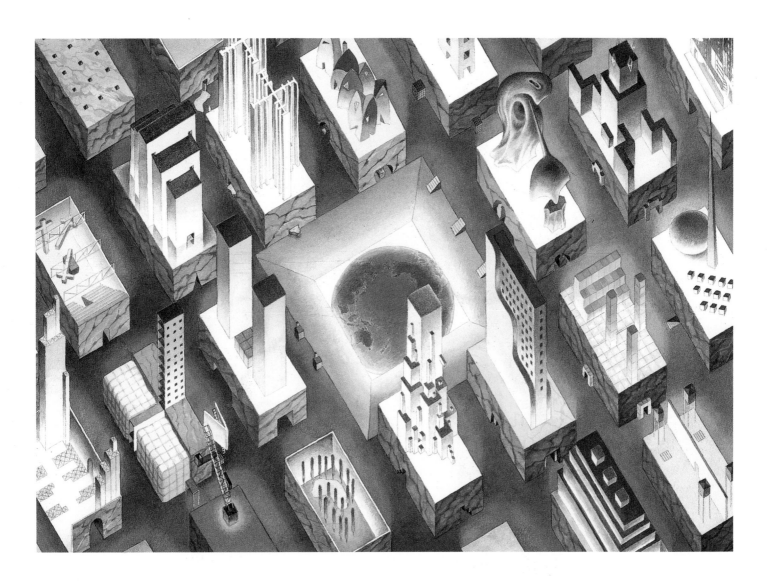

■ *The modern "Professor's Dream"–a Utopian version of the "City with the Imprisoned Globe." By Rem Koolhaas, The Office of Metropolitan Architecture, Rotterdam.*
● *Der moderne «Traum des Professors», eine utopische Vision der «Stadt mit dem gefangen Globus». Rem Koolhaas, The Office of Metropolitan Architecture, Rotterdam.*
▲ *La version moderne du «rêve du professuer», une vision utopique de la «ville au globe captif». Rem Koolhaas, The Office of Metropolitan Architecture, Rotterdam.*

STATISTICAL AND COMPARATIVE

STATISTIKEN UND VERGLEICHE

STATISTIQUES COMPARATIVES

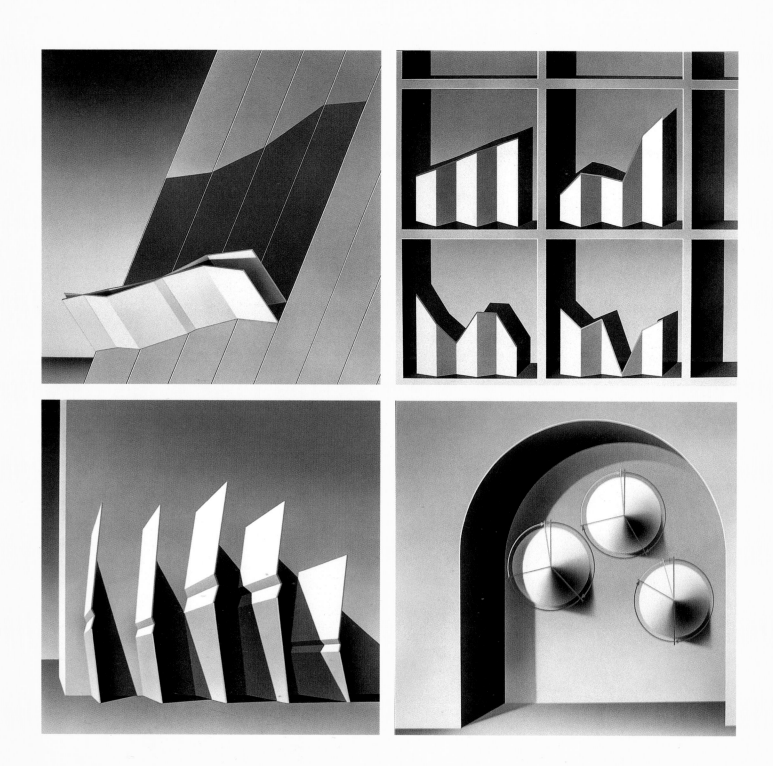

(*PRECEDING SPREAD AND THIS SPREAD*) **WALTER PEPPERLE** *DG HYP*

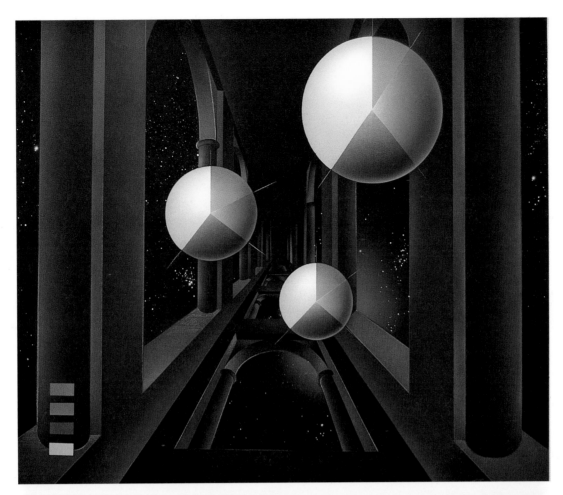

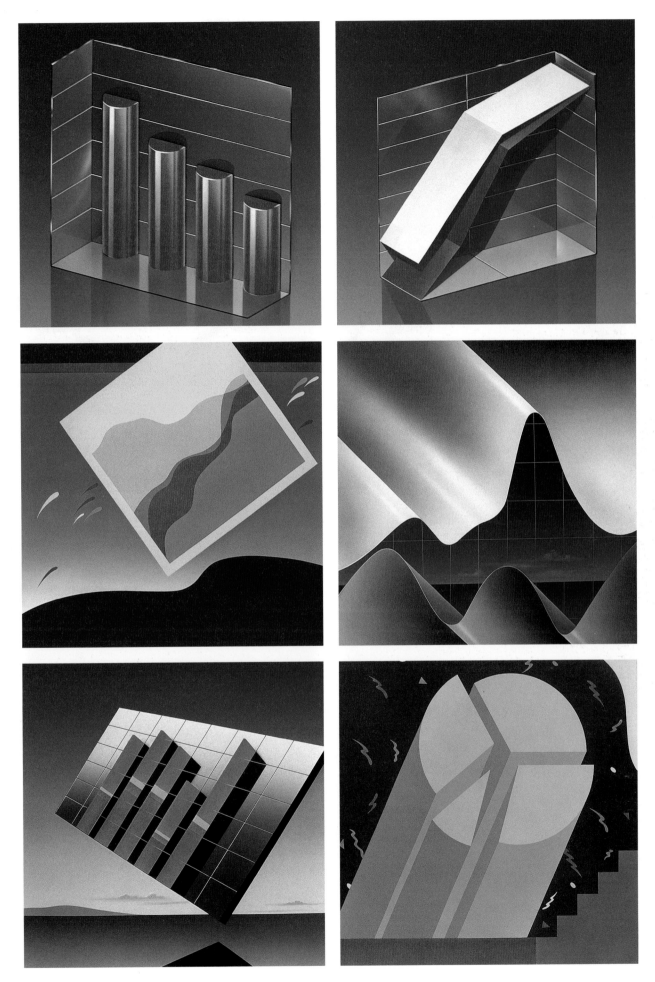

*(This Spread)* **WALTER PEPPERLE** *DG HYP*

1 9     1 9 9 3     9 4

ONE WOMAN 750
EMPLOYEES

NET INCOME

1,451

3,699

4,177

4,077

FIRST QUARTER

SECOND QUARTER

THIRD QUARTER

FOURTH QUARTER

*(THIS SPREAD)* **TOLLESON DESIGN** *Fox River Paper*

# GROWTH

(*This Spread*) **TOLLESON DESIGN** *Fox River Paper*

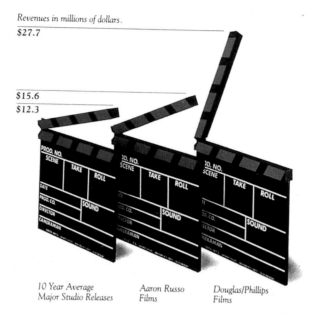

Revenues in millions of dollars.

$27.7

$15.6

$12.3

10 Year Average
Major Studio Releases

Aaron Russo
Films

Douglas/Phillips
Films

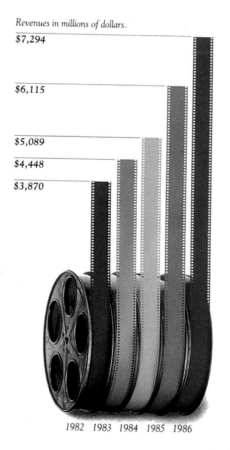

Revenues in millions of dollars.

$7,294

$6,115

$5,089

$4,448

$3,870

1982   1983   1984   1985   1986

**PHILIP GIPS** *HBO/Cinema Plus*

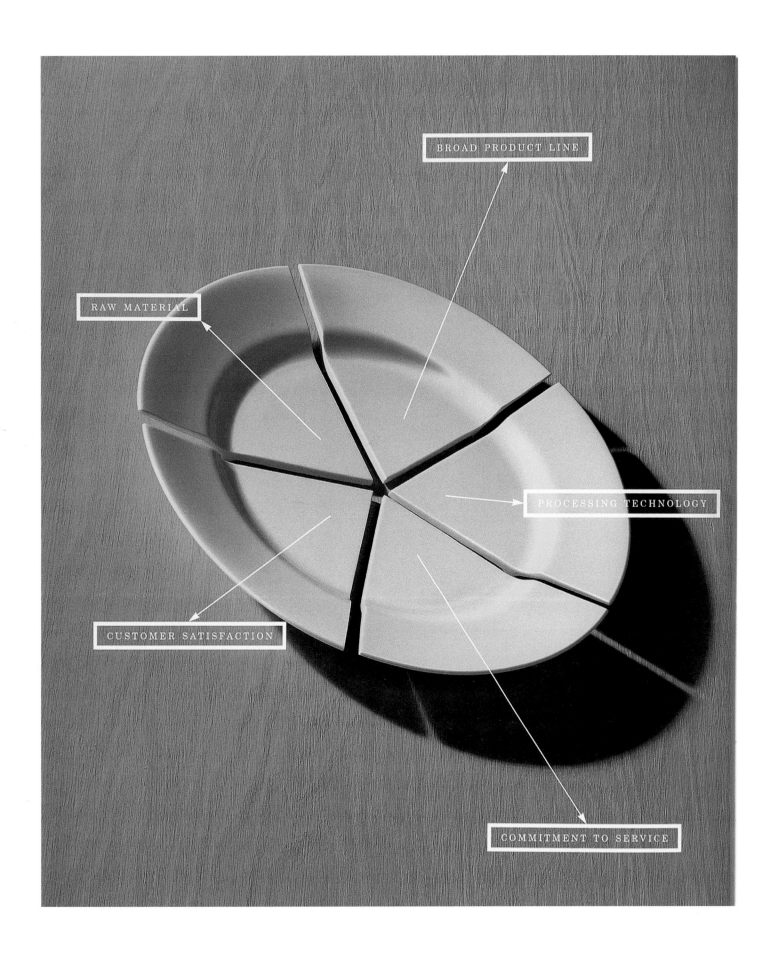

BROAD PRODUCT LINE

RAW MATERIAL

PROCESSING TECHNOLOGY

CUSTOMER SATISFACTION

COMMITMENT TO SERVICE

VSA PARTNERS, INC. Smithfield Foods, Inc.

## NET REVENUES (IN THOUSANDS)

| 5.4 | 10.5 | 12.5 | 14.2 | 15.7 | 23.4 | 29.4 | 42.5 |
|---|---|---|---|---|---|---|---|
| FY94 Q1 | Q2 | Q3 | Q4 | FY95 Q1 | Q2 | Q3 | Q4 |

(y-axis: 45, 36, 27, 18, 9)

## REVENUES (IN THOUSANDS)

| 30.1 | 42.6 | 111.0 |
|---|---|---|
| 93 | 94 | 95 |

(y-axis: 120, 96, 72, 48, 24)

## NET INCOME (IN THOUSANDS)

| (5.4) | 3.8 | 21.2 |
|---|---|---|
| 93 | 94 | 95 |

(y-axis: 20, 15, 10, 5, 0)

## GROSS MARGIN

| 4.5 | 16.6 | 54.6 |
|---|---|---|
| 93 | 94 | 95 |

(y-axis: 55, 44, 33, 22, 11)

## INVESTMENT IN R & D

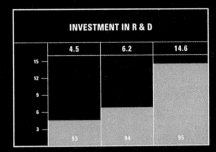

| 4.5 | 6.2 | 14.6 |
|---|---|---|
| 93 | 94 | 95 |

(y-axis: 15, 12, 9, 6, 3)

## NET INCOME (IN THOUSANDS)

| (.9) | .9 | 2.1 | 1.7 | 2.1 | 4.3 | 5.6 | 9.3 |
|---|---|---|---|---|---|---|---|
| FY94 Q1 | Q2 | Q3 | Q4 | FY95 Q1 | Q2 | Q3 | Q4 |

(y-axis: 10, 8, 6, 4, 2, 0)

PRODUCTION

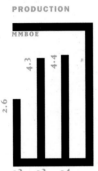

MMBOE

2.6  4.3  4.4

92  93  94

EBITDA

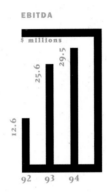

$ millions

12.6  25.6  29.5

92  93  94

OPERATING
CASH FLOW

$ millions

8.8  16.8  16.9

92  93  94

DOWNSTREAM
GROSS PROFIT

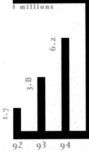

$ millions

1.7  3.8  6.2

92  93  94

UPSTREAM G&A

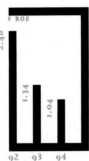

$ BOE

2.48  1.34  1.04

92  93  94

PRODUCTION
EXPENSE

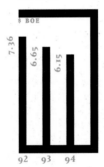

$ BOE

7.36  6.65  6.15

92  93  94

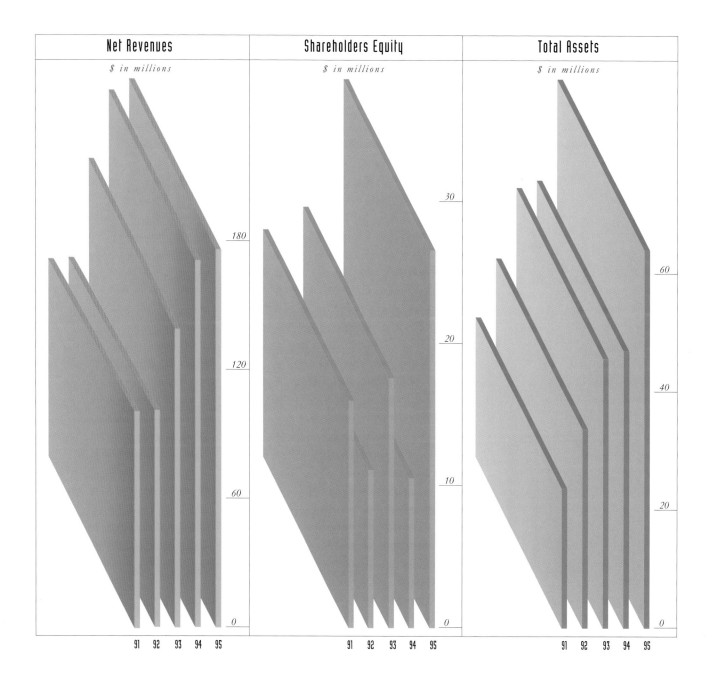

| Net Revenues | Shareholders Equity | Total Assets |
| --- | --- | --- |
| $ in millions | $ in millions | $ in millions |

$446

$378

$100

$100

$100

Dow Jon
Averag
1984

Dow Jones
Average
1994

S&P 5(
1984

S&P 500
1994

1984

1994

Coca-Cola

Coca-Col

**TOR PETTERSEN & PARTNERS LTD.** *RMC Group Services Ltd.*

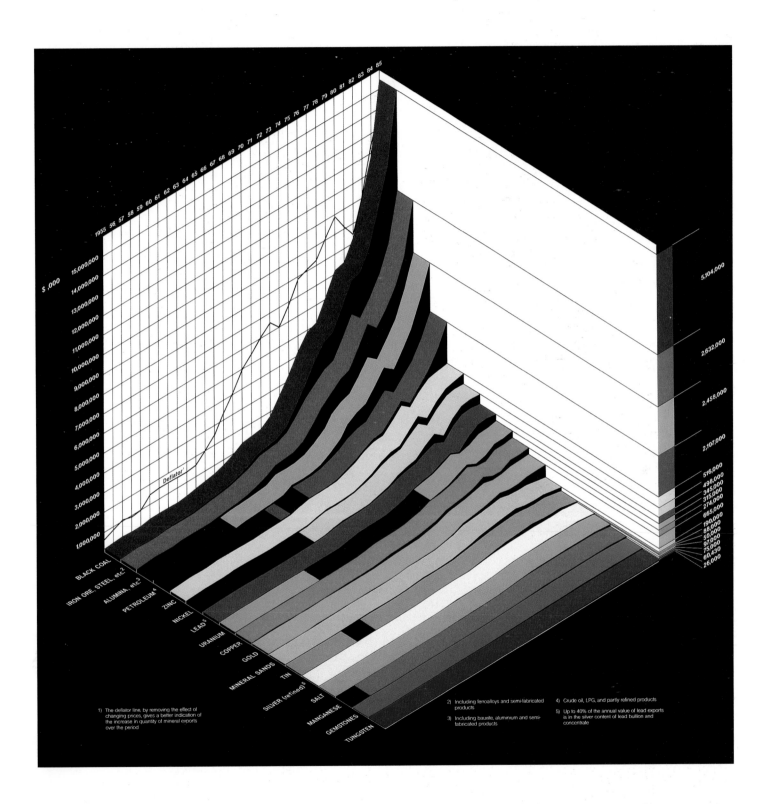

1) The deflator line, by removing the effect of changing prices, gives a better indication of the increase in quantity of mineral exports over the period

2) Including ferroalloys and semi-fabricated products

3) Including bauxite, aluminium and semi-fabricated products

4) Crude oil, LPG, and partly refined products

5) Up to 40% of the annual value of lead exports is in the silver content of lead bullion and concentrate

**CHRISTIAN PREUSCHL-HALDENBURG** *National Library of Australia*

*10 Year Historical Data*

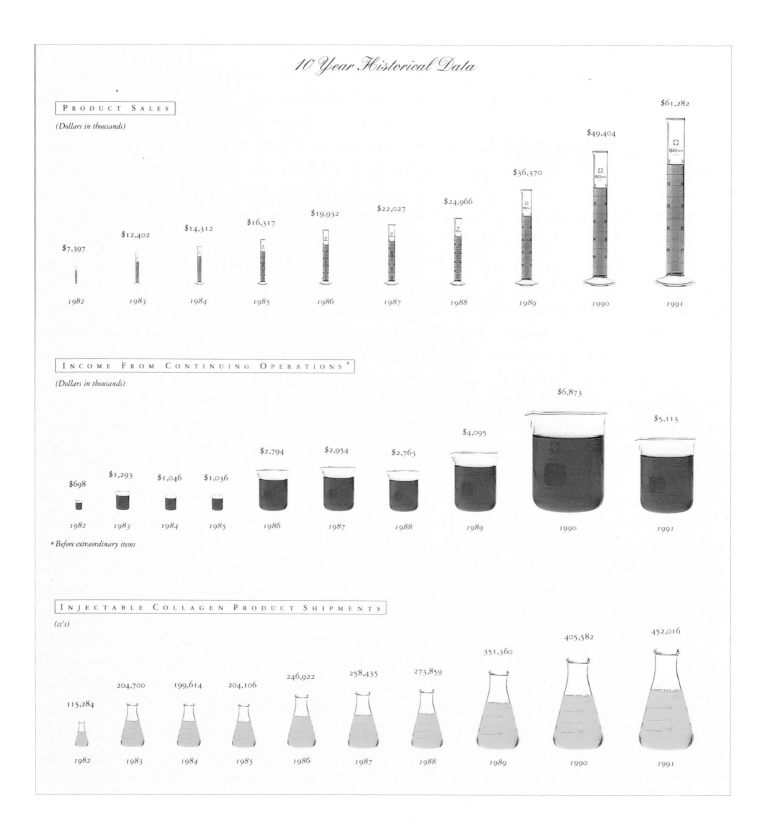

PRODUCT SALES
*(Dollars in thousands)*

$7,397 1982 | $12,402 1983 | $14,312 1984 | $16,317 1985 | $19,932 1986 | $22,027 1987 | $24,966 1988 | $36,370 1989 | $49,404 1990 | $61,282 1991

INCOME FROM CONTINUING OPERATIONS*
*(Dollars in thousands)*

$698 1982 | $1,293 1983 | $1,046 1984 | $1,036 1985 | $2,794 1986 | $2,954 1987 | $2,763 1988 | $4,095 1989 | $6,873 1990 | $5,113 1991

*Before extraordinary items

INJECTABLE COLLAGEN PRODUCT SHIPMENTS
*(cc's)*

115,284 1982 | 204,700 1983 | 199,614 1984 | 204,106 1985 | 246,922 1986 | 258,435 1987 | 273,859 1988 | 351,360 1989 | 405,582 1990 | 452,016 1991

## Research and Development

*Collagen Corporation continuing operations R&D as a percent of revenues*
*---Industry R&D as a percent of revenues (average)**

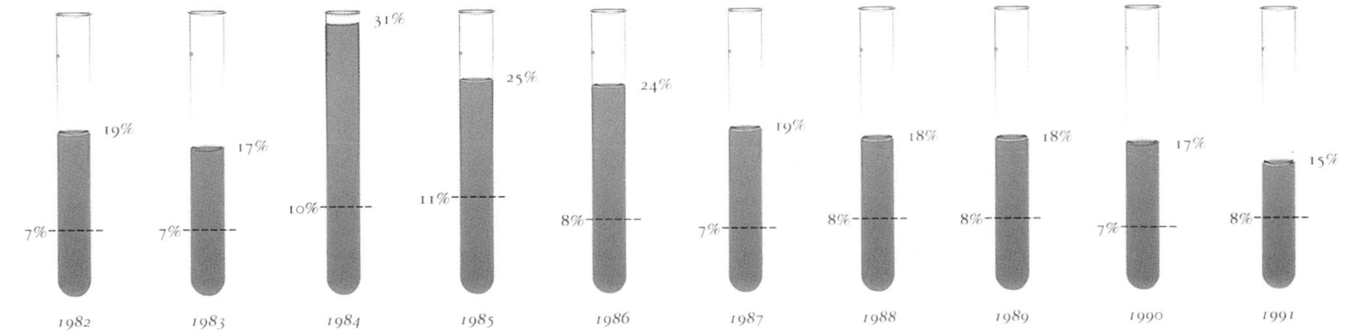
19%
7%
1982
17%
7%
1983
31%
10%
1984
25%
11%
1985
24%
8%
1986
19%
7%
1987
18%
8%
1988
18%
8%
1989
17%
7%
1990
15%
8%
1991

** Industry as a percent of revenues is based upon eight medical device companies.*

## Closing Stock Price Range

*(Dollars)*

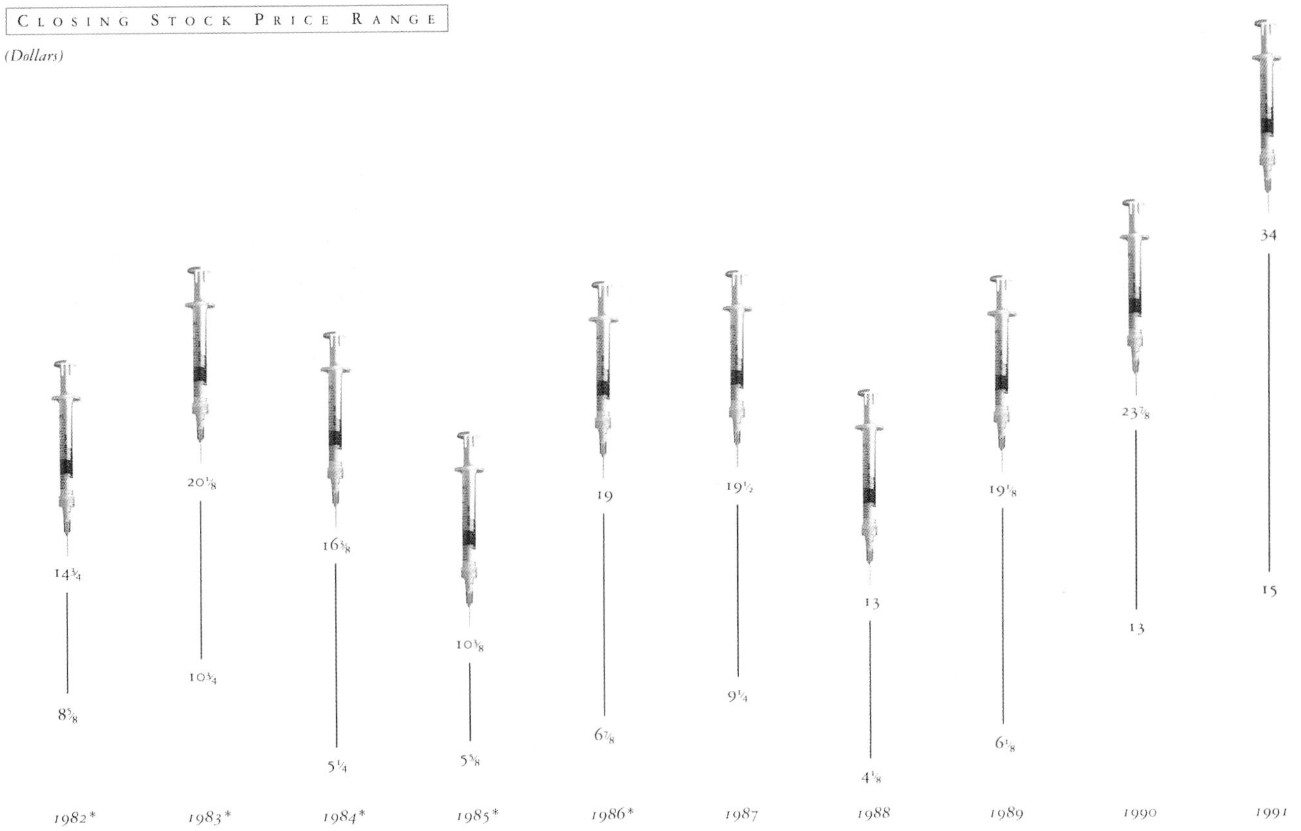
14 3/4
8 5/8
1982*
20 1/8
10 3/4
1983*
16 3/8
5 1/4
1984*
10 3/8
5 5/8
1985*
19
6 7/8
1986*
19 1/2
9 1/4
1987
13
4 1/8
1988
19 1/8
6 1/8
1989
23 7/8
13
1990
34
15
1991

**Reflects a July 1986 3-for-2 stock split.*

*(This Spread)* **GEE + CHUNG DESIGN** *Collagen Corporation*

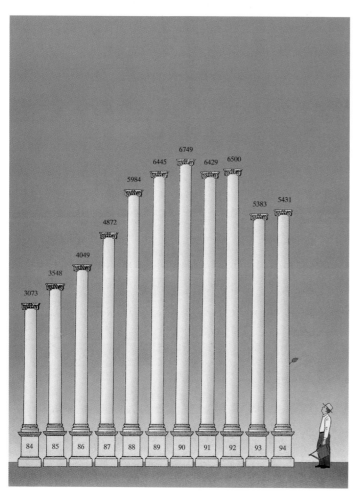

*(This Spread)* **KPMG NATIONAL MARKETING DESIGN GROUP** *KPMG*

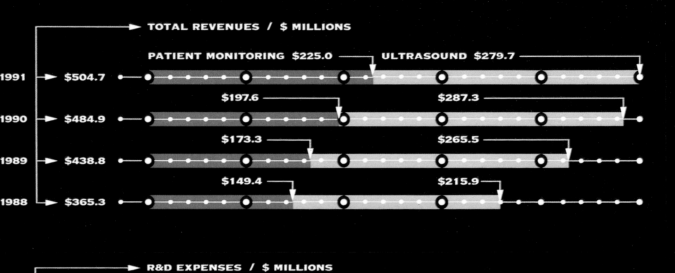

**TOTAL REVENUES / $ MILLIONS**

PATIENT MONITORING $225.0 —— ULTRASOUND $279.7 ——

1991 → $504.7

$197.6 ——— $287.3 ———
1990 → $484.9

$173.3 ——— $265.5 ———
1989 → $438.8

$149.4 ——— $215.9 ———
1988 → $365.3

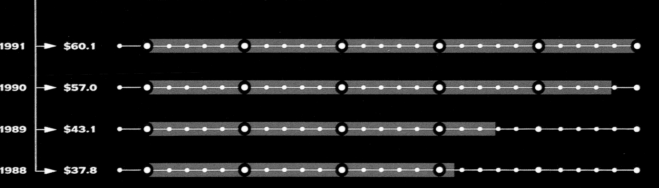

**R&D EXPENSES / $ MILLIONS**

1991 → $60.1

1990 → $57.0

1989 → $43.1

1988 → $37.8

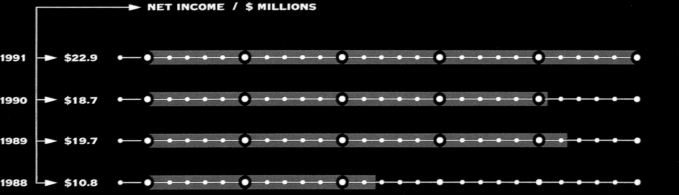

**NET INCOME / $ MILLIONS**

1991 → $22.9

1990 → $18.7

1989 → $19.7

1988 → $10.8

**ACTIVE CUSTOMER BASE**

163,000 · 199,000 · 233,000 · 260,000 · 311,000

1988 1989 1990 1991 1992

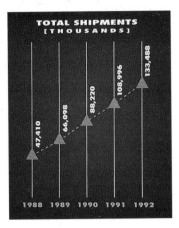

**TOTAL SHIPMENTS** [THOUSANDS]

47,410 · 66,098 · 88,220 · 108,996 · 133,488

1988 1989 1990 1991 1992

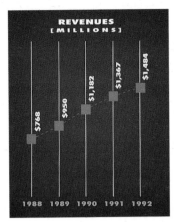

**REVENUES** [MILLIONS]

$768 · $950 · $1,182 · $1,367 · $1,484

1988 1989 1990 1991 1992

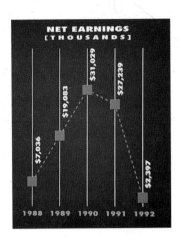

**NET EARNINGS** [THOUSANDS]

$7,036 · $19,083 · $31,029 · $27,239 · $2,397

1988 1989 1990 1991 1992

**Présentation** *Que pensez-vous de la qualité et de la présentation du numéro 0 d'Alliage ?*

▼ *sans réponse*   ▼ *très bon*   ▼ *bon*   ▼ *insuffisant*   ▼ *très insuffisant*

en %

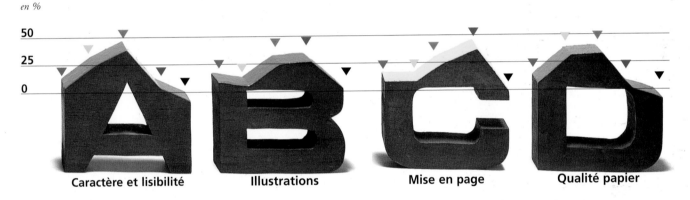

50
25
0

Caractère et lisibilité          Illustrations          Mise en page          Qualité papier

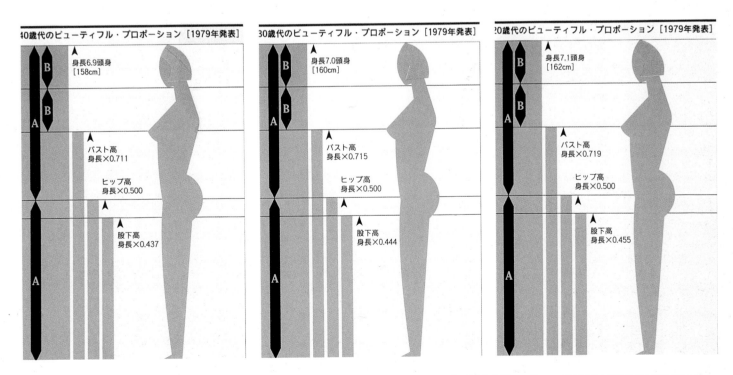

*(Top)* **HORNALL ANDERSON DESIGN WORKS, INC.** *Airborne Express* ■ *(Middle)* **DESIGN DEPT.** *Synthélabo/Alliage* ■ *(Bottom)* **BOLTS & NUTS STUDIO** *Wacoal*

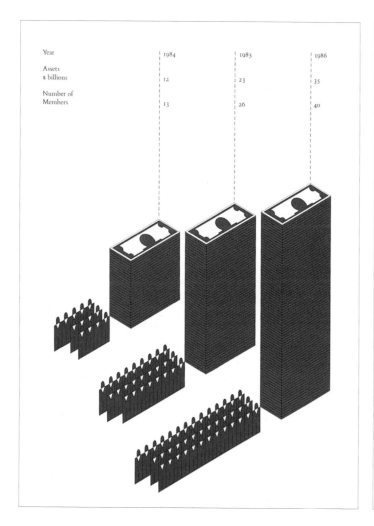

| Year | 1984 | 1985 | 1986 |
|---|---|---|---|
| Assets $ billions | 12 | 23 | 35 |
| Number of Members | 13 | 26 | 40 |

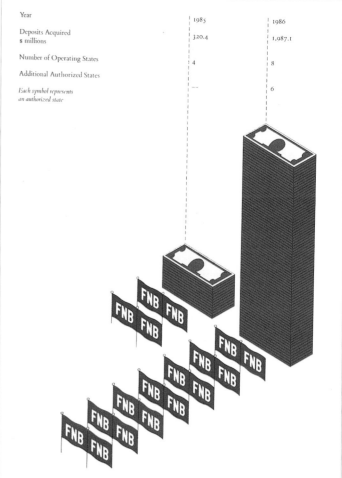

| Year | 1985 | 1986 |
|---|---|---|
| Deposits Acquired $ millions | 320.4 | 1,987.1 |
| Number of Operating States | 4 | 8 |
| Additional Authorized States | -- | 6 |

*Each symbol represents an authorized state*

**EMMETT MORAVA** *First Nationwide Financial Corp.*

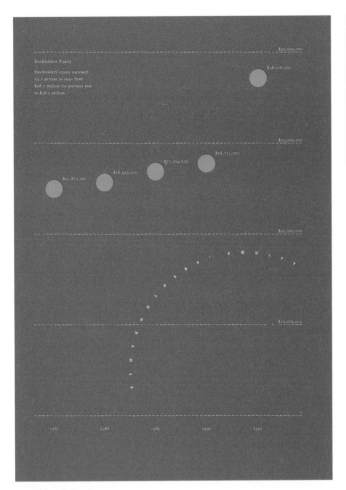

**Stockholders' Equity**

Stockholders' equity increased
53.1 percent in 1991 from
$28.7 million the previous year
to $38.2 million.

$40,000,000

$38,216,000

$30,000,000

$28,711,000

$25,872,000    $26,523,000    $27,754,000

$20,000,000

STOCKHOLDERS' EQUITY

$10,000,000

0

1987        1988        1989        1990        1991

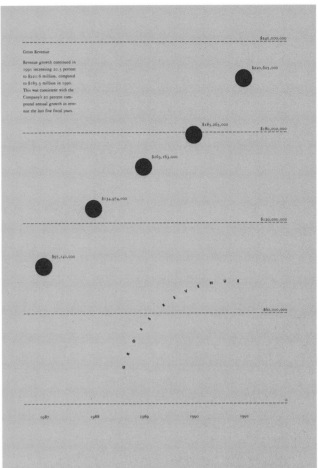

**Gross Revenue**

Revenue growth continued in
1991 increasing 20.3 percent
to $220.6 million, compared
to $183.3 million in 1990.
This was consistent with the
Company's 20 percent com-
pound annual growth in revenue the last five fiscal years.

$240,000,000

$220,625,000

$183,363,000

$180,000,000

$163,163,000

$134,974,000

$120,000,000

$97,140,000

GROSS REVENUE

$60,000,000

0

1987        1988        1989        1990        1991

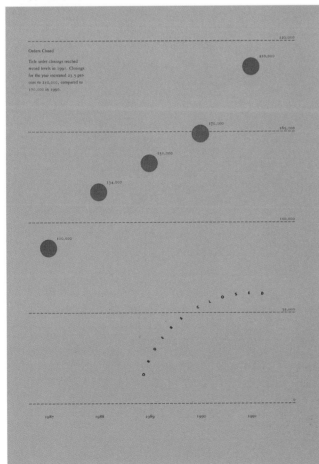

**Orders Closed**

Title order closings reached
record levels in 1991. Closings
for the year increased 23.5 percent to 210,000, compared to
170,000 in 1990.

230,000

210,000

170,000        165,000

151,000

134,000

110,000

100,000

ORDERS CLOSED

55,000

0

1987        1988        1989        1990        1991

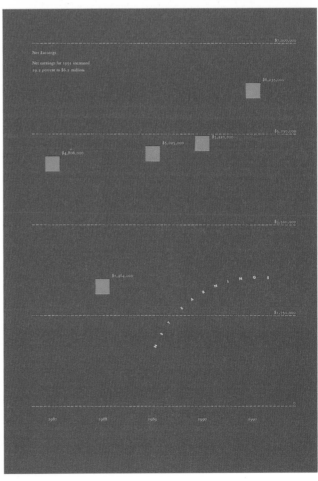

**Net Earnings**

Net earnings for 1991 increased
19.2 percent to $6.2 million.

$7,000,000

$6,255,000

$5,250,000

$5,025,000    $5,220,000

$4,806,000

$3,500,000

$3,464,000

NET EARNINGS

$1,750,000

0

1987        1988        1989        1990        1991

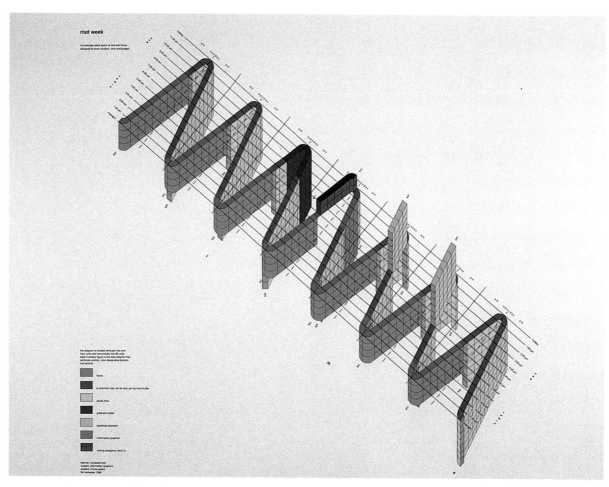

## A meaty potential

The market for prepared petfood in continental Europe is currently growing at a rate of 3% per annum. This rate when set against the overall size of the market represents an exciting opportunity for Spillers Petfoods. As a clear number two with a strong portfolio of major brands and a highly developed distribution network, Spillers Petfoods is well placed to capitalise on the growth potential of the European petfood markets.

*(TOP)* **RONNIE PETERS** *Student project for Rhode Island School of Design* ■ *(BOTTOM)* **TOR PETTERSEN & PARTNERS LTD.** *Lucas Industries Plc.*

# The United States budget deficit

In millions of dollars

■ Denotes the difference between receipts and outlays

■ Denotes the budget deficit

■ Denotes the years where the receipts exceeded outlays

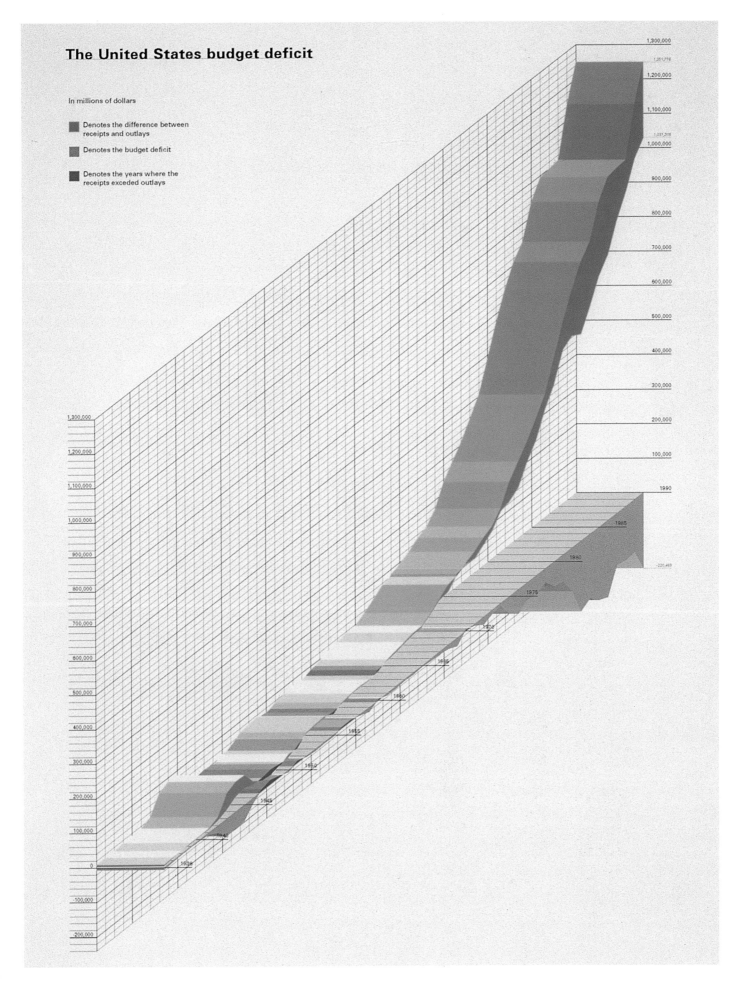

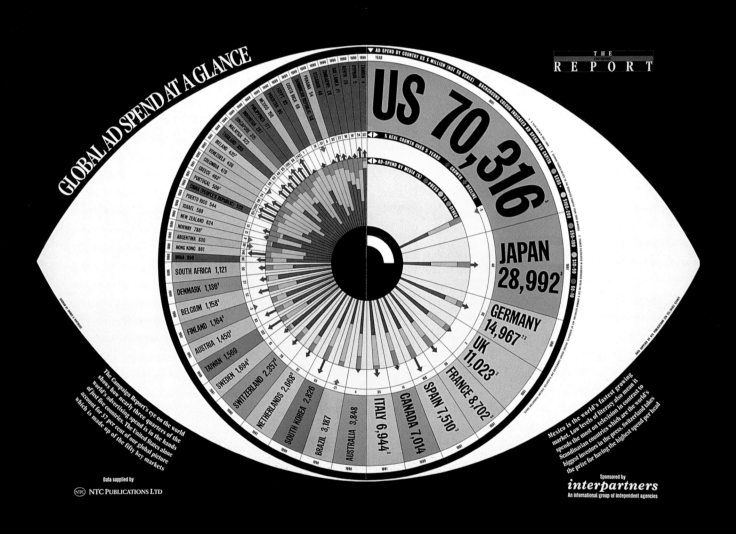

GLOBAL AD SPEND AT A GLANCE

THE
REPORT

The Campaign Report's eye on the world shows how nearly three quarters of the world's advertising spend is in the hands of just five countries. The United States alone accounts for 37 per cent of our global picture which is made up of the fifty key markets

Mexico is the world's fastest growing market. Low levels of literacy also mean it spends the most on television in contrast to Scandinavian countries which are the world's biggest investors in the press. Switzerland takes the prize for having the highest spend per head

Data supplied by
NTC PUBLICATIONS LTD

Sponsored by
interpartners
An international group of independent agencies

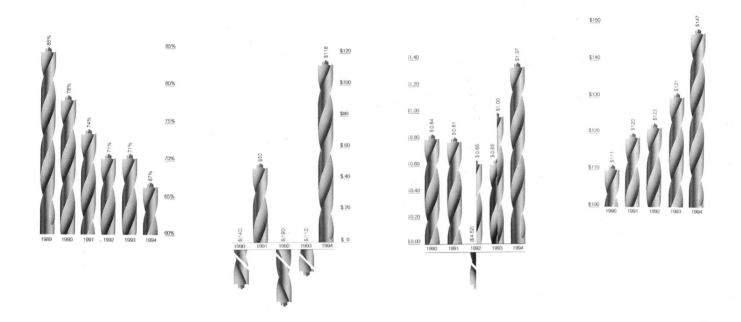

**COOK + SHANOSKY ASSOCIATES, INC.** *Black & Decker Corporation*

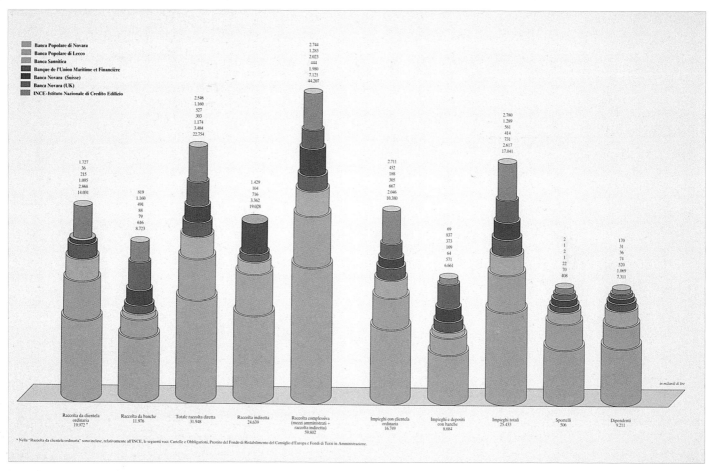

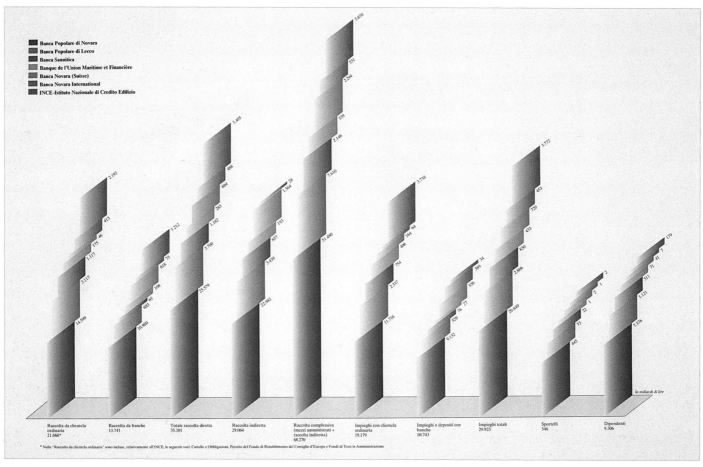

TANGRAM STRATEGIC DESIGN *Banco Popolare di Novara*

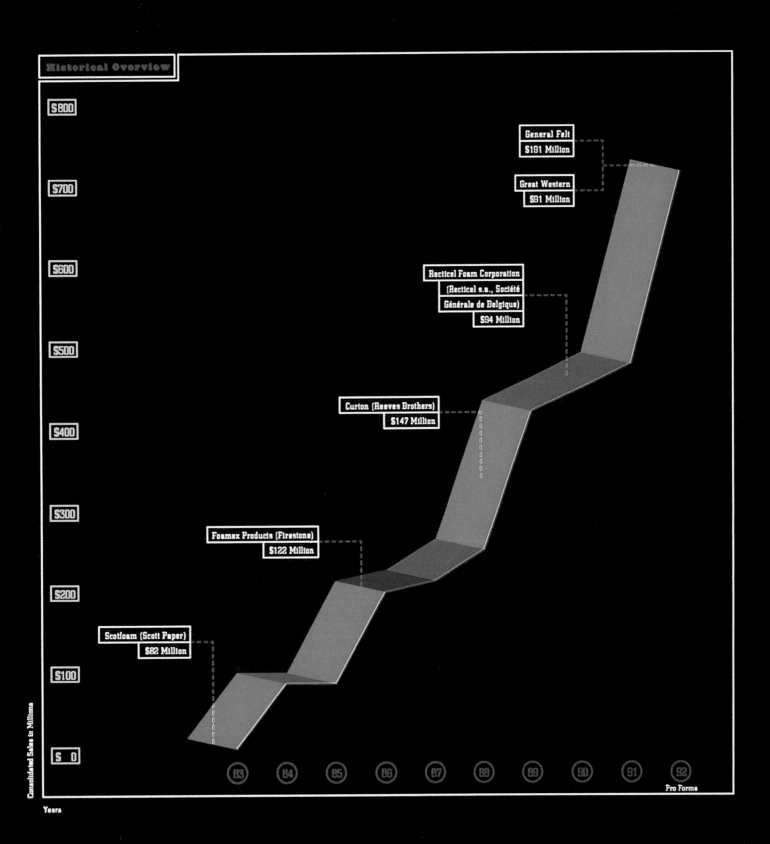

Historical Overview

Consolidated Sales in Millions

$800

$700

$600

$500

$400

$300

$200

$100

$ 0

Years

General Felt
$191 Million

Great Western
$91 Million

Recticel Foam Corporation
(Recticel s.a., Société
Générale de Belgique)
$94 Million

Curton (Reeves Brothers)
$147 Million

Foamex Products (Firestone)
$122 Million

Scotfoam (Scott Paper)
$82 Million

83   84   85   86   87   88   89   90   91   92

Pro Forma

OUR THIN-FILM MEDIA FACTORIES IN THE U.S. AND JAPAN PRODUCED RECORD FINANCIAL RESULTS, REFLECTING UNPRECEDENTED DEMAND, FAVORABLE PRODUCT MIX SHIFTS TOWARD HIGHER DENSITY AND SMALLER DIAMETER DISKS, AND THE SUCCESSFUL EXECUTION OF CONTINUOUS IMPROVEMENT PROGRAMS IN MANUFACTURING.

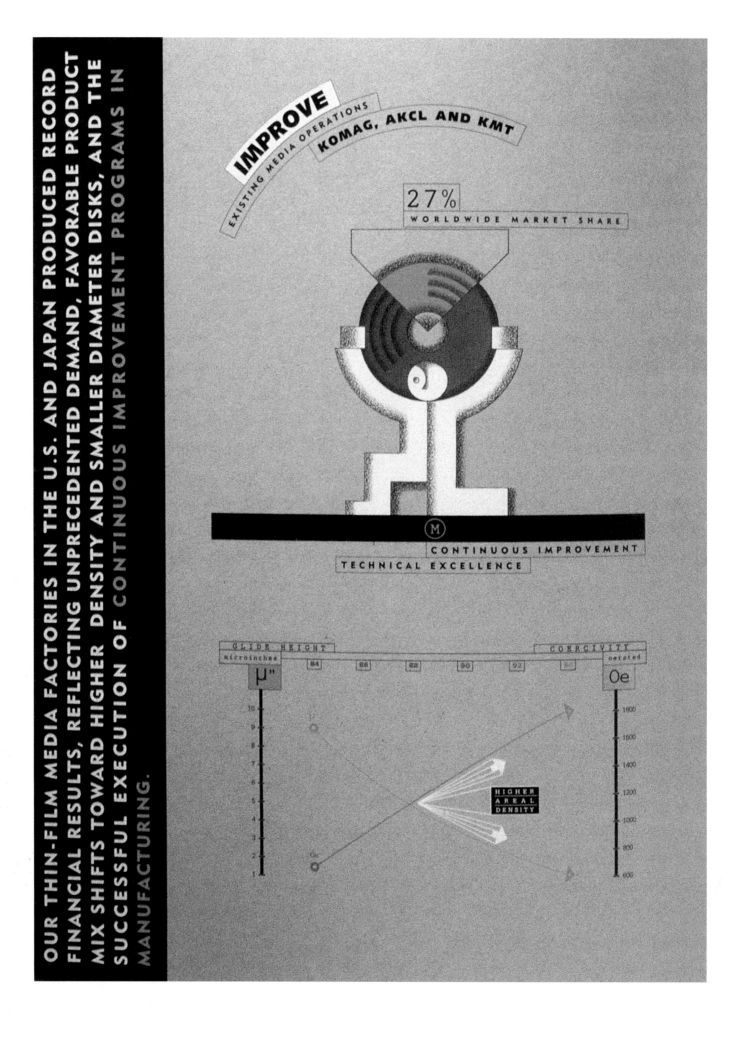

IMPROVE

EXISTING MEDIA OPERATIONS

KOMAG, AKCL AND KMT

27%

WORLDWIDE MARKET SHARE

CONTINUOUS IMPROVEMENT

TECHNICAL EXCELLENCE

GLIDE HEIGHT

microinches

COERCIVITY

oersted

HIGHER AREAL DENSITY

THIN-FILM HEADS PROVIDE A KEY ENABLING TECHNOLOGY FOR THE ADVANCEMENT OF DISK DRIVE RECORDING DENSITIES. AS THE ONLY INDEPENDENT VOLUME SUPPLIER OF BOTH THIN-FILM HEADS AND MEDIA, KOMAG IS IN A UNIQUE POSITION TO UNDERSTAND, CONTROL AND OPTIMIZE BOTH SIDES OF THE CRITICAL HEAD-DISK INTERFACE.

DIVERSIFY
INTO HIGH-GROWTH THIN-FILM HEAD MARKET
DASTEK, INC.

MAGNETORESISTIVE CODEVELOPMENT
HIGHER AREAL DENSITIES

OUR NEW MALAYSIAN FACTORY PROVIDES US WITH THE OPPORTUNITY TO FURTHER REDUCE PRODUCTION COSTS. THIS STRATEGIC EXPANSION GIVES US AN ADDITIONAL ADVANTAGE OVER OUR JAPANESE COMPETITORS AND PROVIDES A LOWER COST ALTERNATIVE FOR OUR DISK DRIVE CUSTOMERS WITH VERTICAL MANUFACTURING STRATEGIES.

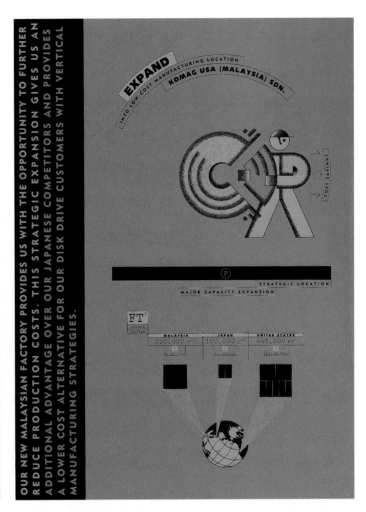

EXPAND
INTO LOW-COST MANUFACTURING LOCATION
KOMAG USA (MALAYSIA) SDN.

STRATEGIC LOCATION
MAJOR CAPACITY EXPANSION

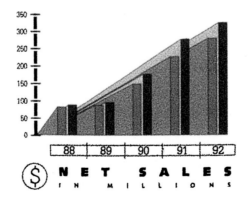

NET SALES
IN MILLIONS

*(THIS SPREAD)* **TOLLESON DESIGN** *Komag, Inc.*

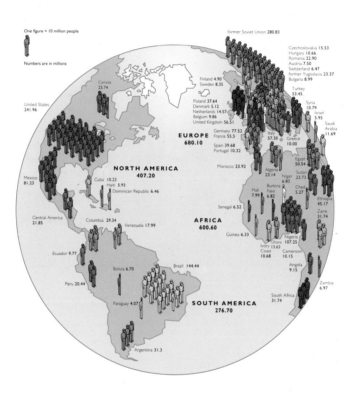

One figure = 10 million people

Numbers are in millions

former Soviet Union 280.83

Czechoslovakia 15.53
Hungary 10.66
Romania 22.90
Austria 7.50
Switzerland 6.47
former Yugoslavia 23.37
Bulgaria 8.99

Canada
25.74

Finland 4.90
Sweden 8.35

Poland 37.64
Denmark 5.12
Netherlands 14.57
Belgium 9.86
United Kingdom 56.51

Turkey
53.45

United States
241.96

EUROPE
680.10

Germany 77.52
France 55.5

Italy
57.30

Greece
10.00

Syria
10.79
Israel
5.95

Saudi
Arabia
11.69

Spain 39.68
Portugal 10.32

Egypt
50.54

NORTH AMERICA
407.20

Morocco 23.92

Algeria
23.14

Sudan
23.73

Mexico
81.23

Cuba 10.23
Haiti 5.93
Dominican Republic 6.46

Niger
6.82

Chad
5.27

Burkina
Faso
6.82

Mali
7.99

Ethiopia
45.17

Central America
21.85

Columbia 29.34

Venezuela 17.99

Senegal 6.52

AFRICA
600.60

Guinea 6.33

Zaire
31.74

Ecuador 9.77

Nigeria
107.25

Cameroon
10.15

Ivory
Coast
10.68

Ghana
13.63

Bolivia 6.70

Brazil 144.44

Peru 20.44

Angola
9.15

Zambia
6.97

Paraguay 4.07

SOUTH AMERICA
276.70

South Africa
31.74

Argentina 31.3

PENTAGRAM DESIGN, INC. *Simpson Paper Company*

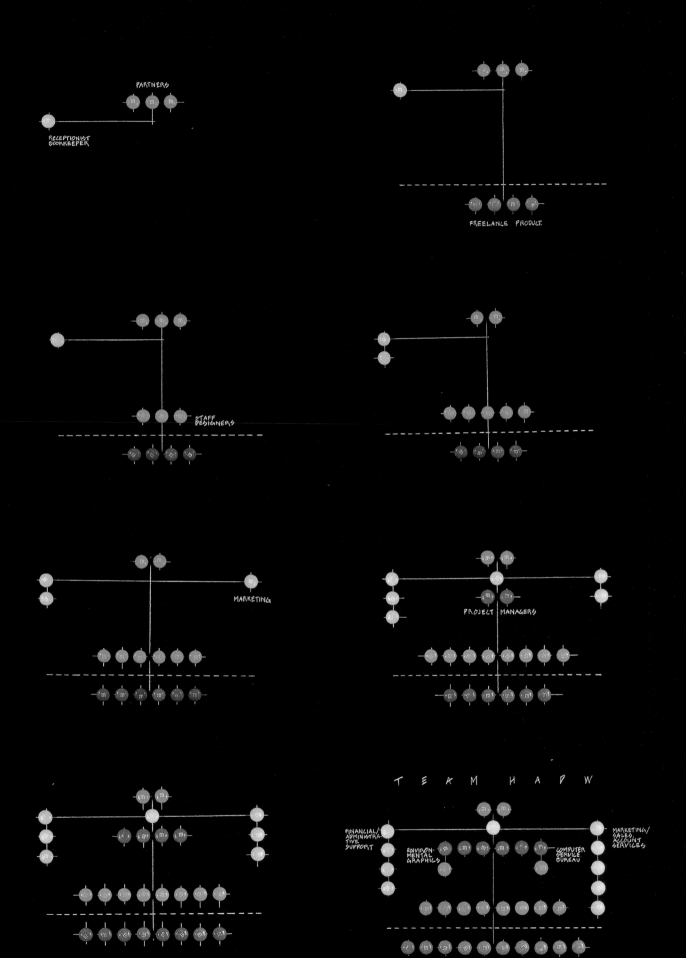

PARTNERS

RECEPTIONIST
BOOKKEEPER

FREELANCE PRODUCT.

STAFF
DESIGNERS

MARKETING

PROJECT MANAGERS

T E A M H A D W

FINANCIAL/
ADMINISTRA-
TIVE
SUPPORT

ENVIRON-
MENTAL
GRAPHICS

COMPUTER
SERVICE
BUREAU

MARKETING/
SALES,
ACCOUNT
SERVICES

**HORNALL ANDERSON DESIGN WORKS** *in-house*

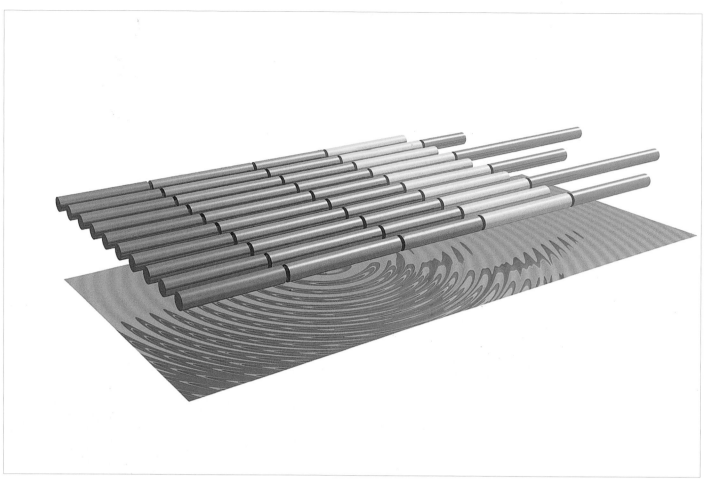

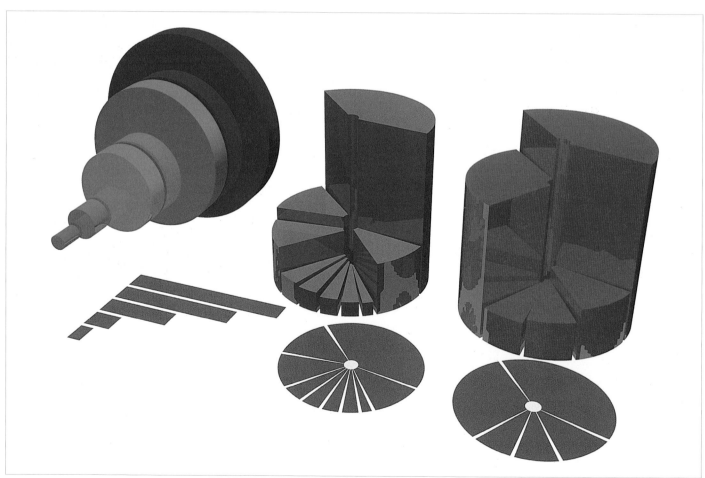

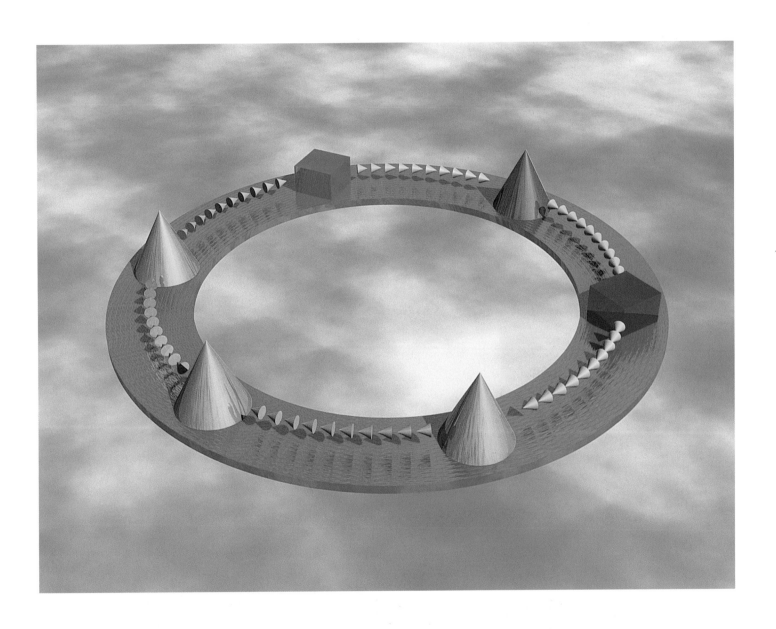

*(This Spread)* **RYUS INC.** *Canon Sales Co., Ltd.*

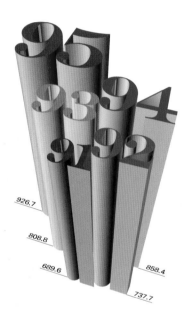

926.7
808.8
689.6
858.4
737.7

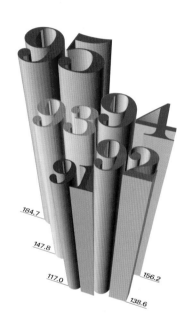

184.7
147.8
117.0
156.2
138.6

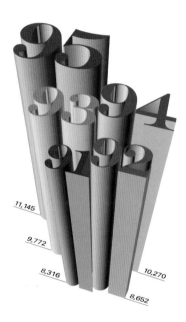

11,145
9,772
8,316
10,270
8,652

**COOK AND SHANOSKY ASSOCIATES, INC.** *Medical Inter-Insurance Exchange*

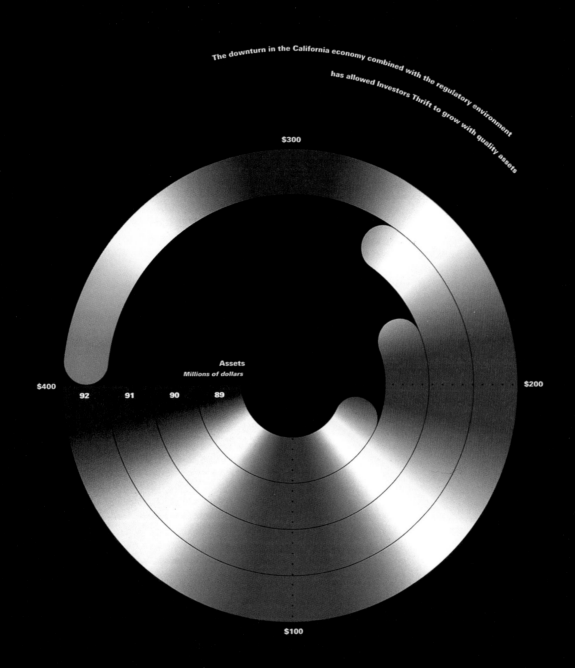

The downturn in the California economy combined with the regulatory environment has allowed Investors Thrift to grow with quality assets

$300

Assets
*Millions of dollars*

$400    92    91    90    89    $200

$100

**CARL SELTZER DESIGN OFFICE** *Fremont General*

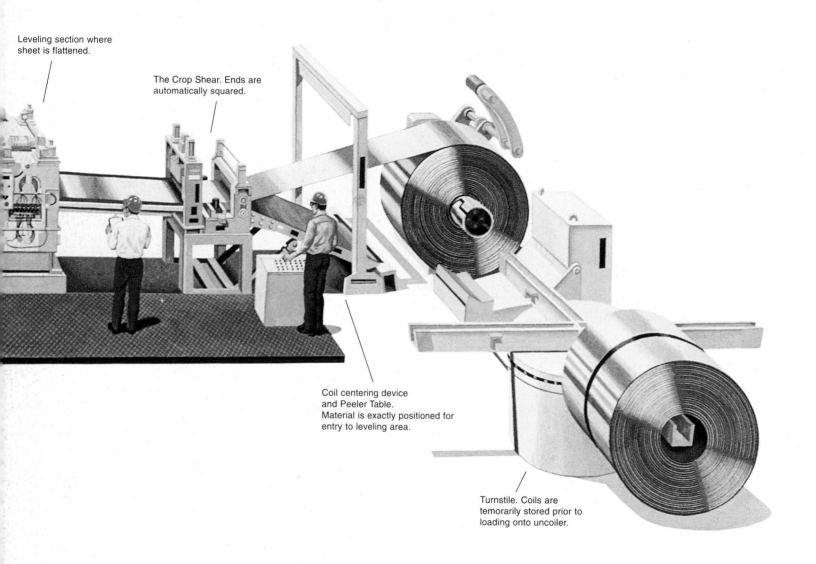

Leveling section where sheet is flattened.

The Crop Shear. Ends are automatically squared.

Coil centering device and Peeler Table. Material is exactly positioned for entry to leveling area.

Turnstile. Coils are temorarily stored prior to loading onto uncoiler.

FLOW AND ORGANIZATIONAL

ABLÄUFE UND GLIEDERUNG

ORGANIGRAMMES

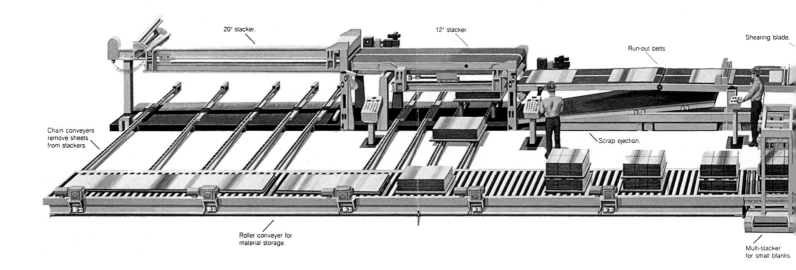

20' stacker.

12' stacker.

Shearing blade.

Run-out belts

Chain conveyers
remove sheets
from stackers.

Scrap ejection.

Roller conveyer for
material storage.

Multi-stacker
for small blanks.

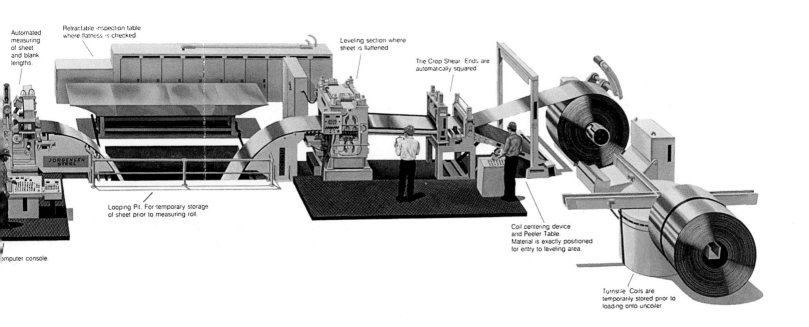

Automated measuring of sheet and blank lengths.

Retractable inspection table where flatness is checked

Leveling section where sheet is flattened

The Crop Shear. Ends are automatically squared

Looping Pit. For temporary storage of sheet prior to measuring roll.

Coil centering device and Peeler Table. Material is exactly positioned for entry to leveling area.

omputer console.

Turnstile. Coils are temporarily stored prior to loading onto uncoiler

*(PRECEDING SPREAD AND THIS SPREAD)* **WILLIAM HAINES GRAPHIC DESIGN** *Earle M. Jorgensen Corp.*

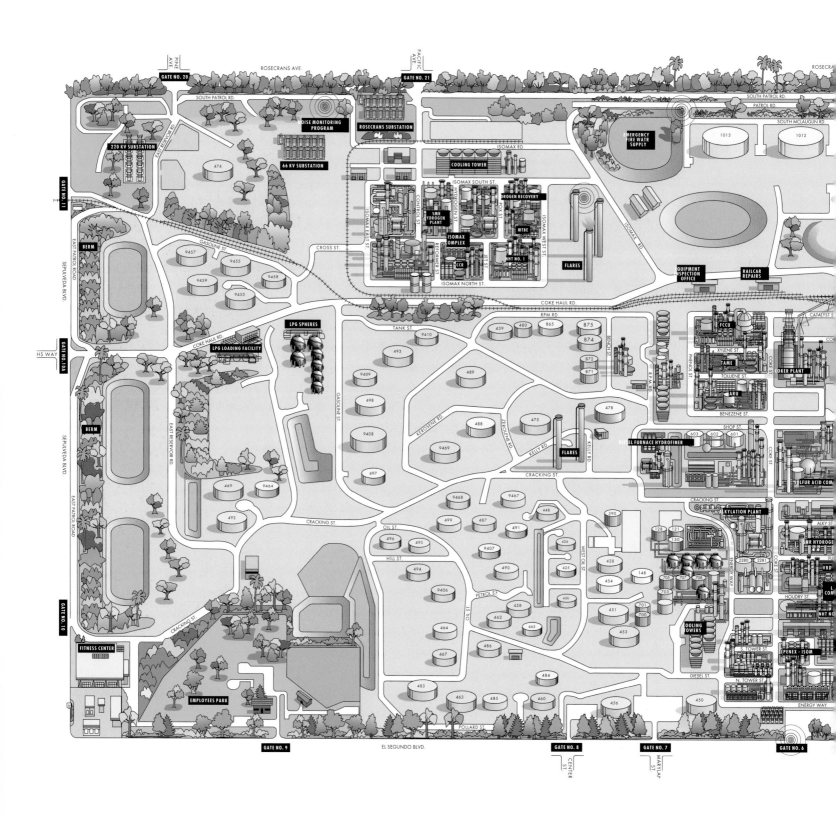

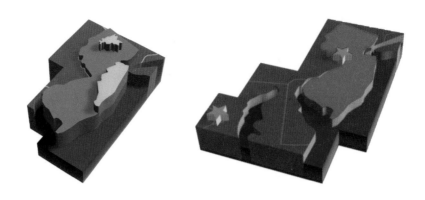

(TOP) **COOK AND SHANOSKY ASSOCIATES, INC.** *New Jersey Natural Gasses* ■ (BOTTOM) **WILLIAM HAINES GRAPHIC DESIGN** *Chevron*

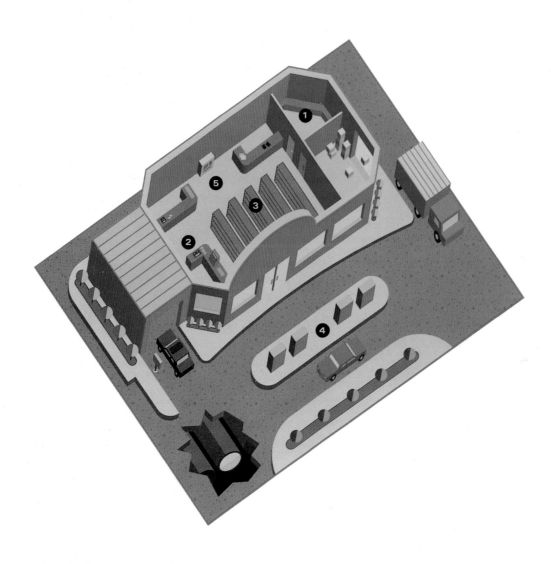

(THIS SPREAD) **EDS CORPORATE COMMUNICATIONS** EDS

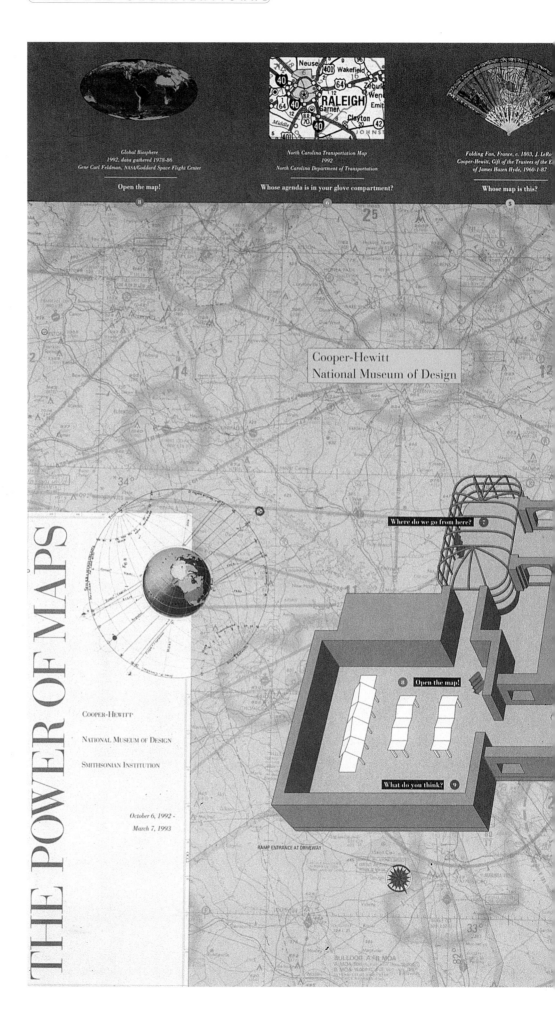

Global Biosphere
1992, data gathered 1978-86
Gene Carl Feldman, NASA/Goddard Space Flight Center

**Open the map!**

North Carolina Transportation Map
1992
North Carolina Department of Transportation

**Whose agenda is in your glove compartment?**

Folding Fan, France, c. 1803, J. LeRo
Cooper-Hewitt, Gift of the Trustees of the E
of James Hazen Hyde, 1960-1-87

**Whose map is this?**

Cooper-Hewitt
National Museum of Design

**Where do we go from here?**

**Open the map!**

**What do you think?**

RAMP ENTRANCE AT DRIVEWAY

THE POWER OF MAPS

COOPER-HEWITT

NATIONAL MUSEUM OF DESIGN

SMITHSONIAN INSTITUTION

October 6, 1992 -
March 7, 1993

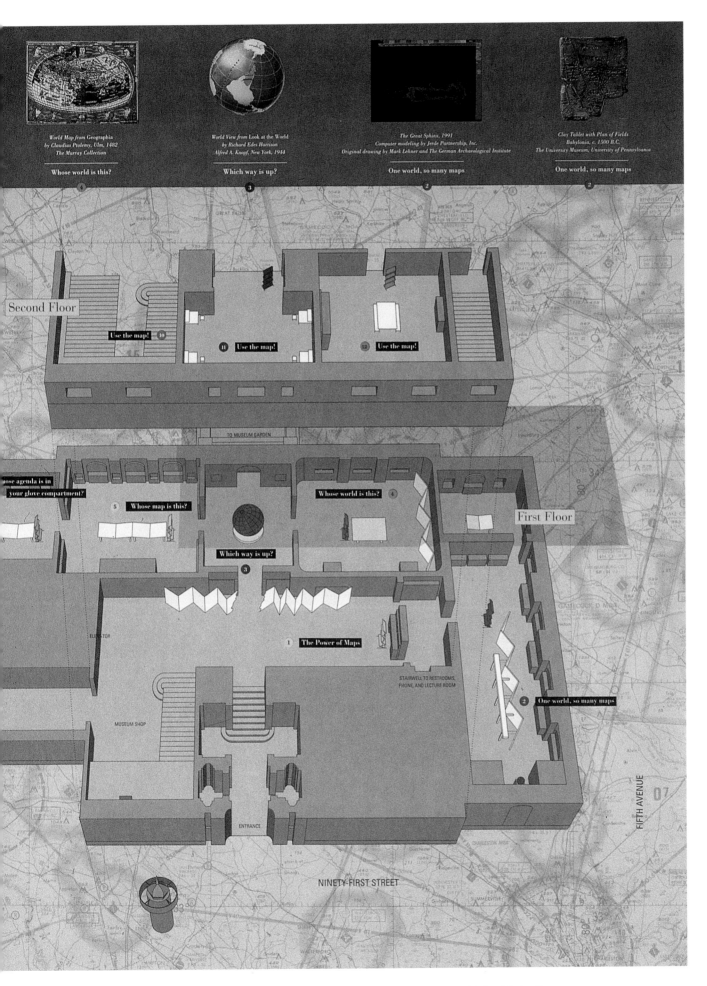

World Map from Geographia
by Claudius Ptolemy, Ulm, 1482
The Murray Collection

**Whose world is this?**

World View from Look at the World
by Richard Edes Harrison
Alfred A. Knopf, New York, 1944

**Which way is up?**

The Great Sphinx, 1991
Computer modeling by Jerde Partnership, Inc.
Original drawing by Mark Lehner and The German Archaeological Institute

**One world, so many maps**

Clay Tablet with Plan of Fields
Babylonia, c. 1500 B.C.
The University Museum, University of Pennsylvania

**One world, so many maps**

Second Floor

Use the map! 10

11 Use the map!

12 Use the map!

TO MUSEUM GARDEN

ose agenda is in
your glove compartment?

5 Whose map is this?

Whose world is this? 4

First Floor

Which way is up?

3

The Power of Maps

1

ELEVATOR

STAIRWELL TO RESTROOMS,
PHONE, AND LECTURE ROOM

One world, so many maps
2

MUSEUM SHOP

FIFTH AVENUE

07

ENTRANCE

NINETY-FIRST STREET

*(THIS SPREAD)* **PENTAGRAM DESIGN** *Cooper-Hewitt National Design Museum*

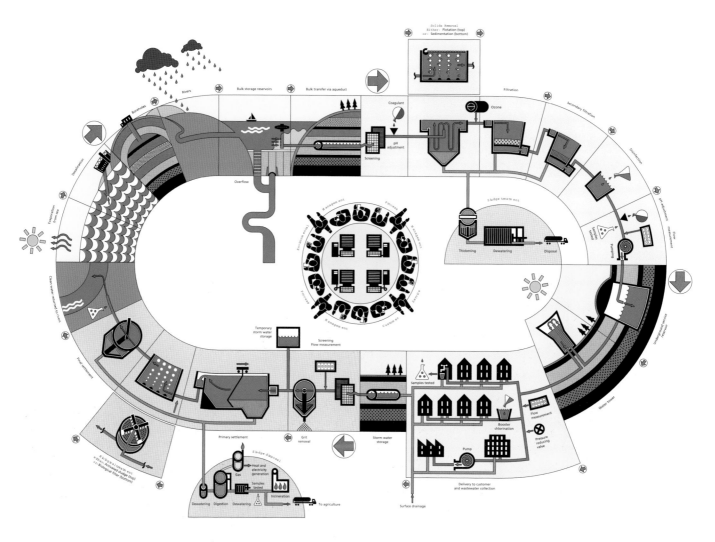

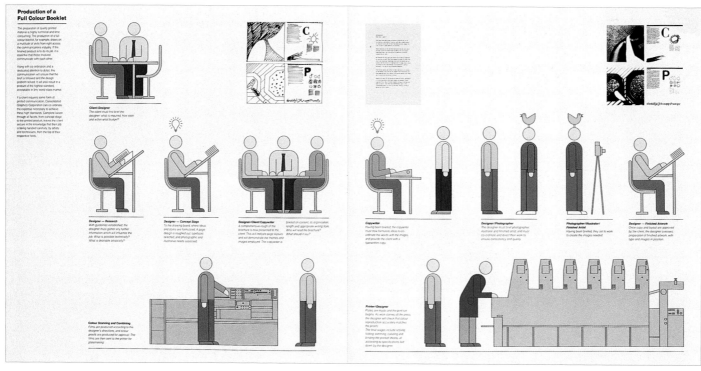

(TOP) **GRUNDY & NORTHEDGE / ADDISON DESIGN GROUP** *Northwest Water* ■ (BOTTOM) **JOHN NOWLAND DESIGN** *Consolidated Graphics Corporation*

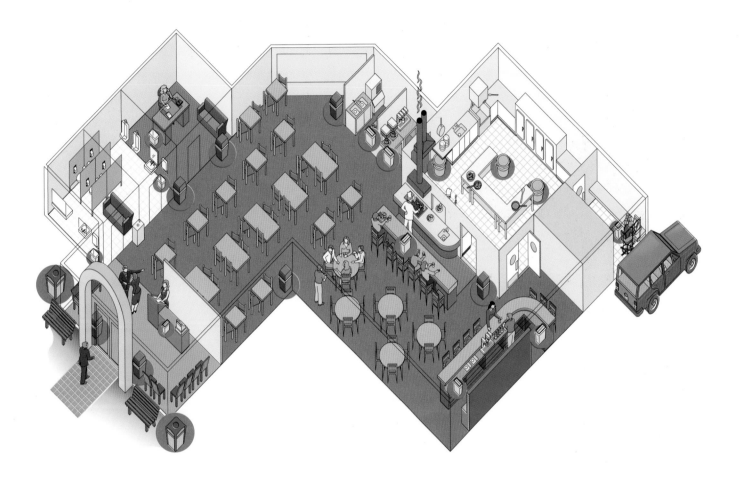

**GORDON BAILEY & ASSOCIATES, INC.** *Penneco Packaging Specialty Products*

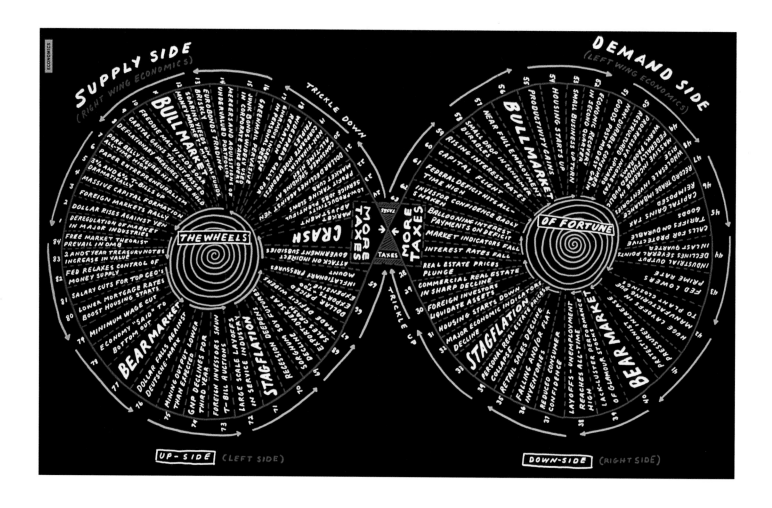

**PENTAGRAM DESIGN** *Champion International Corporation*

375,000 American children are schooled at home—31% of American voters would vote for an atheist president—Number of times George Bush recited the

34% of American school teachers plan to quit within 5 years—1/3 of American high school seniors cannot locate Latin America on a map—1 in 7 Americans have no health insurance—There are 2 dogs or cats for every American child—35 Americans have been killed by pit bulls since 1986—16% of Jewish homes have Christmas trees—87% of Americans who own running shoes don't run—200,000,000 M&Ms are sold every day in U.S.—10% of U.S. adults are opposed to sex education—1% of national scholarships are from the Miss America pageant—The median age of U.S. voters is 45—8 out of 10 presidential candidate winners were taller than their opponent—1 out of 10 bills passed by Congress in 1990 established commemorative days, weeks or months—The U.S. justice system costs $248 per capita—The total amount of NYC driver parking fines is $461,000,000—There is a 1 in 7 chance that a U.S. burglary case will be solved—5,506,720 documents are classified as secret by the U.S. government—There is a 1 in 5 chance that a U.S. working woman will earn more than her husband—6% of American gun owners are black, 88% are white—By the age of 16 the average U.S. child has seen 10,000 murders on TV—29% of U.S. teenagers worry about losing their hair—190 books were published in the 80s with the word "Terrorism" in the title—57% of Iowans say that front porch swings should be brought back—Nancy Reagan's former hairdresser charges $150 for a haircut—6% of Americans didn't like what they got for Christmas—60% of U.S. men would not have sex with Madonna if she asked—Ronald Reagan awarded a Medal of Freedom twice as often as Jimmy Carter—A video tape of Andrei Sakharov's funeral goes for $1,500—7,632,000 condoms were purchased for the armed services in 1989—The B-52 bomber has been developed or manufactured in 50 states—5,600,000 people died in armed conflict in the 80s—40,000 Americans live in communes—Mick Jagger has appeared on the cover of Rolling Stone 15 times—23 countries have been invaded since 1945—12% of the world's legislators are women—The U.S. has invaded or occupied 5 Latin American countries per year on average since 1900—57% of Texans don't consider George Bush to be a "real Texan"—96,738 acres of U.S. land is occupied by shopping malls—There is a 1 in 15 chance that a male North Dakotan is an elk—"Read My Lips" appeared in the Washington Post 135 times during the first 2 years of the Bush presidency—50% of all Americans watch television during dinner—2 of the 3 highest grossing films in the Soviet Union starred Steve Guttenberg—2,400,000 Americans play accordion—36,000,000 Americans read below the eighth grade level—Estimated waiting period for a telephone in Poland as of 1990 is 20 years—70% of Americans earning over $70,000 a year cheat on their wives—Americans spend 165 minutes of each work day earning tax dollars—The national debt will increase by $33,000 in the time it takes to read this line—The S&L bailout will cost northeastern states $41,900,000,000—Drexel Burnham Lambert spent $46,000,000 copying documents for the SEC—125 different colors were featured in the fall 1990 Tweeds catalog—It costs $23,700 to have a body mummified in Salt Lake City—2,600 triangular UFO sightings have been reported in Belgium—87% of Iowans say "it's not the heat it's the humidity"—.003% of all insecticides used in the U.S. actually reach an insect—2,632 new animals and plants have been patented since 1980—8 nuclear reactors are abandoned in ocean—1/3 of Americans don't drink—78% of Americans say they run no risk of getting AIDS—1 in 3 Americans always "feel rushed"—An average adult cries for 6 minutes—U.S. cosmetic surgeons remove 200,000 pounds of fat each year—$52,000,000,000 was spent in the U.S. on private security forces—36% of Americans say God has spoken to them—The Jane Fonda workout video cassette costs $372 in the Moscow black market—250,000 bolts of lightning strike the U.S. every day—40% of all animal species are beetles—1/3 of fourth graders say there is peer pressure to try wine coolers—Human hair grows at .00000001 miles per hour—Barbie's measurements if she were life-size are 39-23-33—20% of Americans say they would rather have a tooth pulled than take a car in for repairs—There are 7,500 astrologers in the U.S.—There are 4,960 astronomers in the U.S.—66% of Americans expect to go to Heaven—There is a 1 in 18 chance that a white, college educated, single, 35-year-old woman will marry—5,500 Americans were conceived in a test tube—Hallmark produces 105 different familial relationship cards—Americans open the refrigerator an average of 22 times per day—Spam controls 3/4 of U.S. luncheon-meat market—Portland, Oregon ranks number 1 in consumption of Grape Nuts—There is a 40% chance of rain on Wednesday.

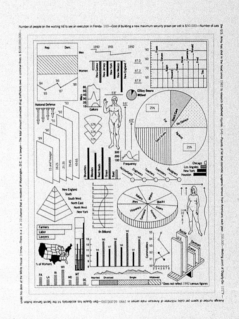

Number of people on the waiting list to see an execution in Florida: 100—Cost of building a new maximum security prison per cell is $50,000—Number of cats

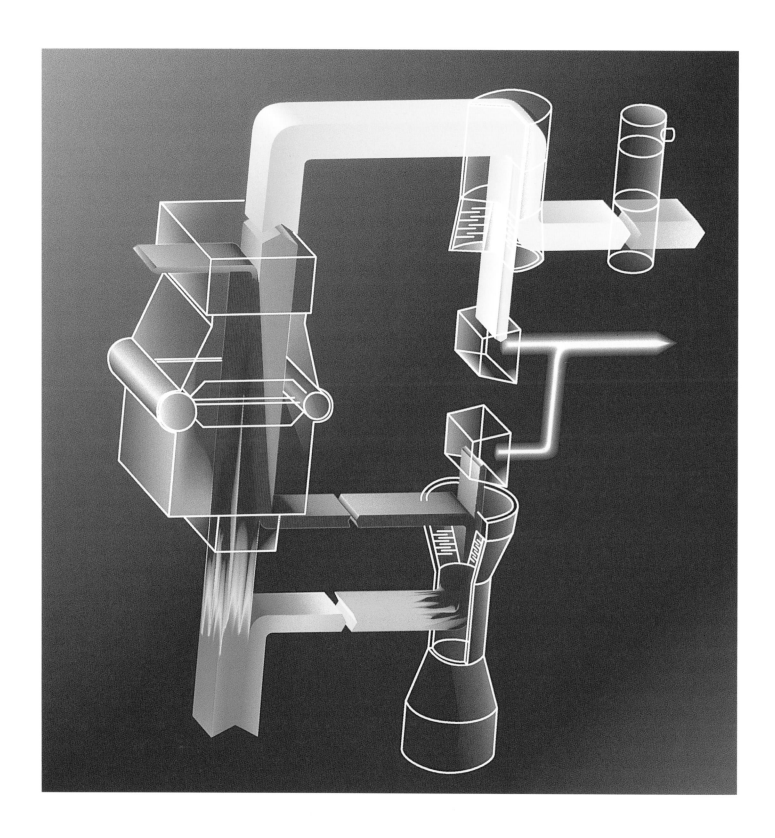

**ARTBEAT DESIGN GMBH** *Lentjes Umweltthechnik*

**ATELIER FRANK BAYER** *Westfalia Becorit*

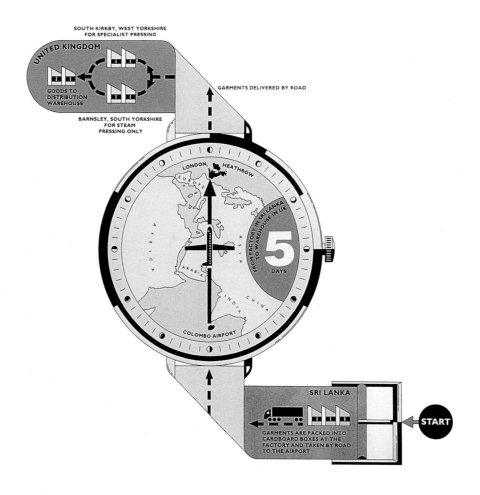

SOUTH KIRKBY, WEST YORKSHIRE
FOR SPECIALIST PRESSING

UNITED KINGDOM

GOODS TO
DISTRIBUTION
WAREHOUSE

BARNSLEY, SOUTH YORKSHIRE
FOR STEAM
PRESSING ONLY

GARMENTS DELIVERED BY ROAD

LONDON, HEATHROW

EUROPE

AFRICA

ASIA

ARABIA

CHINA

INDIA

COLOMBO AIRPORT

FROM FACTORY IN SRI LANKA
TO WAREHOUSE IN UK

5 DAYS

SRI LANKA

START

GARMENTS ARE PACKED INTO
CARDBOARD BOXES AT THE
FACTORY AND TAKEN BY ROAD
TO THE AIRPORT

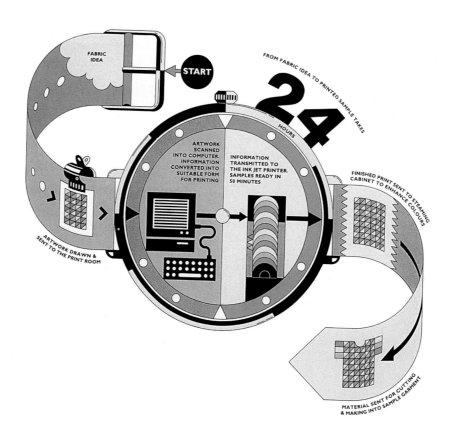

FABRIC
IDEA

START

FROM FABRIC IDEA TO PRINTED SAMPLE TAKES

24 HOURS

ARTWORK
SCANNED
INTO COMPUTER.
INFORMATION
CONVERTED INTO
SUITABLE FORM
FOR PRINTING

INFORMATION
TRANSMITTED TO
THE INK JET PRINTER.
SAMPLES READY IN
50 MINUTES

FINISHED PRINT SENT TO STEAMING
CABINET TO ENHANCE COLOURS

ARTWORK DRAWN &
SENT TO THE PRINT ROOM

MATERIAL SENT FOR CUTTING
& MAKING INTO SAMPLE GARMENT

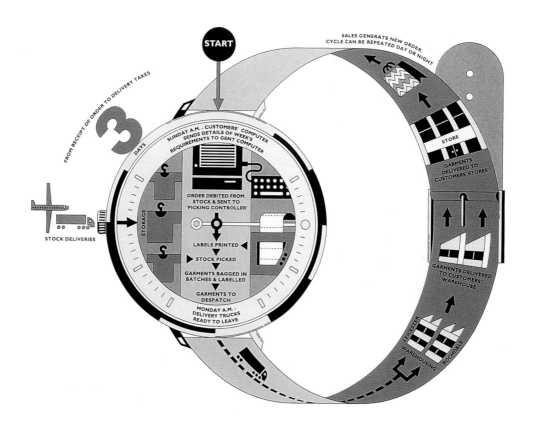

START

SALES GENERATE NEW ORDER.
CYCLE CAN BE REPEATED DAY OR NIGHT

FROM RECEIPT OF ORDER TO DELIVERY TAKES

3 DAYS

SUNDAY A.M. - CUSTOMERS' COMPUTER
SENDS DETAILS OF WEEK'S
REQUIREMENTS TO GENT COMPUTER

ORDER DEBITED FROM
STOCK & SENT TO
'PICKING CONTROLLER'

LABELS PRINTED

STOCK PICKED

GARMENTS BAGGED IN
BATCHES & LABELLED

GARMENTS TO
DESPATCH

MONDAY A.M. -
DELIVERY TRUCKS
READY TO LEAVE

STORAGE

STOCK DELIVERIES

STORE

GARMENTS
DELIVERED TO
CUSTOMERS' STORES

GARMENTS DELIVERED
TO CUSTOMERS'
WAREHOUSE

LEICESTER
WAREHOUSING
ROCHDALE

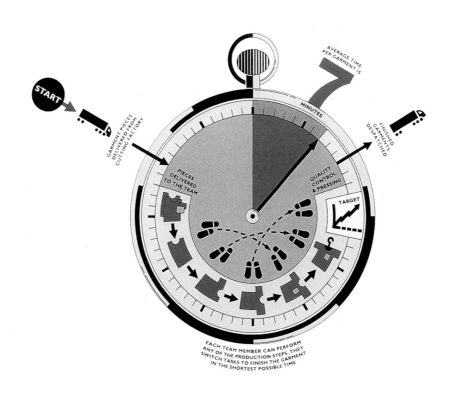

START

GARMENT PIECES
DELIVERED FROM
CUTTING FACTORY

AVERAGE TIME
PER GARMENT IS

7 MINUTES

FINISHED
GARMENTS
DESPATCHED

PIECES
DELIVERED
TO THE TEAM

QUALITY
CONTROL
& PRESSING

TARGET

EACH TEAM MEMBER CAN PERFORM
ANY OF THE PRODUCTION STEPS. THEY
SWITCH TASKS TO FINISH THE GARMENT
IN THE SHORTEST POSSIBLE TIME

(THIS SPREAD) **GRUNDY & NORTHEDGE / ADDISON DESIGN GROUP** *S.R. Gent*

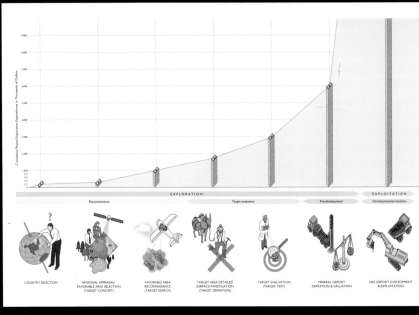

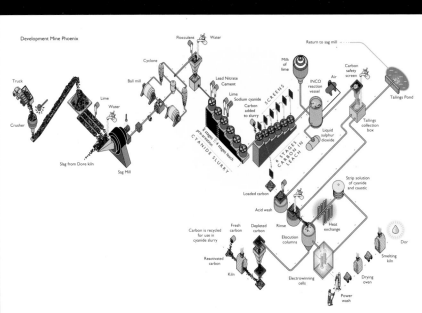

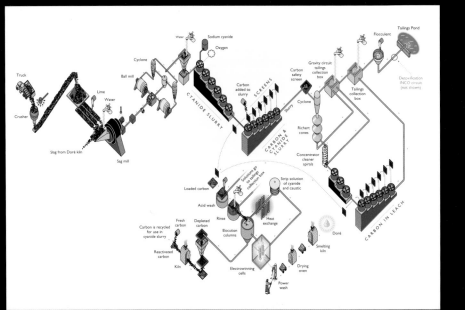

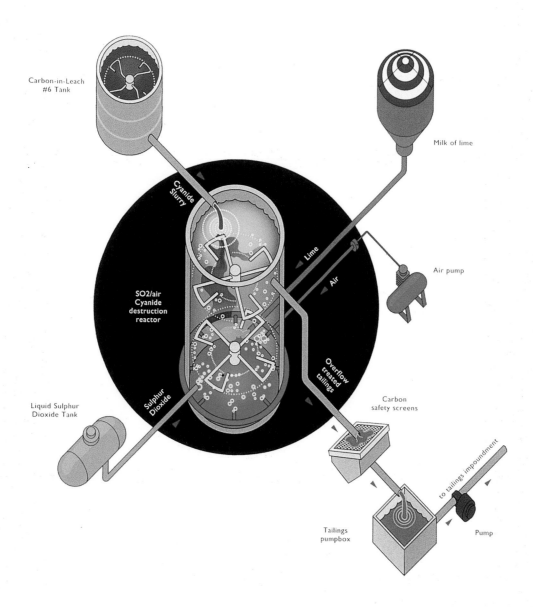

Carbon-in-Leach
#6 Tank

Milk of lime

Cyanide
Slurry

Lime

Air

SO2/air
Cyanide
destruction
reactor

Air pump

Liquid Sulphur
Dioxide Tank

Sulphur
Dioxide

Overflow
treated
tailings

Carbon
safety screens

to tailings impoundment

Tailings
pumpbox

Pump

*(THIS SPREAD)* **GLUTH WEAVER DESIGN** *Battle Mountain Gold*

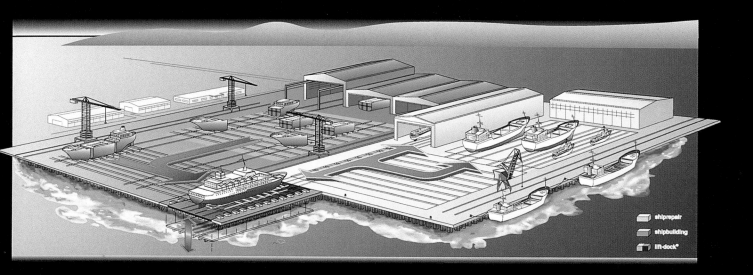

shiprepair
shipbuilding
lift-dock®

*(TOP)* **ARTBEAT DESIGN GMBH** *Schiess de Fries* ■ *(BOTTOM)* **KURT HEINEMANN** *ICPR Intern (Commission for the Protection of the Rhine)*

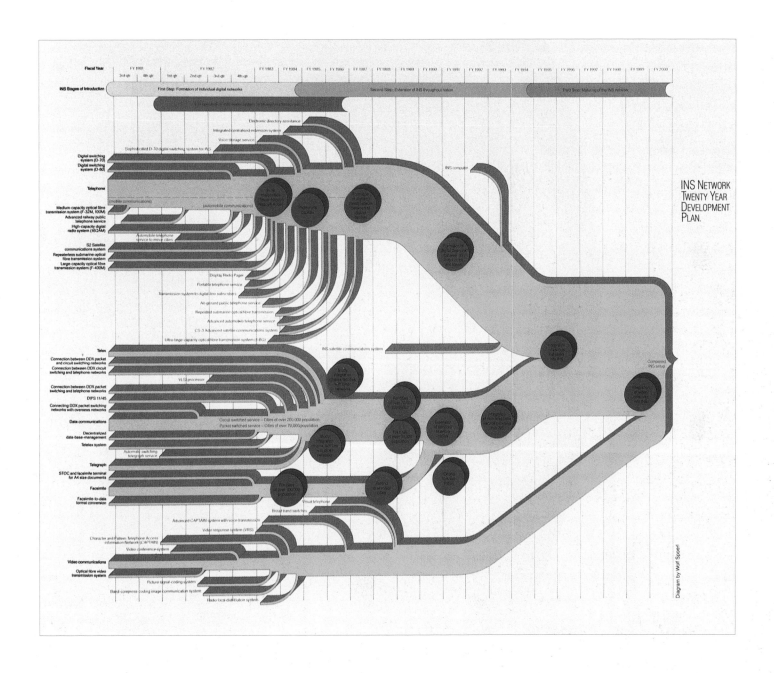

INS NETWORK
TWENTY YEAR
DEVELOPMENT
PLAN.

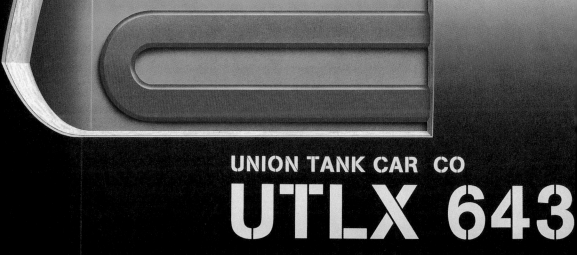

UNION TANK CAR CO
UTLX 643

2 INCH HF COMP SHOES

TECHNICAL AND FUNCTIONAL

TECHNIK

TECHNIQUE

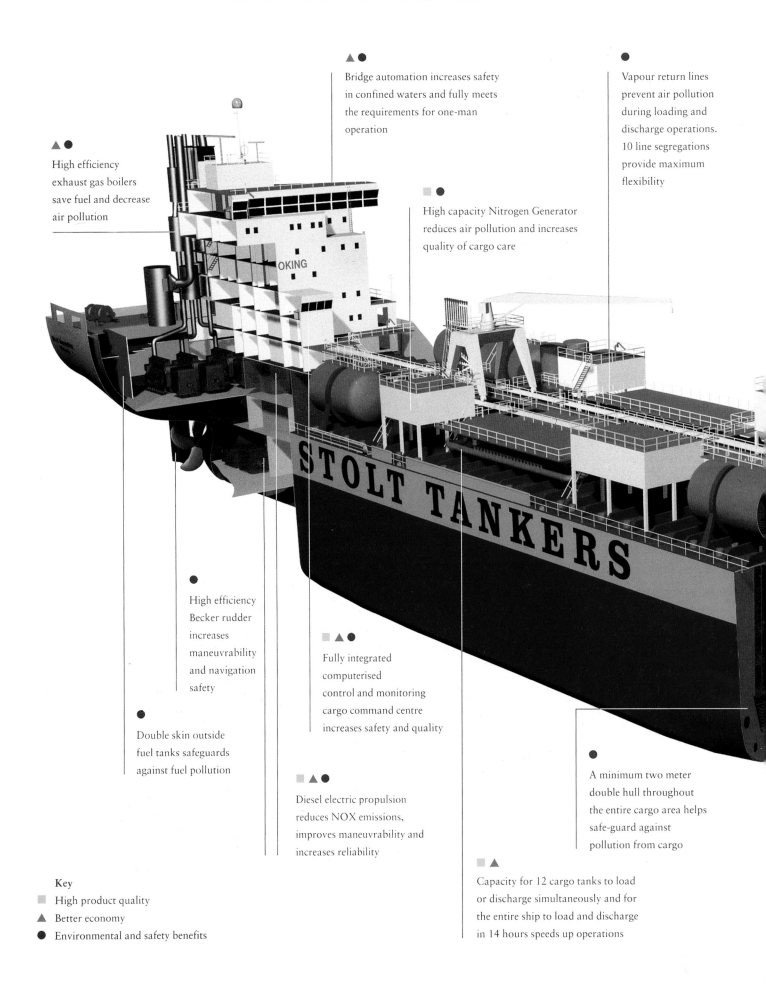

Bridge automation increases safety in confined waters and fully meets the requirements for one-man operation

Vapour return lines prevent air pollution during loading and discharge operations. 10 line segregations provide maximum flexibility

High efficiency exhaust gas boilers save fuel and decrease air pollution

High capacity Nitrogen Generator reduces air pollution and increases quality of cargo care

High efficiency Becker rudder increases maneuvrability and navigation safety

Fully integrated computerised control and monitoring cargo command centre increases safety and quality

Double skin outside fuel tanks safeguards against fuel pollution

A minimum two meter double hull throughout the entire cargo area helps safe-guard against pollution from cargo

Diesel electric propulsion reduces NOX emissions, improves maneuvrability and increases reliability

Capacity for 12 cargo tanks to load or discharge simultaneously and for the entire ship to load and discharge in 14 hours speeds up operations

**Key**
■ High product quality
▲ Better economy
● Environmental and safety benefits

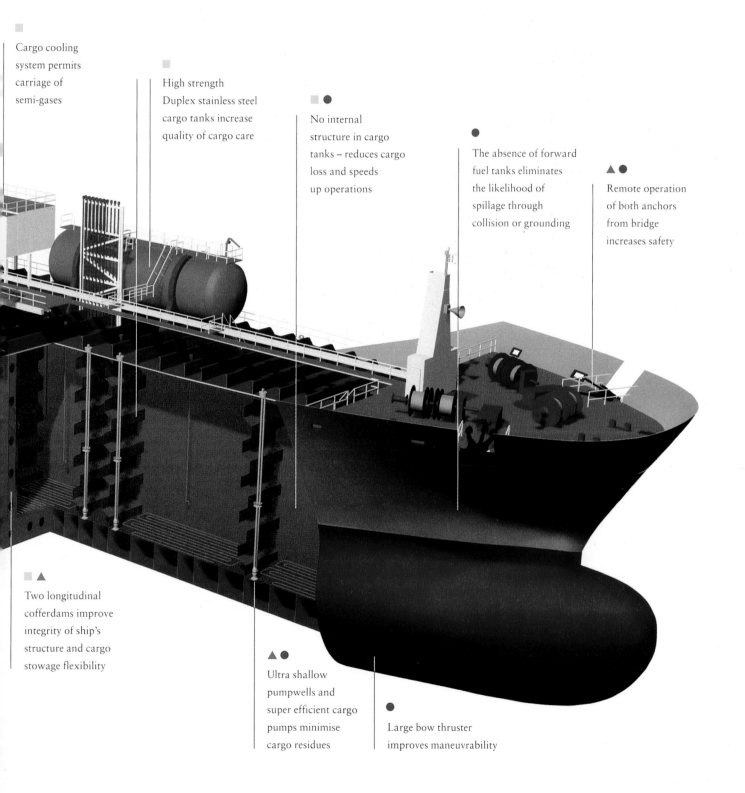

Cargo cooling system permits carriage of semi-gases

High strength Duplex stainless steel cargo tanks increase quality of cargo care

No internal structure in cargo tanks – reduces cargo loss and speeds up operations

The absence of forward fuel tanks eliminates the likelihood of spillage through collision or grounding

Remote operation of both anchors from bridge increases safety

Two longitudinal cofferdams improve integrity of ship's structure and cargo stowage flexibility

Ultra shallow pumpwells and super efficient cargo pumps minimise cargo residues

Large bow thruster improves maneuvrability

(PRECEDING SPREAD) **SX2 ESSEX TWO INCORPORATED** *The Marmon Group, Inc.* ■ (THIS SPREAD) **TOR PETTERSEN & PARTNERS LTD** *Stolt-Nielsen S.A.*

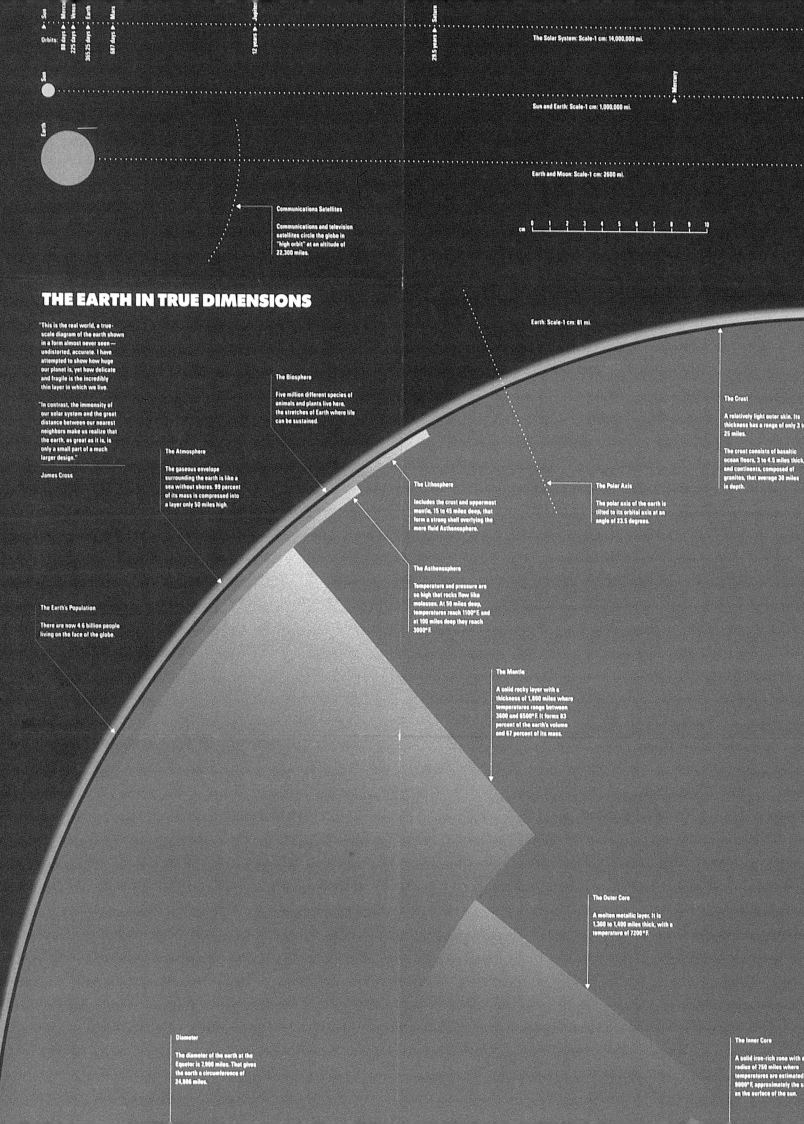

Sun ▲ Mercury

Sun and Earth: Scale-1 cm: 1,000,000 mi.

Earth

Earth and Moon: Scale-1 cm: 2600 mi.

cm   0   1   2   3   4   5   6   7   8   9   10

**Communications Satellites**

Communications and television
satellites circle the globe in
"high orbit" at an altitude of
22,300 miles.

Earth: Scale-1 cm: 81 mi.

# THE EARTH IN TRUE DIMENSIONS

"This is the real world, a true-
scale diagram of the earth shown
in a form almost never seen —
undistorted, accurate. I have
attempted to show how huge
our planet is, yet how delicate
and fragile is the incredibly
thin layer in which we live.

"In contrast, the immensity of
our solar system and the great
distance between our nearest
neighbors make us realize that
the earth, as great as it is, is
only a small part of a much
larger design."

James Cross

**The Biosphere**

Five million different species of
animals and plants live here,
the stretches of Earth where life
can be sustained.

**The Atmosphere**

The gaseous envelope
surrounding the earth is like a
sea without shores. 99 percent
of its mass is compressed into
a layer only 50 miles high.

**The Crust**

A relatively light outer skin. Its
thickness has a range of only 3 to
25 miles.

The crust consists of basaltic
ocean floors, 3 to 4.5 miles thick,
and continents, composed of
granites, that average 30 miles
in depth.

**The Lithosphere**

Includes the crust and uppermost
mantle, 15 to 45 miles deep, that
form a strong shell overlying the
more fluid Asthenosphere.

**The Polar Axis**

The polar axis of the earth is
tilted to its orbital axis at an
angle of 23.5 degrees.

**The Asthenosphere**

Temperature and pressure are
so high that rocks flow like
molasses. At 50 miles deep,
temperatures reach 1100°F, and
at 100 miles deep they reach
3000°F.

**The Earth's Population**

There are now 4.6 billion people
living on the face of the globe.

**The Mantle**

A solid rocky layer with a
thickness of 1,800 miles where
temperatures range between
3600 and 6500°F. It forms 83
percent of the earth's volume
and 67 percent of its mass.

**The Outer Core**

A molten metallic layer. It is
1,300 to 1,400 miles thick, with a
temperature of 7200°F.

**Diameter**

The diameter of the earth at the
Equator is 7,900 miles. That gives
the earth a circumference of
24,906 miles.

**The Inner Core**

A solid iron-rich zone with a
radius of 750 miles where
temperatures are estimated at
9000°F, approximately the same
as the surface of the sun.

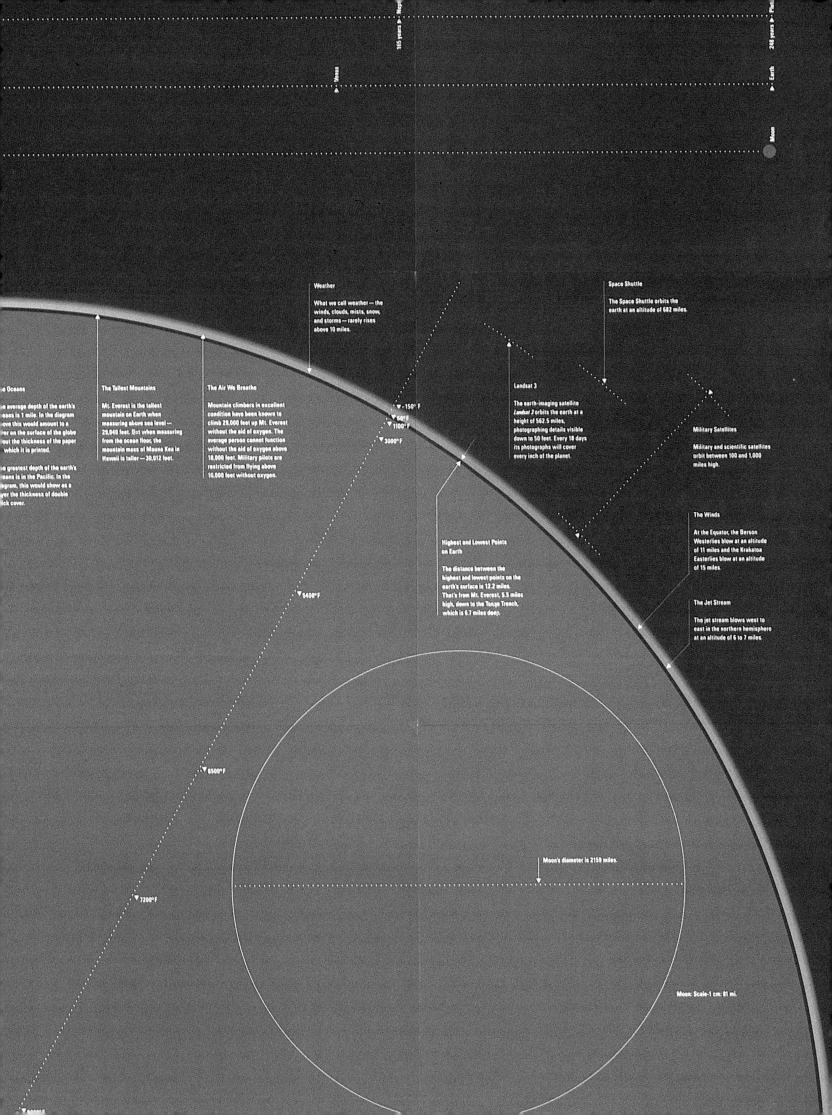

165 years ▲ Nep

248 years ▶ Plu

Mars ▲

▲ Earth ▶

Moon ●

### Weather

What we call weather — the winds, clouds, mists, snow, and storms — rarely rises above 10 miles.

### Space Shuttle

The Space Shuttle orbits the earth at an altitude of 682 miles.

### Oceans

e average depth of the earth's eans is 1 mile. In the diagram ove this would amount to a er on the surface of the globe out the thickness of the paper which it is printed.

e greatest depth of the earth's eans is in the Pacific. In the gram, this would show as a er the thickness of double ick cover.

### The Tallest Mountains

Mt. Everest is the tallest mountain on Earth when measuring above sea level — 29,040 feet. But when measuring from the ocean floor, the mountain mass of Mauna Kea in Hawaii is taller — 30,012 feet.

### The Air We Breathe

Mountain climbers in excellent condition have been known to climb 29,000 feet up Mt. Everest without the aid of oxygen. The average person cannot function without the aid of oxygen above 18,000 feet. Military pilots are restricted from flying above 10,000 feet without oxygen.

### Landsat 3

The earth-imaging satellite *Landsat 3* orbits the earth at a height of 562.5 miles, photographing details visible down to 50 feet. Every 18 days its photographs will cover every inch of the planet.

### Military Satellites

Military and scientific satellites orbit between 100 and 1,000 miles high.

▼ -150° F
▼ 60° F
▼ 1100° F
▼ 3000° F

### The Winds

At the Equator, the Berson Westerlies blow at an altitude of 11 miles and the Krakatoa Easterlies blow at an altitude of 15 miles.

### Highest and Lowest Points on Earth

The distance between the highest and lowest points on the earth's surface is 12.2 miles. That's from Mt. Everest, 5.5 miles high, down to the Tonga Trench, which is 6.7 miles deep.

### The Jet Stream

The jet stream blows west to east in the northern hemisphere at an altitude of 6 to 7 miles.

▼ 5400° F

▼ 6500° F

▼ 7200° F

Moon's diameter is 2159 miles.

Moon: Scale–1 cm: 81 mi.

▼ 8000° F

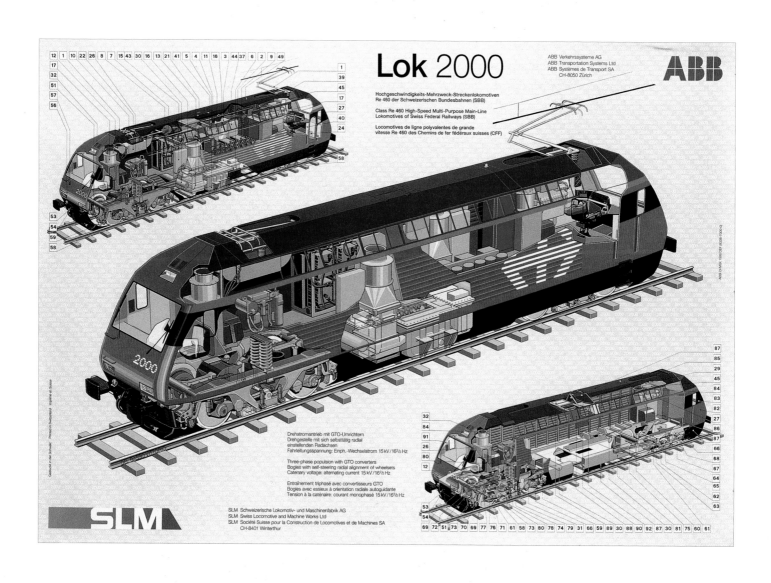

(PRECEDING SPREAD) **CROSS ASSOCIATES** *Simpson Paper Company* ■ (THIS PAGE) **VITTORIO DEL BASSO** *ABB Transportation Systems Ltd./SLM Swiss Locomotive and Machine Works Ltd.*

104

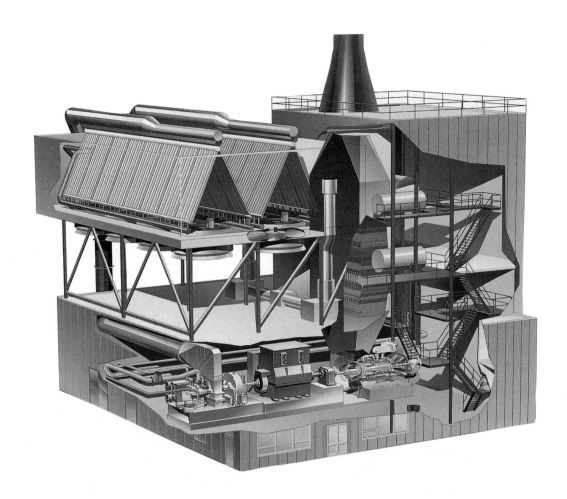

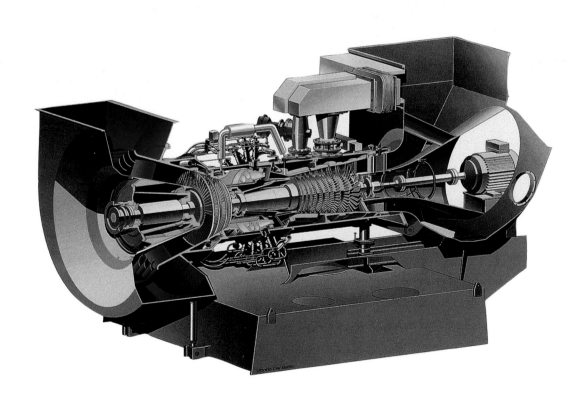

**VITTORIO DEL BASSO** *ABB Stal Support*

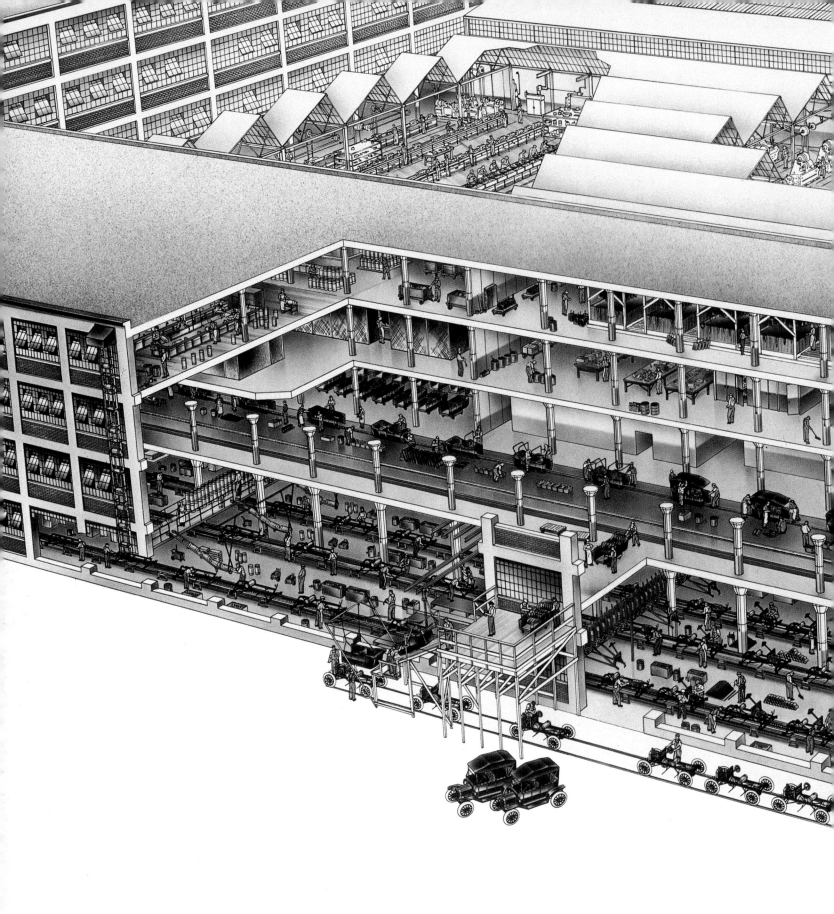

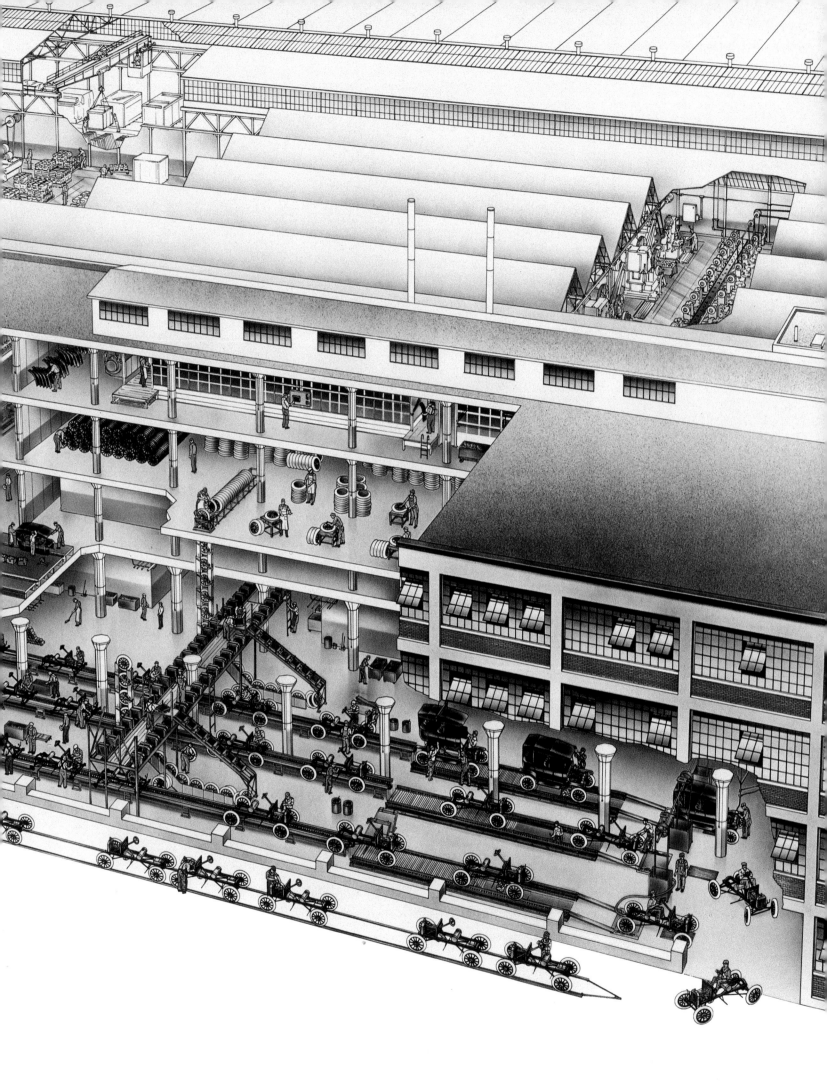

# THE SOLAR SYSTEM
## OUR SUN'S FAMILY

MERCURY ☿

VENUS ♀

EARTH ⊕
● Earth's moon

MARS ♂
· Phobos
· Deimos

JUPITER ♃

· Metis
· Adrastea
· Amalthea
· Thebe
● Io
● Europa
● Ganymede
● Callisto
· Leda
· Himalia
· Lysithea
· Elara
· Ananke
· Carme
· Pasiphae
· Sinope

SATURN ♄

· Atlas
· Prometheus
· Pandora
· Janus
· Epimetheus
· Mimas
· Enceladus
· Tethys
· Telesto
· Calypso
· Dione
· Helene
· Rhea
● Titan
· Hyperion
· Iapetus
· Phoebe

URANUS ♅

· Cordelia
· Ophelia
· Bianca
· Cressida
· Desdemona
· Juliet
· Portia
· Rosalind
· Belinda
· Puck
· Miranda
· Ariel
· Umbriel
· Titania
· Oberon

NEPTUNE ♆

· Naiad
· Thalassa
· Despoina
· Galatea
· Larissa
· Proteus
● Triton
· Nereid

PLUTO ♇
· Charon

SUNSPOTS

### SUN
The gravitational attraction of this medium-size star, our sun, controls the orbits of the planets. A rotating nuclear furnace, mostly of hydrogen and helium, it constantly emits energy. Periodically magnetic fields emerge from its surface in areas called sunspots, darker because they are less hot. Associated with these disturbances, which may last for weeks, are arching streams of gas called prominences and brilliant regions called flares. Such activity affects Earth's magnetic field, its atmosphere, and possibly its climate. Maximum sunspot activity occurs during 11-year cycles; the most recent one peaked in 1990. PERIOD OF ROTATION: 25 days at equator. DIAMETER: 1,400,000 km. MASS: 333,000 x that of Earth. TEMPERATURE: 15,000,000°C in core; 5,500°C at surface.

The images of the planets, taken from space, and the photograph of the sun, taken from Earth, are shown to scale. An image of Neptune's moon Triton, believed to be similar to Pluto, represents that planet, which has not been visited by spacecraft. Astronomical symbols accompany the planet names.

### MERCURY
Heavily cratered and nearly airless, this dead planet—much like Earth's moon—has changed little since volcanism ceased perhaps three billion years ago. A very thin atmosphere of sodium and helium remains. DISTANCE FROM SUN: 57,900,000 km. REVOLUTION AROUND SUN: 88 days. ROTATION: 59 days. DIAMETER: 4,880 km. DENSITY: 5.4 x that of water. MASS: 0.055 x that of Earth. SURFACE TEMPERATURE: 430°C on dayside, minus 180°C on nightside.

### JUPITER
The largest planet, one-tenth the diameter of the sun, is a whirling ball of gas compressed to liquid in the interior. Jupiter's Great Red Spot, an intense windstorm three times larger than Earth, was first observed 300 years ago. Among Jupiter's satellites, Io alone has an atmosphere—albeit a tenuous one—and volcanoes. The most violent eruptions eject sulfur and sulfur compounds hundreds of kilometers above the surface and may feed particles into the faint ring that encircles Jupiter. Another satellite, Europa, is covered with a layer of ice, which may overlie oceans of liquid water. DISTANCE FROM SUN: 778,300,000 km. REVOLUTION AROUND SUN: 11.86 years. ROTATION: 9.9 hours. DIAMETER: 142,800 km. DENSITY: 1.3 x that of water. MASS: 318 x that of Earth. TEMPERATURE: minus 130°C at cloud tops.

### SATURN
Countless orbiting icy particles make up the majestic ring system of the second largest planet. Of its moons, only Titan has a dense atmosphere, mostly nitrogen. Although less conspicuous than those on Jupiter, raging storms disturb Saturn's hydrogen-rich atmosphere. DISTANCE FROM SUN: 1,427,000,000 km. REVOLUTION AROUND SUN: 29.46 years. ROTATION: 10.7 hours. DIAMETER: 120,600 km. DENSITY: 0.7 x that of water. MASS: 95 x that of Earth. TEMPERATURE: minus 185°C at cloud tops.

### URANUS
Rotating on an axis tilted 98 degrees, Uranus resembles Neptune in color. Its atmosphere, like Neptune's, contains methane, which absorbs red wavelengths of sunlight, resulting in a greenish blue color. Narrow rings are probably held in place by tiny moons. Of the planet's satellites, Miranda is one of the oddest objects in the solar system. Deep scars and a jumbled surface indicate that Miranda may have been shattered by collisions and then reassembled under the force of gravity. DISTANCE FROM SUN: 2,870,000,000 km. REVOLUTION AROUND SUN: 84 years. ROTATION: 17.2 hours. DIAMETER: 51,300 km. DENSITY: 1.3 x that of water. MASS: 14.4 x that of Earth. TEMPERATURE: minus 200°C at cloud tops.

### NEPTUNE
Like Uranus, Neptune has an atmosphere containing methane, and like Jupiter it is disturbed by great storms. Embedded within the outermost of its rings are three bright arc segments, whose structure remains unexplained. Triton, the largest of eight satellites, has a thin atmosphere dominated by nitrogen. (The six inner moons bear provisional names.) Geyser-like plumes jet some ten kilometers above the sparkling nitrogen frost that covers Triton's frigid surface. DISTANCE FROM SUN: 4,497,000,000 km. REVOLUTION AROUND SUN: 165 years. ROTATION: 16.1 hours. DIAMETER: 49,100 km. DENSITY: 1.6 x that of water. MASS: 17.2 x that of Earth. TEMPERATURE: minus 200°C at cloud tops.

BORN IN THE DARKNESS of interstellar space some 4.6 billion years ago, our solar system emerged from a contracting molecular cloud of dust and gas. When the core of this cloud became dense enough, gravity triggered the collapse of its inner layers. Matter fell inward for perhaps a million years. Internal heat, trapped by the gases, fired up a protosun and ignited thermonuclear reactions. Rotation drew the material into a swirling nebular disk. Its hot innermost constituents drifted farther inward, enlarging the protosun. A powerful gaseous outflow from the solar inferno blasted away the infalling material, unveiling our newborn sun in all its brilliance. The cooler, more distant portions of the nebula contained the raw material of a planetary system.

Tiny dust grains in the disk consist solid carbon, silicates, and metals as as ices of volatile materials such as w carbon dioxide, methane, and amm that had condensed as the solar ula continued to cool. These particle alesced into rocky or icy clumps—a oids or comets—called planetesimals building blocks of planets and their s lites. Since planetesimals aggregate different distances from the sun's and light, the composition of the pla varies. Those nearer the sun are r rocky, those farther away more icy.

Four terrestrial, or earthlike, pla inhabit the inner realm of the solar tem: Mercury, Venus, Earth, and M Each is a solid sphere with a metallic

Earth's near twin...
greenhouse effect kee...
the thick sulfuric acid...
large volcanoes, som...
108,200,000 km. REV...
TION 243 days DIAM...
MASS: 0.8 x that o...

♈ Vernal Equinox

MARS A.D. 2000

Ascending ☊ Node

♈ Vernal Equinox

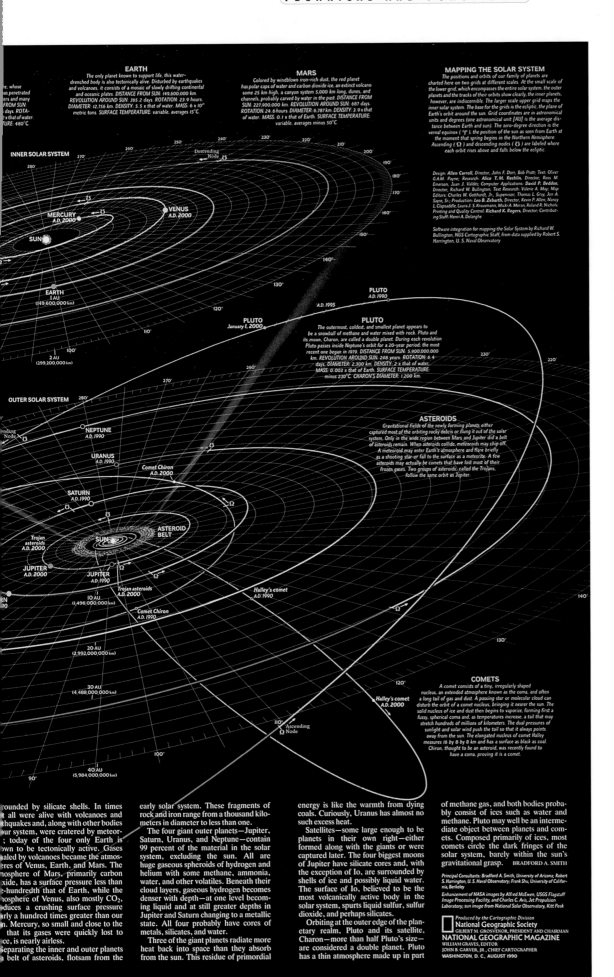

## EARTH
The only planet known to support life, this water-drenched body is also tectonically alive. Disturbed by earthquakes and volcanoes, it consists of a mosaic of slowly drifting continental and oceanic plates. DISTANCE FROM SUN: 149,600,000 km. REVOLUTION AROUND SUN: 365.2 days. ROTATION: 23.9 hours. DIAMETER: 12,756 km. DENSITY: 5.5 x that of water. MASS: 6 x 10²¹ metric tons. SURFACE TEMPERATURE: variable, averages 15°C.

## MARS
Colored by windblown iron-rich dust, the red planet has polar caps of water and carbon dioxide ice, an extinct volcano some 25 km high, a canyon system 5,000 km long, dunes, and channels, probably carved by water in the past. DISTANCE FROM SUN: 227,900,000 km. REVOLUTION AROUND SUN: 687 days. ROTATION: 24.6 hours. DIAMETER: 6,787 km. DENSITY: 3.9 x that of water. MASS: 0.1 x that of Earth. SURFACE TEMPERATURE: variable, averages minus 50°C.

## MAPPING THE SOLAR SYSTEM
The positions and orbits of our family of planets are charted here on two grids at different scales. At the small scale of the lower grid, which encompasses the entire solar system, the outer planets and the tracks of their orbits show clearly; the inner planets, however, are indiscernible. The larger scale upper grid maps the inner solar system. The base for the grids is the ecliptic, the plane of Earth's orbit around the sun. Grid coordinates are in astronomical units and degrees (one astronomical unit [AU] is the average distance between Earth and sun). The zero-degree direction is the vernal equinox ( ♈ ), the position of the sun as seen from Earth at the moment that spring begins in the Northern Hemisphere. Ascending ( ☊ ) and descending nodes ( ☋ ) are labeled where each orbit rises above and falls below the ecliptic.

Design: Allen Carroll, Director, John F. Dorr, Bob Pratt; Text: Oliver G.A.M. Payne; Research: Alice T. M. Rechlin, Director, Ross M. Emerson, Juan J. Valdés; Computer Applications: David P. Beddoe, Director, Richard W. Bullington; Text Research: Valerie A. May; Map Editors: Charles W. Gotthardt, Jr., Supervisor, Thomas L. Gray, Jon A. Sayre, Sr.; Production: Leo B. Zebarth, Director, Kevin P. Allen, Nancy L. Clapsaddle, Laura J. S. Krausmann, Micki A. Moran, Roland R. Nichols; Printing and Quality Control: Richard K. Rogers, Director; Contributing Staff: Henri A. Delanghe.

Software integration for mapping the Solar System by Richard W. Bullington, NGS Cartographic Staff, from data supplied by Robert S. Harrington, U. S. Naval Observatory.

INNER SOLAR SYSTEM
OUTER SOLAR SYSTEM

MERCURY A.D. 2000
VENUS A.D. 2000
SUN
EARTH 1 AU (149,600,000 km)
2 AU (299,200,000 km)

NEPTUNE A.D. 1990
URANUS A.D. 1990
Comet Chiron A.D. 2000
SATURN A.D. 1990
Trojan asteroids A.D. 2000
SUN
JUPITER A.D. 2000
JUPITER A.D. 1990
Trojan asteroids A.D. 2000
Comet Chiron A.D. 1990
ASTEROID BELT

10 AU (1,496,000,000 km)
20 AU (2,992,000,000 km)
30 AU (4,488,000,000 km)
40 AU (5,984,000,000 km)

PLUTO A.D. 1990
A.D. 1995
PLUTO January 1, 2000

## PLUTO
The outermost, coldest, and smallest planet appears to be a snowball of methane and water mixed with rock. Pluto and its moon, Charon, are called a double planet. During each revolution Pluto passes inside Neptune's orbit for a 20-year period; the most recent one began in 1979. DISTANCE FROM SUN: 5,900,000,000 km. REVOLUTION AROUND SUN: 248 years. ROTATION: 6.4 days. DIAMETER: 2,300 km. DENSITY: 2 x that of water. MASS: 0.003 x that of Earth. SURFACE TEMPERATURE: minus 230°C. CHARON'S DIAMETER: 1,200 km.

## ASTEROIDS
Gravitational fields of the newly forming planets either captured most of the orbiting rocky debris or flung it out of the solar system. Only in the wide region between Mars and Jupiter did a belt of asteroids remain. When asteroids collide, meteoroids may chip off. A meteoroid may enter Earth's atmosphere and flare briefly as a shooting star or fall to the surface as a meteorite. A few asteroids may actually be comets that have lost most of their frozen gases. Two groups of asteroids, called the Trojans, follow the same orbit as Jupiter.

Halley's comet A.D. 1990
Halley's comet A.D. 2000
Ascending Node

## COMETS
A comet consists of a tiny, irregularly shaped nucleus, an extended atmosphere known as the coma, and often a long tail of gas and dust. A passing star or molecular cloud can disturb the orbit of a comet nucleus, bringing it nearer the sun. The solid nucleus of ice and dust then begins to vaporize, forming first a fuzzy, spherical coma and, as temperatures increase, a tail that may stretch hundreds of millions of kilometers. The dual pressures of sunlight and solar wind push the tail so that it always points away from the sun. The elongated nucleus of comet Halley measures 16 by 8 km and has a surface as black as coal. Chiron, thought to be an asteroid, was recently found to have a coma, proving it is a comet.

rounded by silicate shells. In times ... all were alive with volcanoes and thquakes and, along with other bodies ur system, were cratered by meteor-; today of the four only Earth is wn to be tectonically active. Gases aled by volcanoes became the atmos-ees of Venus, Earth, and Mars. The nosphere of Mars, primarily carbon xide, has a surface pressure less than -hundredth that of Earth, while the nosphere of Venus, also mostly CO₂, duces a crushing surface pressure rly a hundred times greater than our n. Mercury, so small and close to the that its gases were quickly lost to ce, is nearly airless. eparating the inner and outer planets belt of asteroids, flotsam from the

early solar system. These fragments of rock and iron range from a thousand kilometers in diameter to less than one.

The four giant outer planets—Jupiter, Saturn, Uranus, and Neptune—contain 99 percent of the material in the solar system, excluding the sun. All are huge gaseous spheroids of hydrogen and helium with some methane, ammonia, water, and other volatiles. Beneath their cloud layers, gaseous hydrogen becomes denser with depth—at one level becoming liquid and at still greater depths in Jupiter and Saturn changing to a metallic state. All four probably have cores of metals, silicates, and water.

Three of the giant planets radiate more heat back into space than they absorb from the sun. This residue of primordial

energy is like the warmth from dying coals. Curiously, Uranus has almost no such excess heat.

Satellites—some large enough to be planets in their own right—either formed along with the giants or were captured later. The four biggest moons of Jupiter have silicate cores and, with the exception of Io, are surrounded by shells of ice and possibly liquid water. The surface of Io, believed to be the most volcanically active body in the solar system, spurts liquid sulfur, sulfur dioxide, and perhaps silicates.

Orbiting at the outer edge of the planetary realm, Pluto and its satellite, Charon—more than half Pluto's size—are considered a double planet. Pluto has a thin atmosphere made up in part

of methane gas, and both bodies probably consist of ices such as water and methane. Pluto may well be an intermediate object between planets and comets. Composed primarily of ices, most comets circle the dark fringes of the solar system, barely within the sun's gravitational grasp.    BRADFORD A. SMITH

Principal Consultants: Bradford A. Smith, University of Arizona; Robert S. Harrington, U. S. Naval Observatory; Frank Shu, University of California, Berkeley

Enhancement of NASA images by Alfred McEwen, USGS Flagstaff Image Processing Facility, and Charles C. Avis, Jet Propulsion Laboratory; sun image from National Solar Observatory, Kitt Peak

Produced by the Cartographic Division
National Geographic Society
GILBERT M. GROSVENOR, PRESIDENT AND CHAIRMAN
NATIONAL GEOGRAPHIC MAGAZINE
WILLIAM GRAVES, EDITOR
JOHN B. GARVER, JR., CHIEF CARTOGRAPHER
WASHINGTON, D. C., AUGUST 1990

For complete map list write to the National Geographic Society, Washington, D. C. 20036.

## 12. Montafoner Damen-Skiweltcup Golm

START
Abfahrt
2089 m

Restaurant
Grüneck

**Anita Wachter-
Weltcupstrecke
Golm Alpboden**

| | |
|---|---|
| Starthöhe | 2089 m |
| Zielhöhe | 1494 m |
| Höhendifferenz | 595 m |
| Streckenlänge | 2220 m |

Prölleck

START
Slalom

Hagelgraben

Golmerhaus

Matschwitz

**ZIEL**

1494 m

Grafik Zündel
Quelle: SC Montafon

## Spektakulärer Unfall bei A 14-Auffahrt Dornbirn-Süd

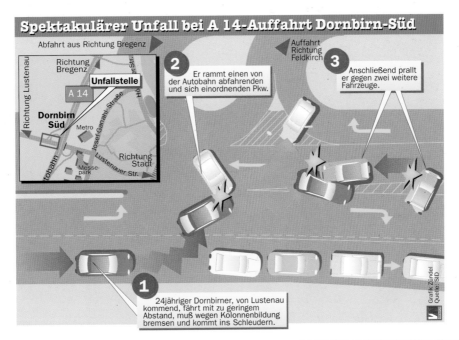

Abfahrt aus Richtung Bregenz

Auffahrt Richtung Feldkirch

**2** Er rammt einen von der Autobahn abfahrenden und sich einordnenden Pkw.

**3** Anschließend prallt er gegen zwei weitere Fahrzeuge.

Richtung Lustenau

Richtung Bregenz

**Unfallstelle**

A 14

**Dornbirn Süd**

Metro

Richtung Stadt

Josef Ganahl-Straße

Lustenauer Str.

Messe-park

**1** 24jähriger Dornbirner, von Lustenau kommend, fährt mit zu geringem Abstand, muß wegen Kolonnenbildung bremsen und kommt ins Schleudern.

Grafik Zündel Quelle: SID

## Neugeplante Überbauung Bahnhofsareal Bregenz

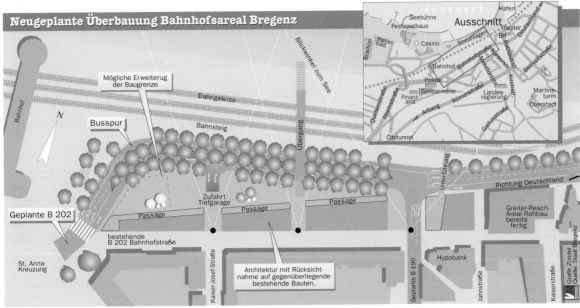

BODENSEE

Ausschnitt

Seebühne Festspielhaus

Hafen

Stadion

Haller-bad

Casino

Seeanlagen

Theater BH

Deutschland

Bahnhof Bahnhofstraße Kaiserstr.

Belruptstraße

Polizei

Montfortstr.

Kirchstr.

Quellenstraße

Rheinstraße

Gendarmerie

Römerstraße

Landes-regierung

Martins-turm

Oberstadt

Finanz amt

Arlberg

Gallusstraße

Citytunnel

Mögliche Erweiterug der Baugrenze

Blickwinkel zum See

Bahngeleise

Bahnhof

N

Busspur

Bahnsteig

Übergang

Unterführung

Richtung Deutschland

Geplante B 202

Zufahrt Tiefgarage

Passage

Passage

Greiter-Resch-Areal Rohbau bereits fertig

Passage

bestehende B 202 Bahnhofstraße

Kaiser-Josef-Straße

Geplante B 190

Hypobank

Kaiserstraße

St. Anna Kreuzung

Architektur mit Rücksicht-nahme auf gegenüberliegende bestehende Bauten.

Jahnstraße

Grafik Zündel Quelle: Stadt Bregenz

## Lauberhornrennen Wengen 1992

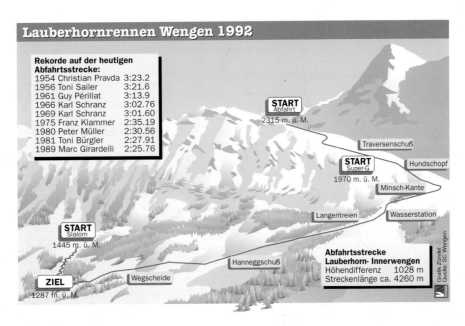

**Rekorde auf der heutigen Abfahrtsstrecke:**

| | | |
|---|---|---|
| 1954 | Christian Pravda | 3:23.2 |
| 1956 | Toni Sailer | 3:21.6 |
| 1961 | Guy Périllat | 3:13.9 |
| 1966 | Karl Schranz | 3:02.76 |
| 1969 | Karl Schranz | 3:01.60 |
| 1975 | Franz Klammer | 2:35.19 |
| 1980 | Peter Müller | 2:30.56 |
| 1981 | Toni Bürgler | 2:27.91 |
| 1989 | Marc Girardelli | 2:25.76 |

**START** Abfahrt
2315 m. ü. M.

Traversenschuß

**START** Super-G
1970 m. ü. M.

Hundschopf

Minsch-Kante

Wasserstation

Langentreien

**START** Slalom
1445 m. ü. M.

Hanneggschuß

**ZIEL**
1287 m. ü. M.

Wegscheide

**Abfahrtsstrecke Lauberhorn- Innerwengen**
Höhendifferenz 1028 m
Streckenlänge ca. 4260 m

Grafik Zündel Quelle: SC Wengen

*(THIS SPREAD)* **RUDOLF ZÜNDEL** *Vorarlberger Nachrichten*

(THIS SPREAD) **COOK + SHANOSKY ASSOCIATES, INC.** *Black & Decker Corporation*

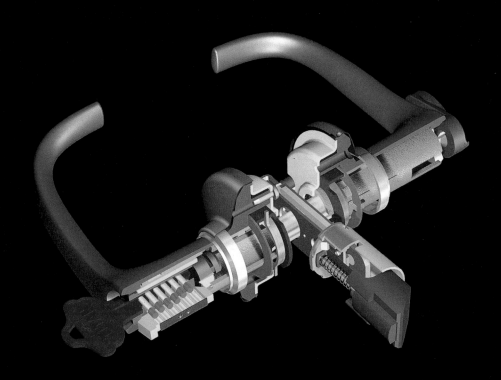

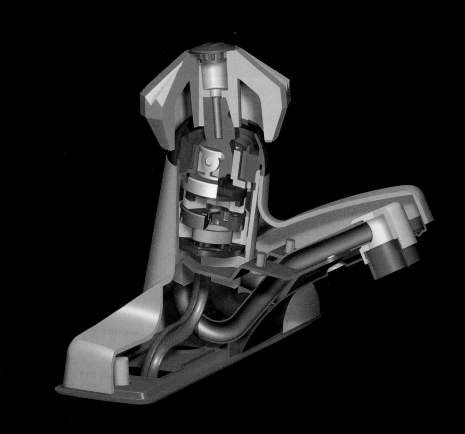

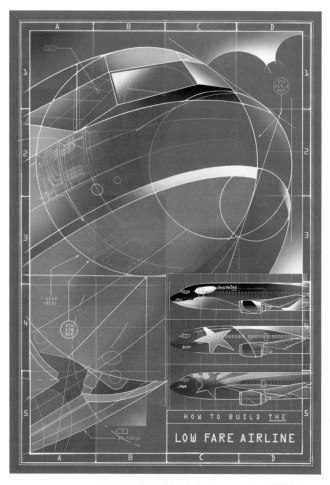

HOW TO BUILD THE
LOW FARE AIRLINE

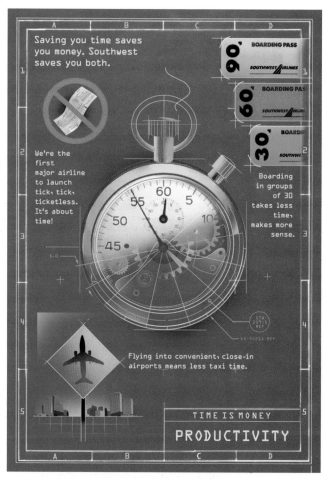

Saving you time saves you money. Southwest saves you both.

We're the first major airline to launch tick, tick, ticketless. It's about time!

Boarding in groups of 30 takes less time, makes more sense.

Flying into convenient, close-in airports means less taxi time.

TIME IS MONEY
PRODUCTIVITY

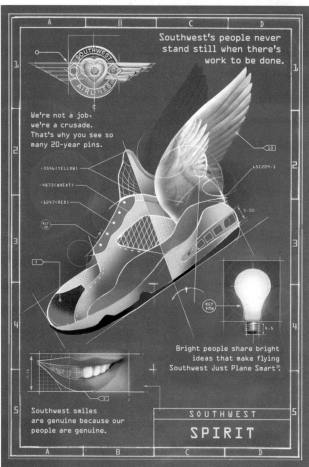

Southwest's people never stand still when there's work to be done.

We're not a job, we're a crusade. That's why you see so many 20-year pins.

Bright people share bright ideas that make flying Southwest Just Plane Smart™.

Southwest smiles are genuine because our people are genuine.

SOUTHWEST
SPIRIT

HOW WE BUILT THE
LOW FARE AIRLINE

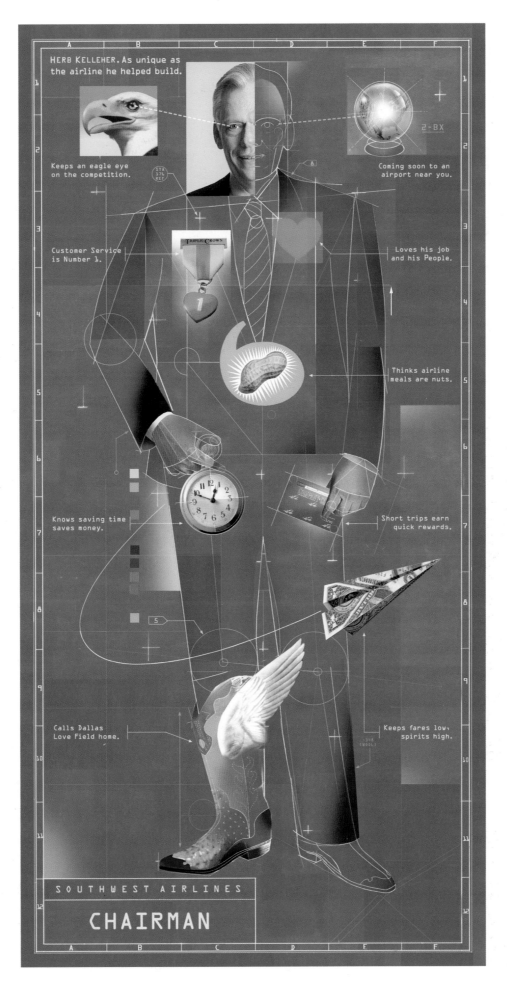

SOUTHWEST AIRLINES

# CHAIRMAN

HERB KELLEHER. As unique as the airline he helped build.

Keeps an eagle eye on the competition.

Coming soon to an airport near you.

Customer Service is Number 1.

Loves his job and his People.

Thinks airline meals are nuts.

Knows saving time saves money.

Short trips earn quick rewards.

Calls Dallas Love Field home.

Keeps fares low, spirits high.

(THIS SPREAD) **SIBLEY/PETEET DESIGN** *Southwest Airlines*

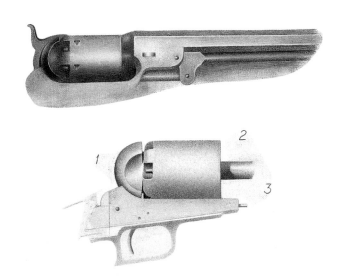

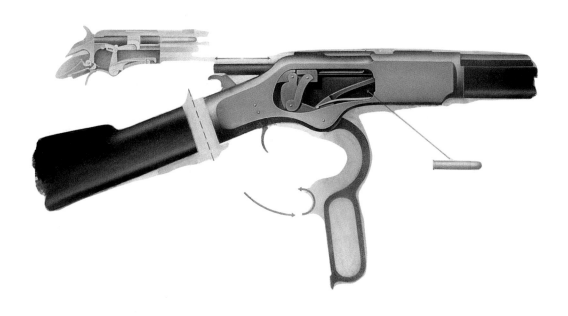

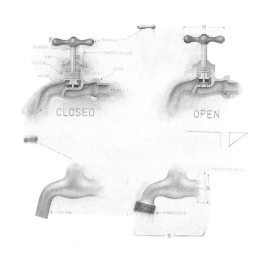

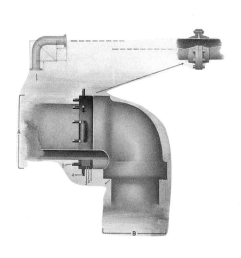

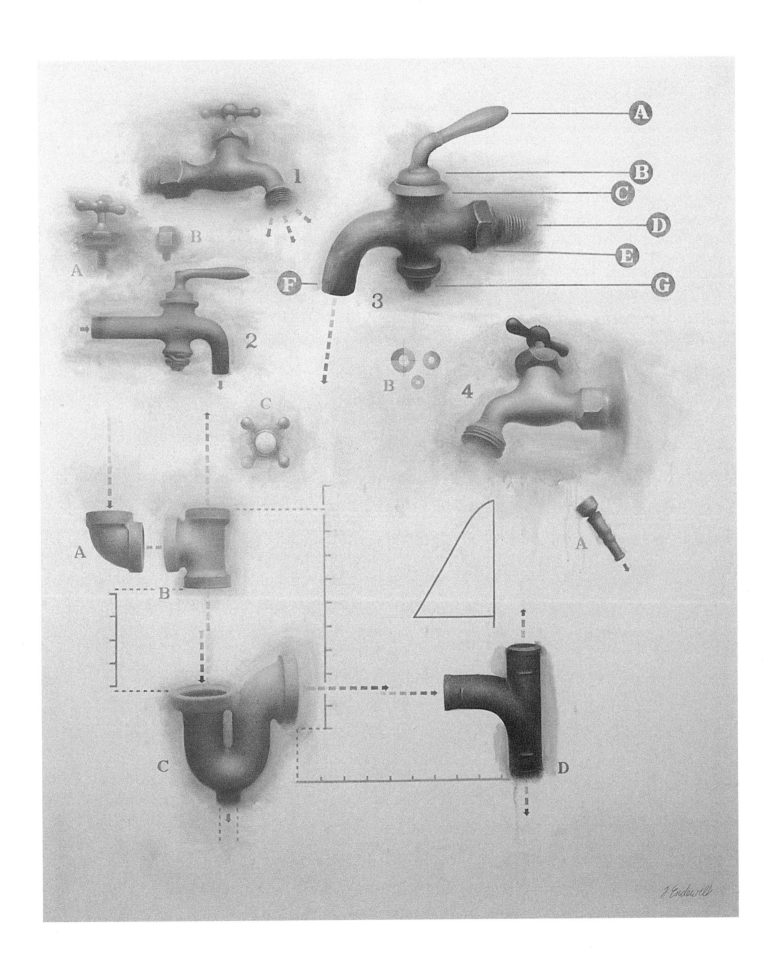

*(THIS SPREAD)* **JACK ENDEWELT** *self-promotion*

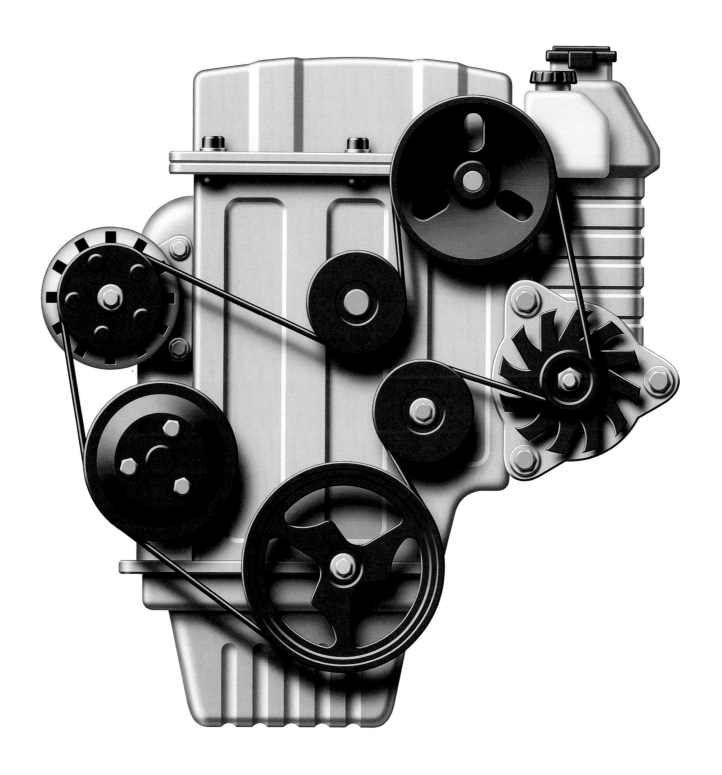

(ABOVE) **PETER KRÄMER** *Texaco* ■ (OPPOSITE, TOP) **PETER KRÄMER** *Deutsche Lufthansa AG* ■ (OPPOSITE, BOTTOM) **TOR PETTERSEN & PARTNERS LTD.** *Lucas Industries Plc.*

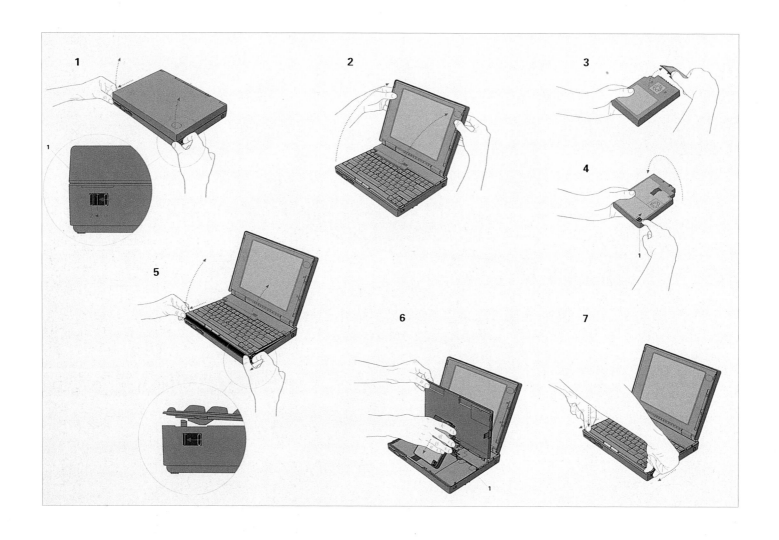

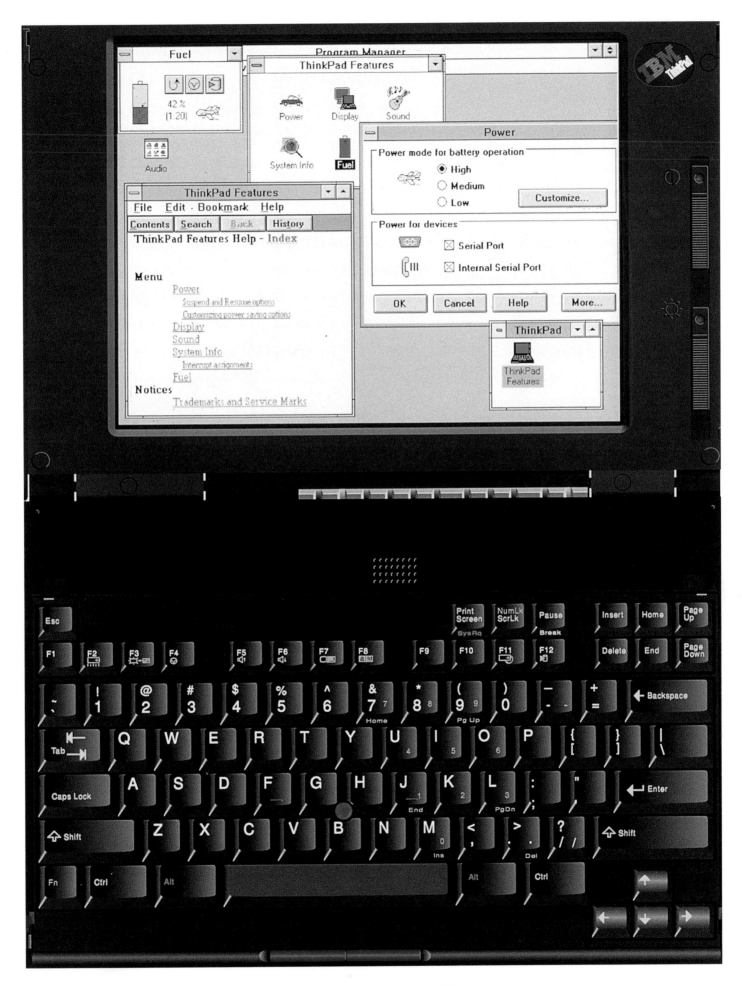

(THIS SPREAD) **RONNIE PETERS** IBM

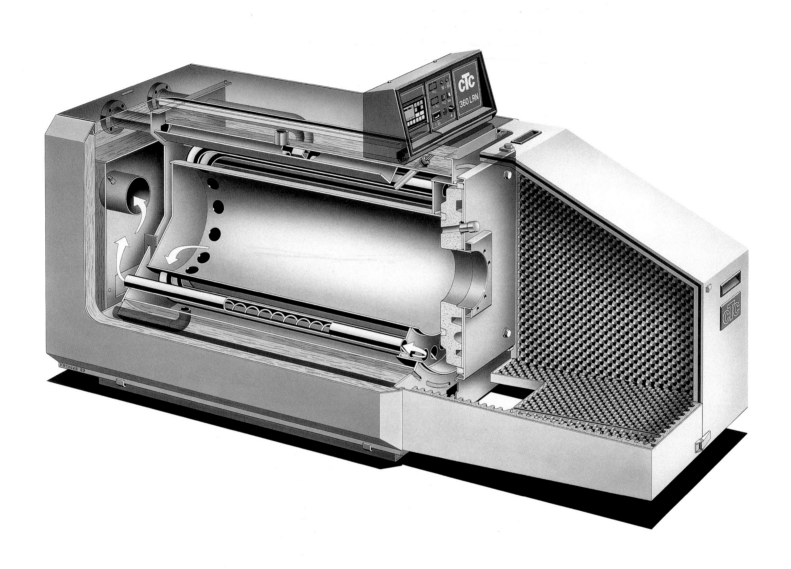

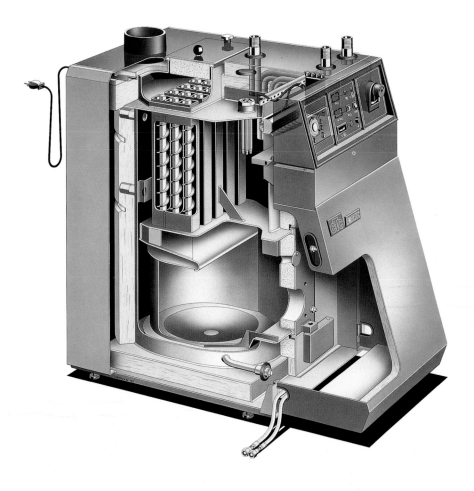

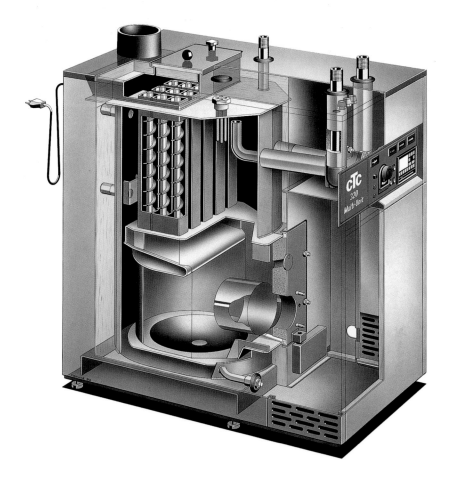

*(This Spread)* **FRANKE TECHN. GRAFIK** *CTC Wärme AG*

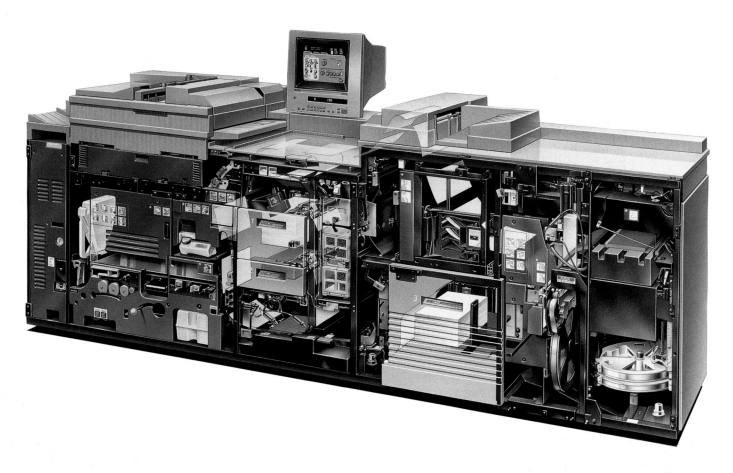

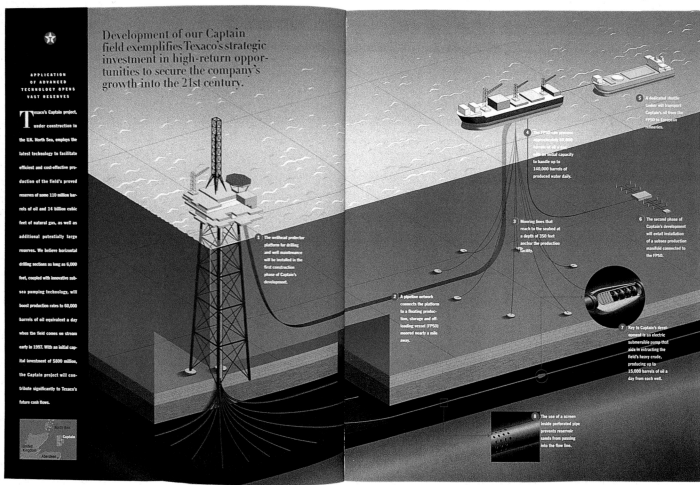

(TOP) **STUDIO LIDDELL** *Rank Zerox* ■ (BOTTOM) **PENTAGRAM DESIGN** *Texaco Inc.*

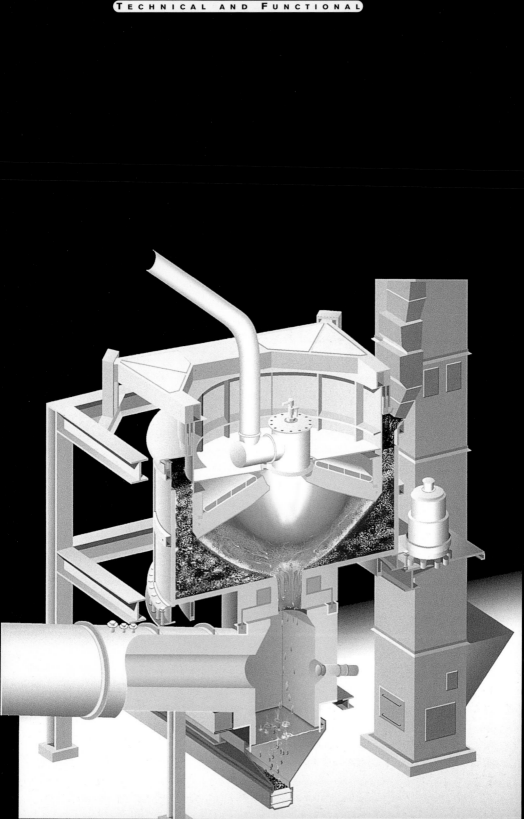

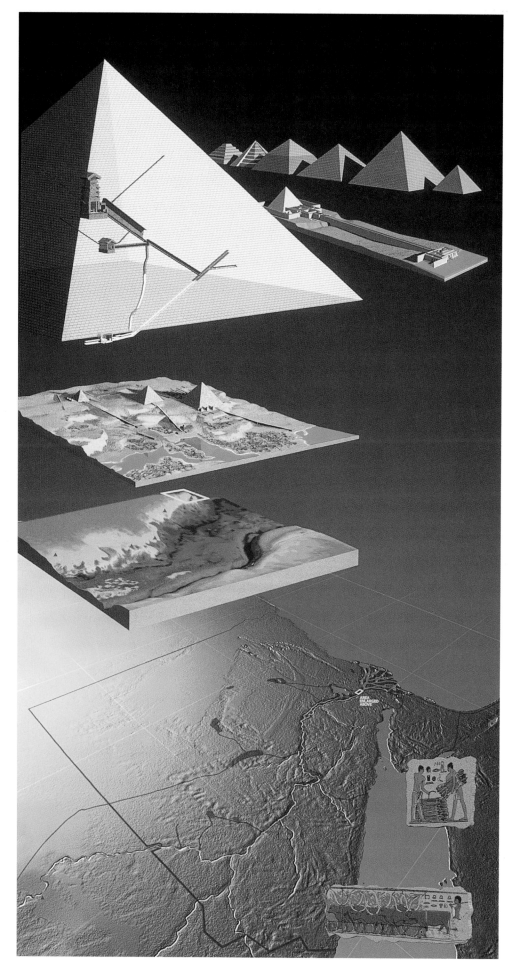

**NATIONAL GEOGRAPHIC SOCIETY** *in-house*

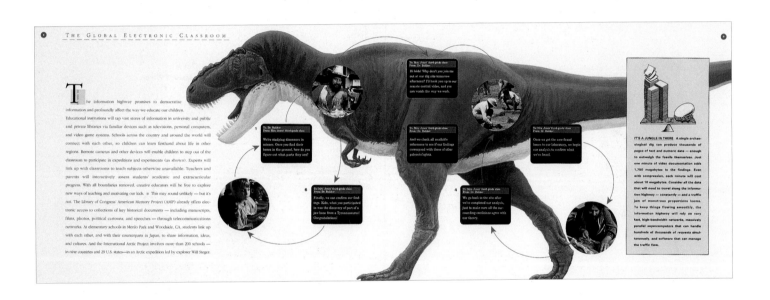

# DIVING ON MONTJUIC

Located on the side of Montjuic, the diving venue has offered television viewers some breathtaking views of divers with Barcelona in the background. The competitors seem to fall from miles high.

**1) Wall** built to reduce wind on the divers.

**2) Structure** above dive platform was built to be covered with canvas to furthur control wind, but wasn't needed.

**3)** 10-meter **platform** is as high as a three story building.

**4)** Seven **judges**, from nations other than those of the competitors, sit in tall seats at poolside, three on one side and four on the other.

**5) Jacuzzi** keeps divers warm and muscles loose.

**6)** Warmup **mats.**

**7)** Three-meter **springboards**. During practice, most divers have prefered the "feel" of board (a) to the other two, but any may be used during competition. This has caused long lines and a few of the stronger divers that prefer not to wait have practiced on board (b) and will likely use this board during competition. Moveable **fulcrum** (inset) enables divers to adjust the spring. Rolled forward (c), the board is tighter and gives the diver less power, but more control. Timing becomes critical. Rolled to the back (d) allows more spring and power, but not as much control.

**8)** Television **camera** positions. Because the diving venue is located on the hillside of Montjuic, the camera at the bottom of the diagram captures dramatic views of divers with Barcelona in the background.

**9)** Stadium **seats** 6,500.

**10)** Water **spray** allows divers to gauge their entry point both visually and audibly.

**11) Impact reduce**r for practice. Pool is equipped with powerful bubble makers that aerate the water under a diver to a thickness of about three feet. This allows divers a softer impact when trying new dives.

**12)** One meter **practice boards**, (a) platform, (b) springboards

**13)** Gaudi's **cathedral** Sagrada Familia.

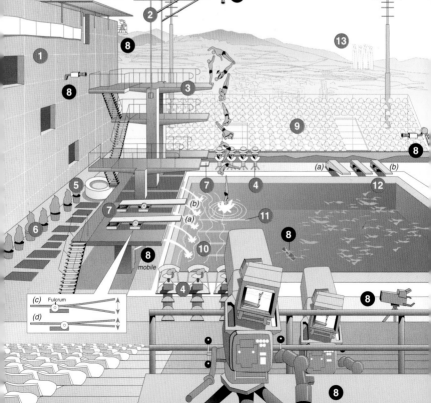

# YACHTING

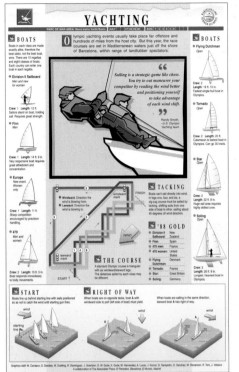

**BOATS** · Olympic yachting events usually take place far offshore and hundreds of miles from the host city. But this year, the race courses are set in Mediterranean waters just off the shore of Barcelona, within range of landlubber spectators.

> Sailing is a strategic game like chess. You try to out maneuver your competitor by reading the wind better and positioning yourself to take advantage of each wind shift.
>
> — Randy Smyth, U.S. Olympic Yachting team

**BOATS** — Flying Dutchman, Tornado, Star, Soling, Finn, Europe, 470, Division II Sailboard

**TACKING**

**THE COURSE**

**'88 GOLD** — Division II Sailboard: New Zealand; Finn: Spain; 470 women: France; 470 men: United States; Flying Dutchman: Denmark; Tornado: France; Star: Great Britain; Soling: Germany

**START** · **RIGHT OF WAY**

# CYCLING

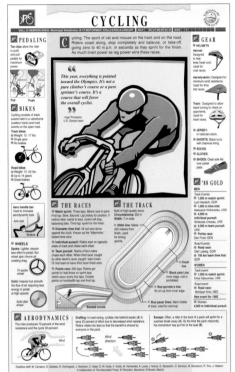

**PEDALING** · Cycling: The sport of cat and mouse on the track and on the road. Riders coast along, stop completely and balance, or take-off, going zero to 40 m.p.h. in seconds as they sprint for the finish. As much brain power as leg power wins these races.

> This year, everything is pointed toward the Olympics. It's not a pure climber's course or a pure sprinter's course. It's a course that will favor the overall cyclist.
>
> —Inga Thompson, U.S. Olympic team

**BIKES** — Track bikes, Road bikes

**THE RACES** · **THE TRACK**

**AERODYNAMICS**

# RUNNING

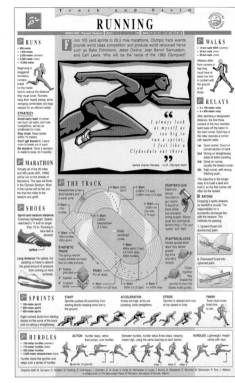

**RUNS** · From 100 yard sprints to 26.2 mile marathons, Olympic track events provide world class competition and produce world renowned heros such as Babe Didrickson, Jesse Owens, Joan Benoit Samuelson, and Carl Lewis. Who will be the heros of the 1992 Olympiad?

> I always look at myself as too big to run a sprint. I feel like a Clydesdale out there.
>
> Jackie Joyner-Kersee, —U.S. Olympic team

**WALKS** · **RELAYS** · **MARATHON**

**THE TRACK** · **SHOES**

**SPRINTS** · **HURDLES**

# ARCHERY

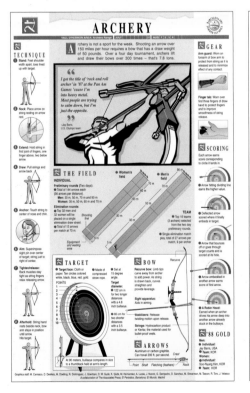

**TECHNIQUE** · Archery is not a sport for the weak. Shooting an arrow over 150 miles per hour requires a bow that has a draw weight of 50 pounds. Over a four day tournament, archers lift and draw their bows over 300 times – that's 7.8 tons.

> I got the title of 'rock and roll archer' in '87 at the Pan Am Games 'cause I'm into heavy metal. Most people are trying to calm down, but I'm just the opposite.
>
> —Jay Barrs, U.S. Olympic team

**GEAR** · **SCORING**

**THE FIELD**

**TARGET** · **BOW** · **ARROWS**

**'88 GOLD**

# WEIGHTLIFTING

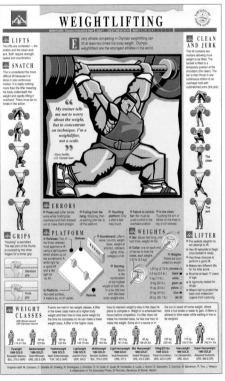

**LIFTS** · Two lifts are contested — the snatch and the clean-and-jerk. Both require strength, speed and coordination.

> My trainer tells me not to worry about the weight, but to concentrate on technique. I'm a weightlifter, not a scale.
>
> —Dave Saville, U.S. Olympic team

**SNATCH** · **CLEAN AND JERK**

**ERRORS** · **GRIPS** · **PLATFORM** · **WEIGHTS** · **LIFTER**

**WEIGHT CLASSES**

# THROWING

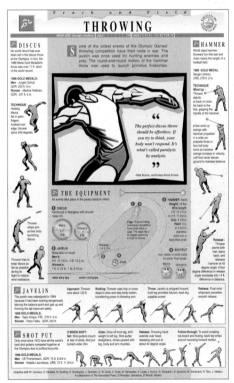

**DISCUS** · Some of the oldest events of the Olympic Games' throwing competition have their roots in war. The javelin was once used for hunting enemies and prey. The round-and-round motion of the hammer throw was used to launch primitive firebombs.

> The perfect discus throw should be effortless. If you try to think, your body isn't called paralysis by analysis.
>
> —Mike Buncic, world-class discus thrower

**HAMMER** · **JAVELIN** · **SHOT PUT**

**TECHNIQUE** · **THE EQUIPMENT**

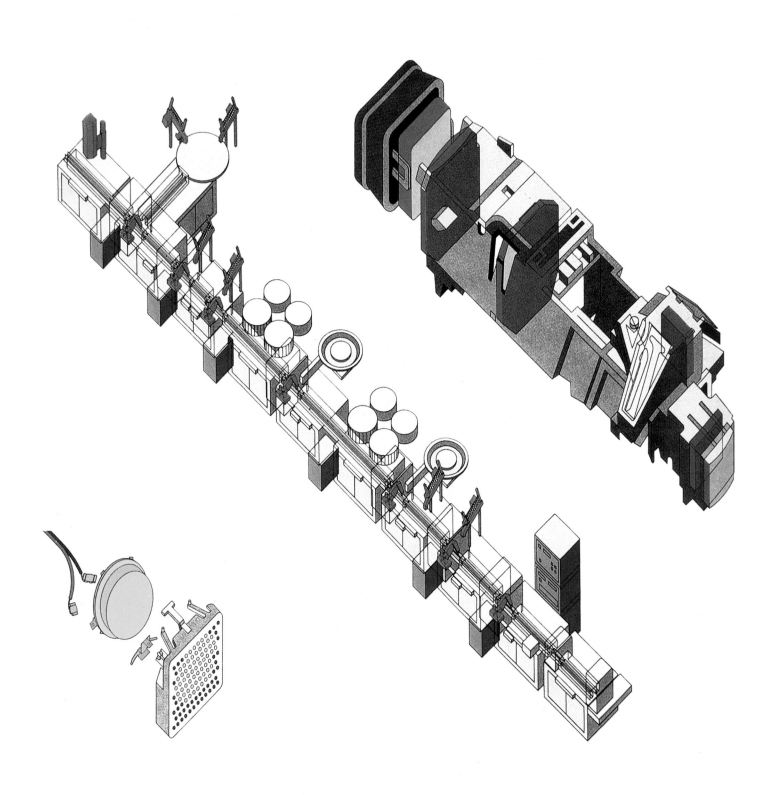

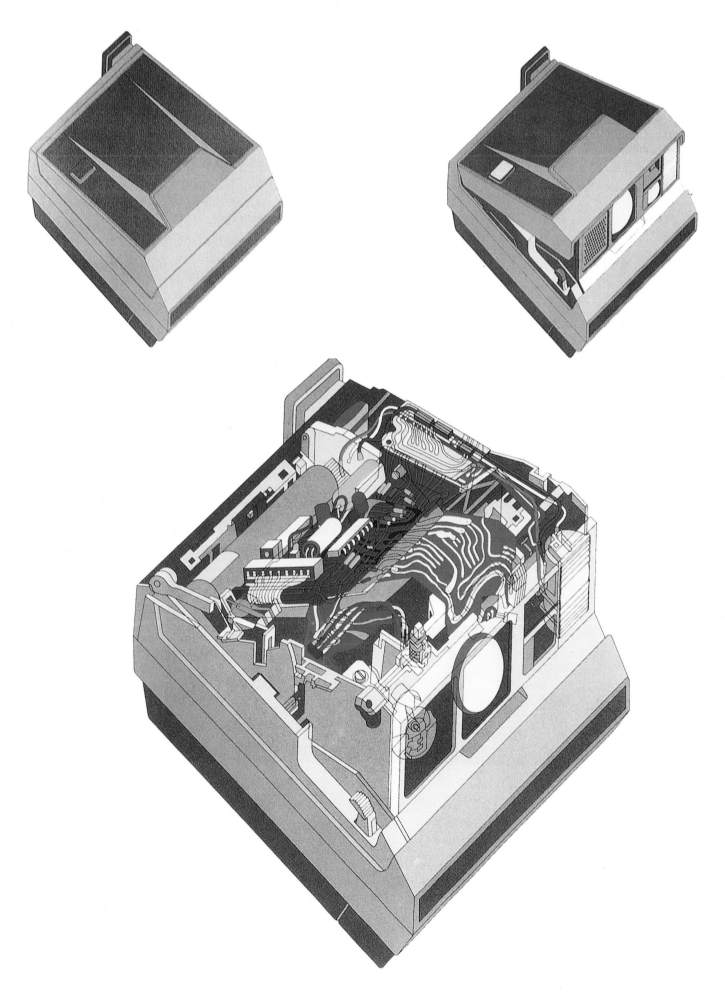

*(THIS SPREAD)* **POLAROID CORPORATION** *in-house*

PUERTO RICO

Virgin Gorda

St. Martin

St. Barthelemy

St. Kitts

Iles des Saintes

MARTINIQUE

ST. LUCIA

Bequia

Tobago Cays

Carriacou

GRENADA

Aruba

Curacao

Bonaire

Los Testigos

Isla de Margarita

VENEZUELA

Puerto la Cruz

MAPS AND PLANS

KARTEN UND PLÄNE

CARTES ET PLANS

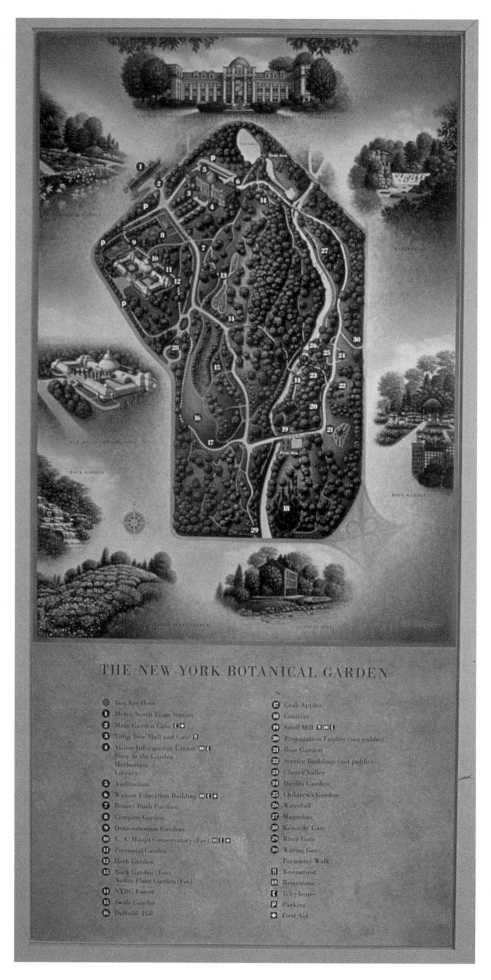

# THE NEW YORK BOTANICAL GARDEN

- ● You Are Here
- ❶ Metro-North Train Station
- ❷ Main Garden Gate
- ❸ Tulip Tree Mall and Cafe
- ❹ Visitor Information Center
  Shop in the Garden
  Herbarium
  Library
- ❺ Auditorium
- ❻ Watson Education Building
- ❼ Beauty Bush Pavilion
- ❽ Compton Garden
- ❾ Demonstration Gardens
- ❿ E. A. Haupt Conservatory (Fee)
- ⓫ Perennial Garden
- ⓬ Herb Garden
- ⓭ Rock Garden (Fee)
  Native Plant Garden (Fee)
- ⓮ NYBG Forest
- ⓯ Snuff Gazebo
- ⓰ Daffodil Hill

- ⓱ Crab Apples
- ⓲ Conifers
- ⓳ Snuff Mill
- ⓴ Propagation Facility (not public)
- 21 Rose Garden
- 22 Service Buildings (not public)
- 23 Cherry Valley
- 24 Daylily Garden
- 25 Children's Garden
- 26 Waterfall
- 27 Magnolias
- 28 Kennedy Gate
- 29 River Gate
- 30 Waring Gate
  Perimeter Walk
- 🍴 Restaurant
- 🚻 Restrooms
- ☎ Telephone
- 🅿 Parking
- ✚ First Aid

(*PRECEDING SPREAD*) **HORNALL ANDERSON DESIGN WORKS, INC.** *Windstar Cruises*

VISITOR INFORMATION CENTER · LIBRARY · SHOP IN THE GARDEN · HERBARIUM

Twin Lakes

Picnic Area

PERENNIAL GARDEN

WATERFALL

E. A. HAUPT CONSERVATORY

ROSE GARDEN

ROCK GARDEN

Snuff Mill Road

Picnic Area

N

NATIVE PLANT GARDEN

SNUFF MILL

(*THIS SPREAD*) **CLIFFORD SELBERT DESIGN, INC.** *New York Botanical Gardens*

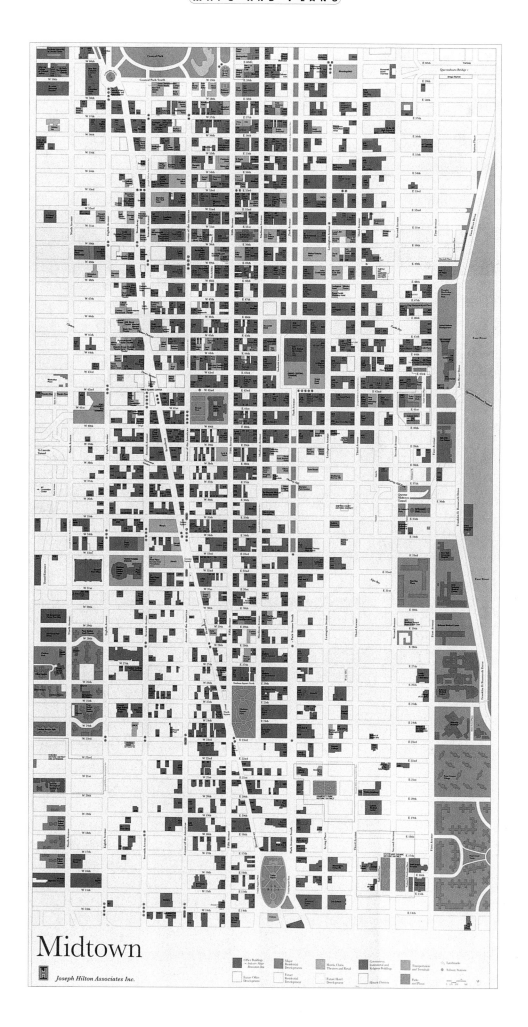

# Midtown

Joseph Hilton Associates Inc.

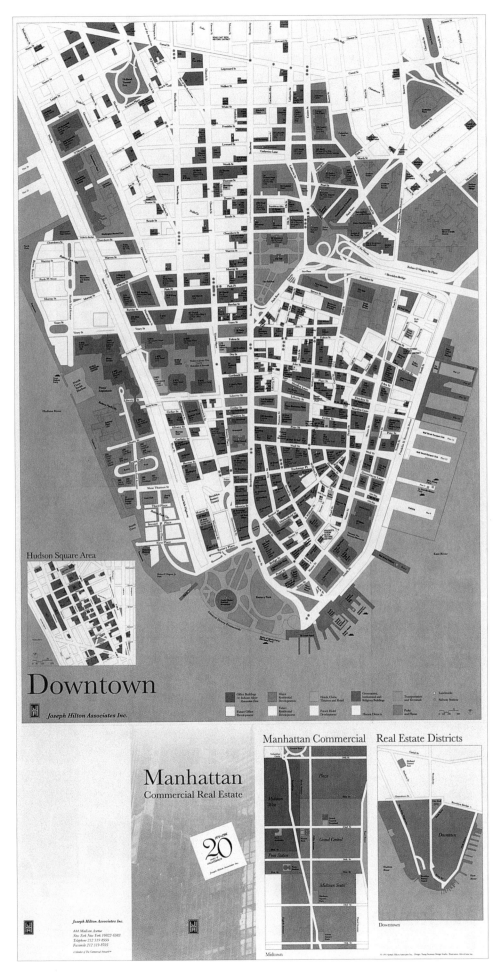

Hudson Square Area

# Downtown

Joseph Hilton Associates Inc.

# Manhattan
Commercial Real Estate

Joseph Hilton Associates Inc.

Manhattan Commercial   Real Estate Districts

(THIS SPREAD) **TSANG SEYMOUR DESIGN** Joseph Hilton Associates

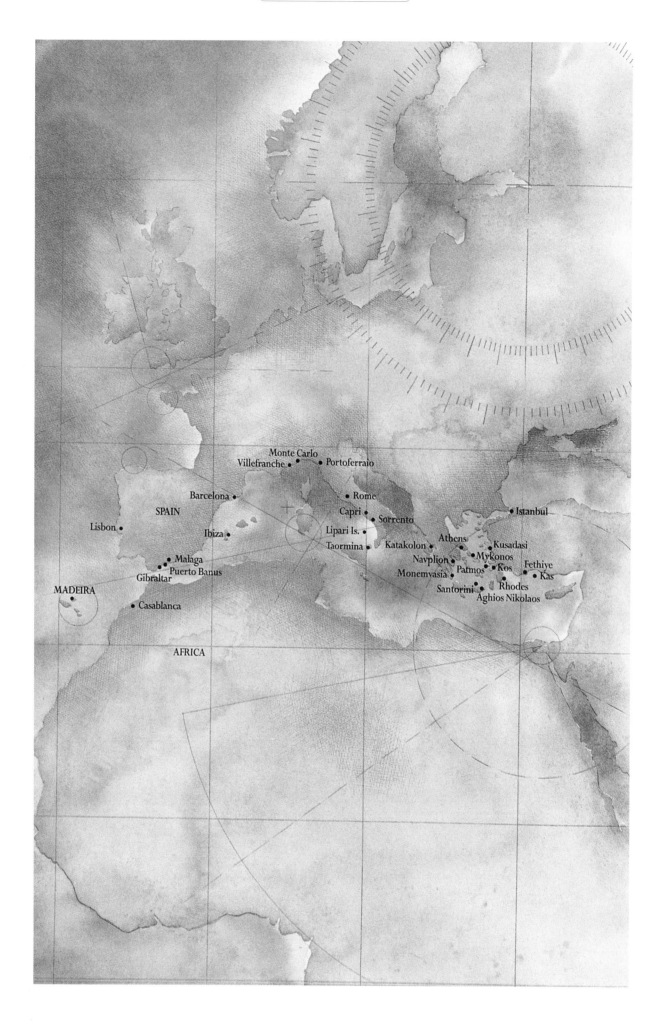

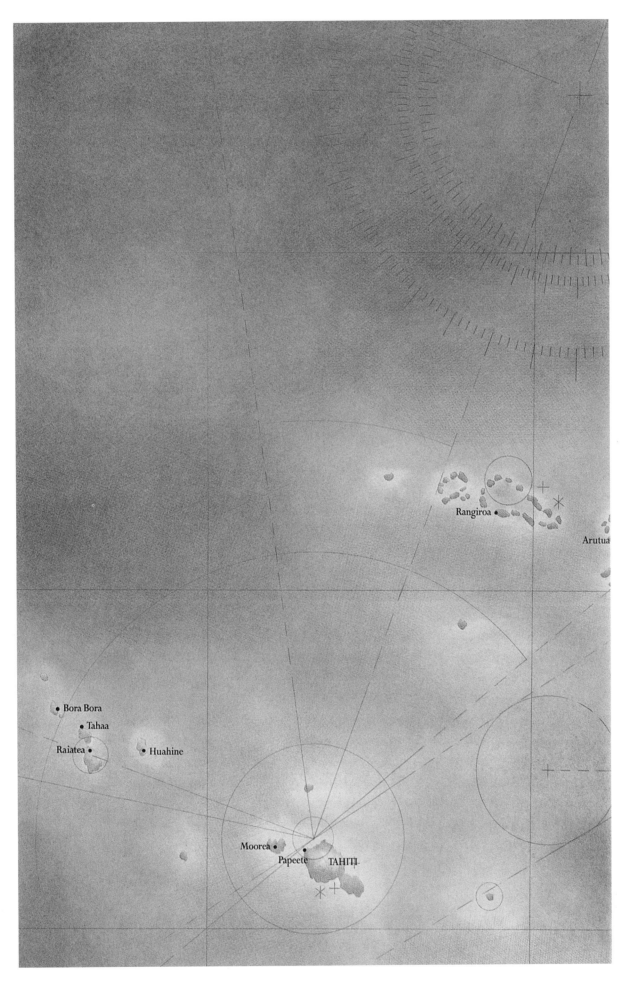

(THIS SPREAD) **HORNALL ANDERSON DESIGN WORKS, INC.** Windstar Cruises

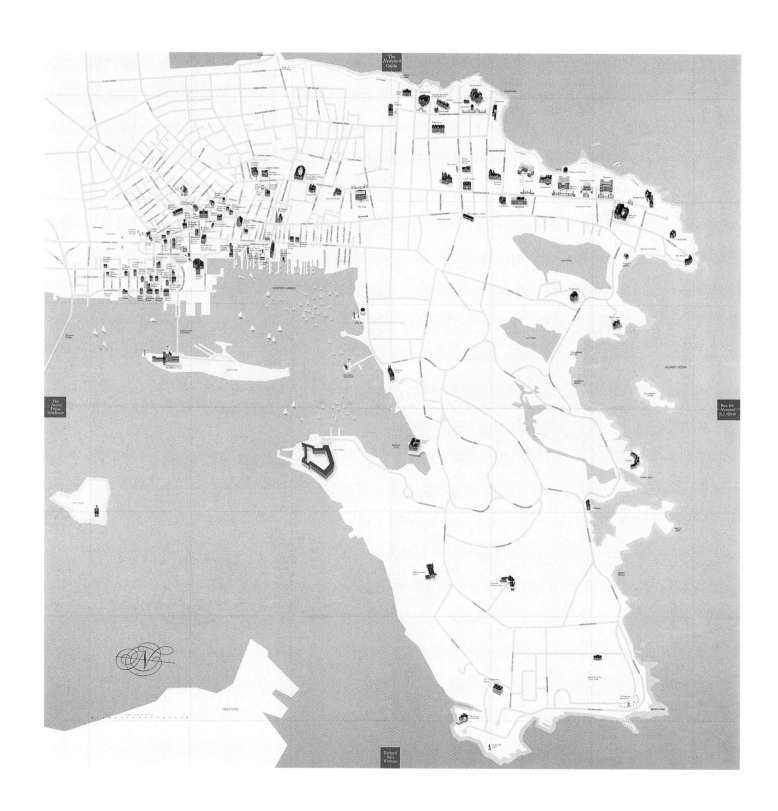

**RICHARD SAUL WURMAN** *The Initial Press Syndicate*

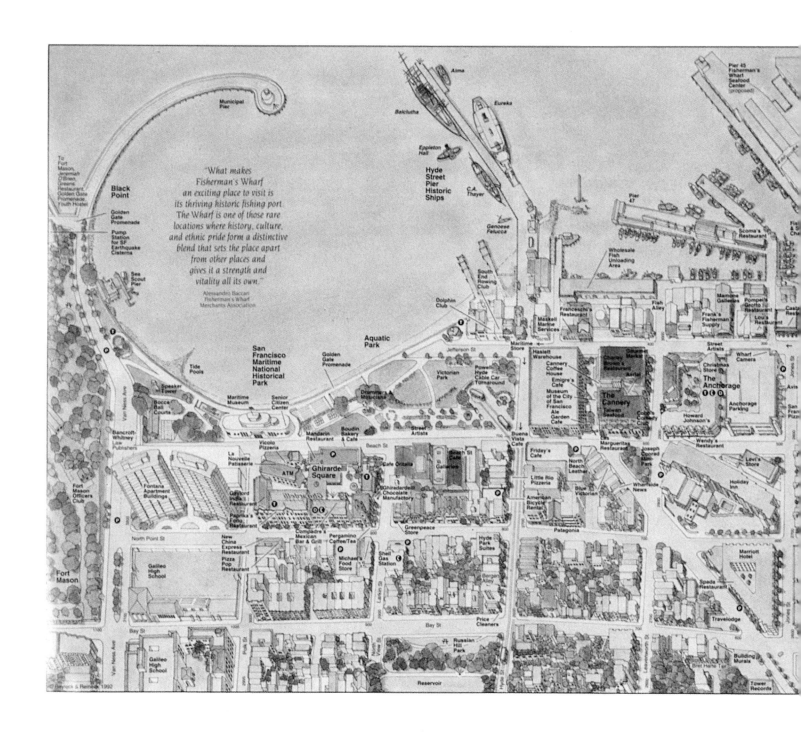

*"What makes Fisherman's Wharf an exciting place to visit is its thriving historic fishing port. The Wharf is one of those rare locations where history, culture, and ethnic pride form a distinctive blend that sets the place apart from other places and gives it a strength and vitality all its own."*

Alessandro Baccari
Fisherman's Wharf
Merchants Association

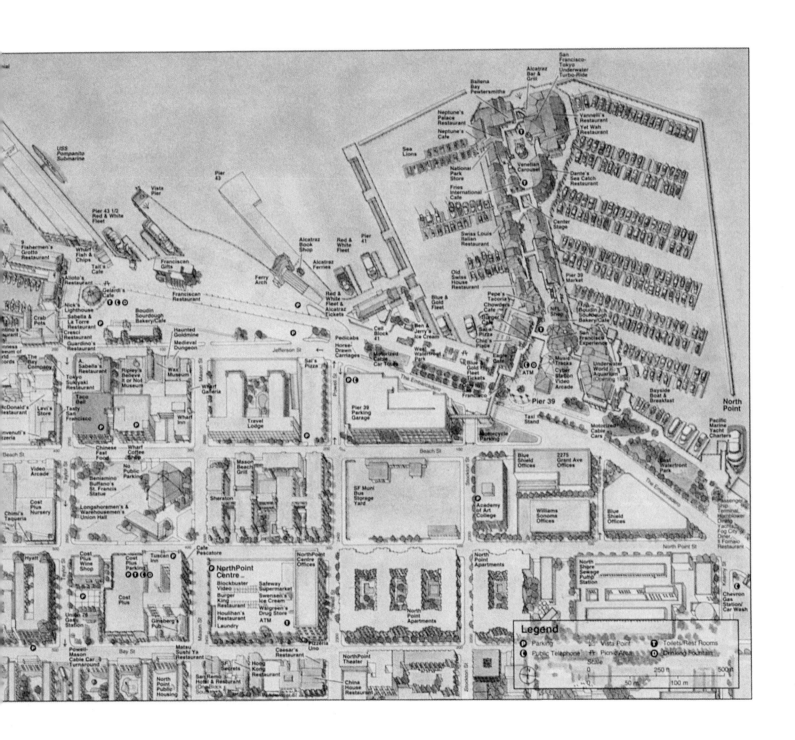

*(THIS SPREAD)* **REINECK & REINECK** *Rufus Graphics*

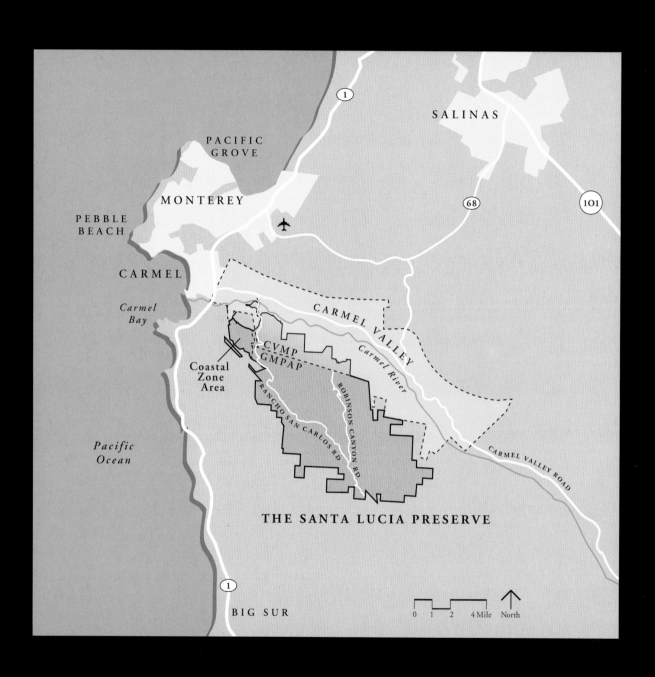

PACIFIC
GROVE

SALINAS

MONTEREY

PEBBLE
BEACH

CARMEL

*Carmel
Bay*

CARMEL VALLEY

*Carmel River*

CVMP
GMPAP

Coastal
Zone
Area

RANCHO SAN CARLOS RD

ROBINSON CANYON RD

CARMEL VALLEY ROAD

*Pacific
Ocean*

THE SANTA LUCIA PRESERVE

BIG SUR

0  1  2      4 Mile    North

**CRONAN DESIGN** *Robert Lamb Hart*

**REINECK & REINECK** *Rufus Graphics*

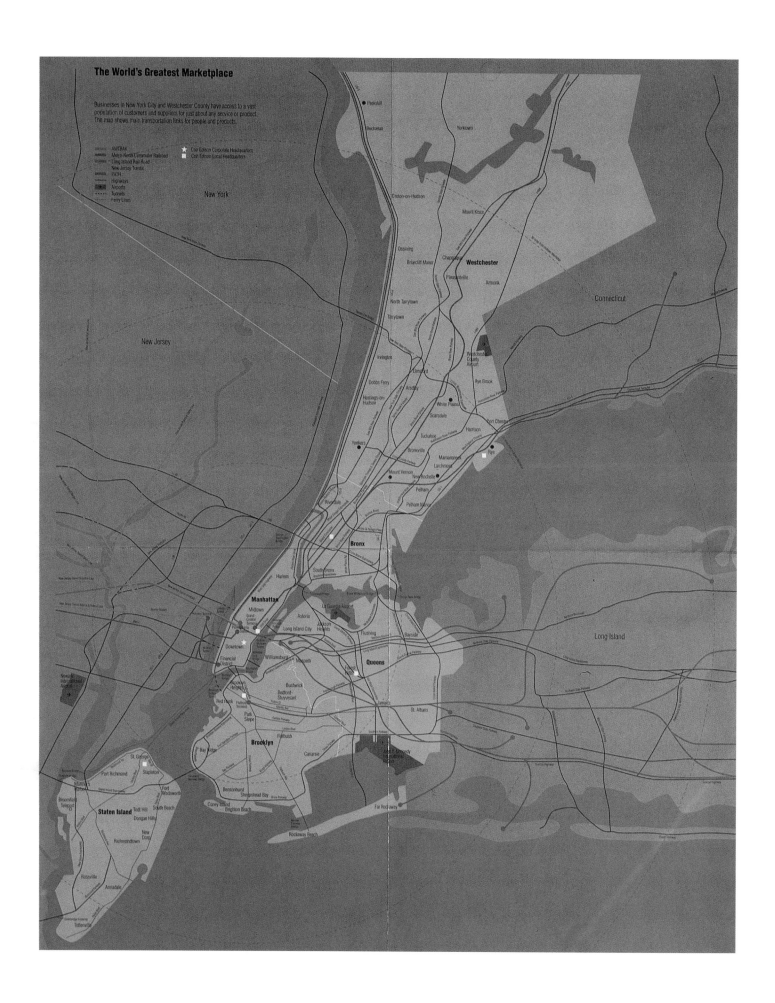

**The World's Greatest Marketplace**

Businesses in New York City and Westchester County have access to a vast population of customers and suppliers for just about any service or product. The map shows main transportation links for people and products.

AMTRAK
Metro-North Commuter Railroad
Long Island Rail Road
New Jersey Transit
PATH
Highways
Airports
Tunnels
Ferry Lines

★ Con Edison Corporate Headquarters
□ Con Edison Local Headquarters

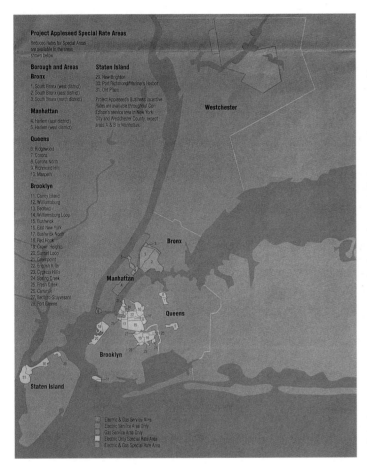

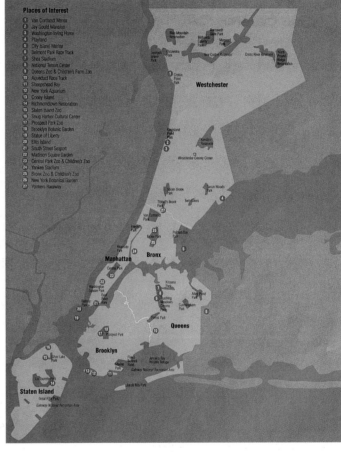

*(This Spread)* **BEAU GARDNER ASSOCIATES** *Consolidated Edison*

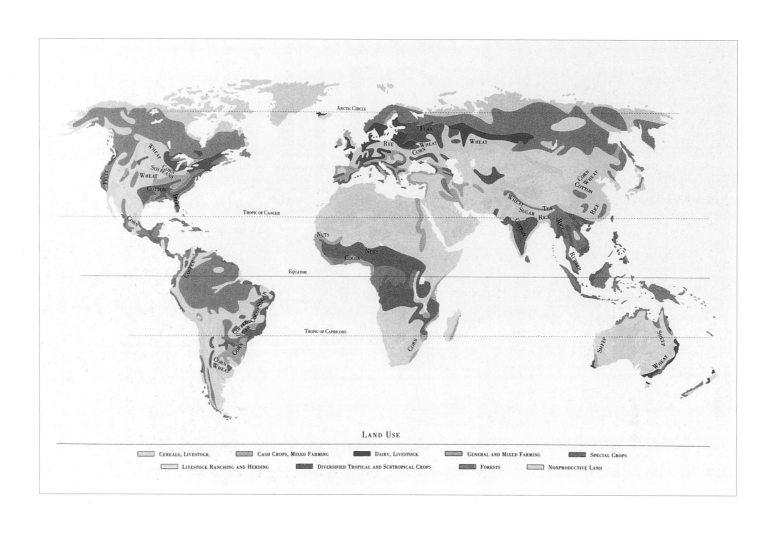

LAND USE

CEREALS, LIVESTOCK    CASH CROPS, MIXED FARMING    DAIRY, LIVESTOCK    GENERAL AND MIXED FARMING    SPECIAL CROPS

LIVESTOCK RANCHING AND HERDING    DIVERSIFIED TROPICAL AND SUBTROPICAL CROPS    FORESTS    NONPRODUCTIVE LAND

(THIS SPREAD) **PENTAGRAM DESIGN** Hammond Inc.

*(THIS SPREAD)* **PENTAGRAM DESIGN** *Hammond Inc.*

AREA OF
OPTIMIZATION
The red band which
surrounds this map
defines the "Area of
Optimization." Within
this bounding curve is
the most accurate
conformal map that can
be made of the region.
Outside the optimized
area, distortion increases
rapidly, and tears or
other irregularities in
the grid may occur.
(See page 11 for
additional information.)

© Copyright by HAMMOND INCORPORATED, Maplewood, N.J.

POPULATION OF CITIES AND TOWNS

| ▣ OVER 3,000,000 | ● 500,000 - 999,999 | ○ UNDER 100,000 |
| ▨ 1,000,000 - 2,999,999 | ● 100,000 - 499,999 | |

SCALE 1:24,000,000    OPTIMAL CONFORMAL PROJECTION

MILES  0        400        800        1200

KILOMETERS  0    400        800    1200

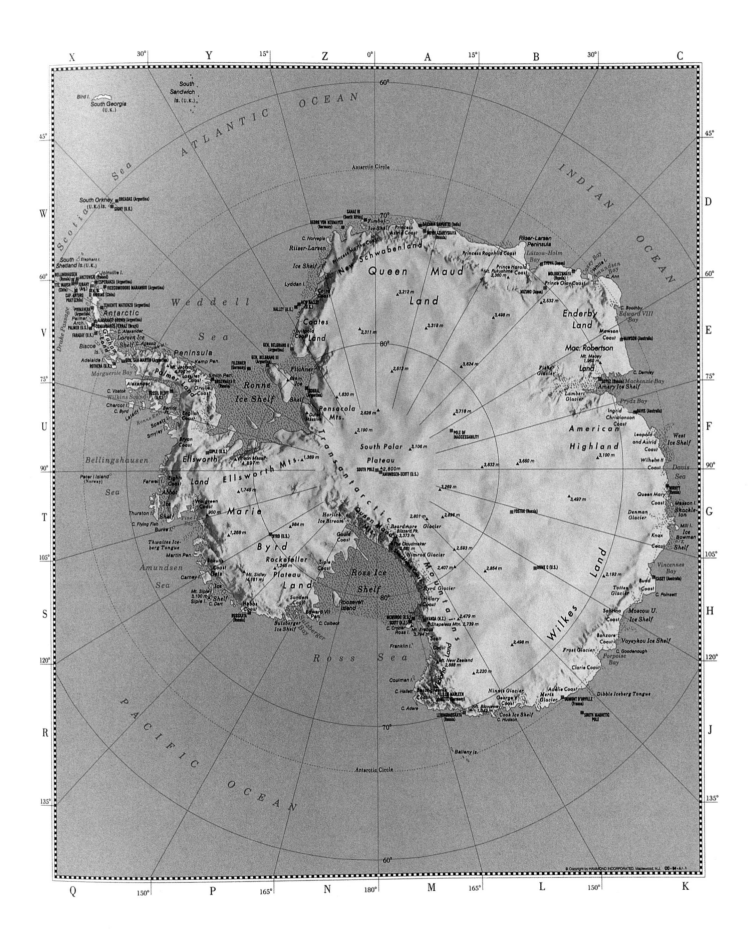

(THIS SPREAD) **PENTAGRAM DESIGN** *Hammond Inc.*

BRAMI DESIGN *New England Chapter, Society of Office and Industrial Realtors*

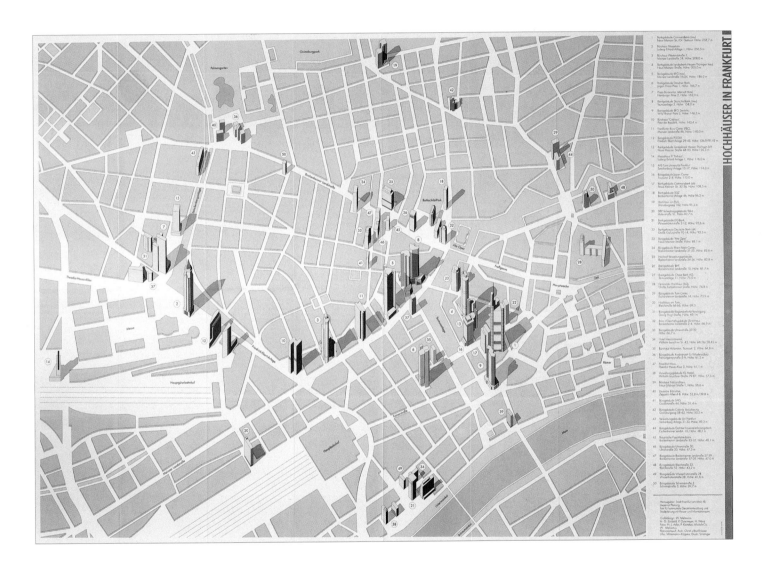

**WILHELM MALKEMUS** *Stadt Frankfurt am Main*

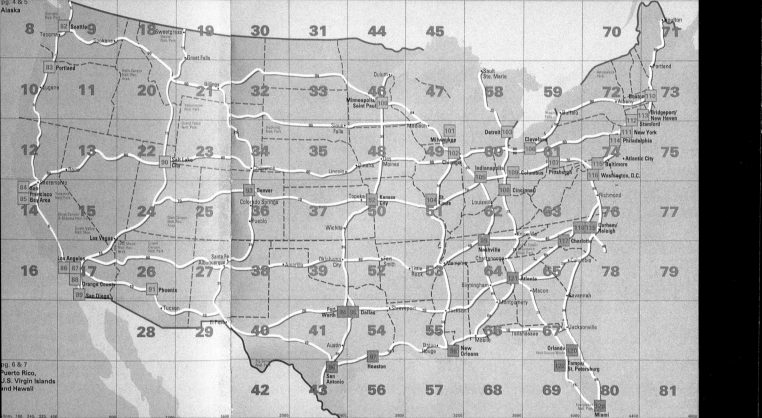

(THIS SPREAD) **RICHARD SAUL WURMAN** *ACCESS Press/H.M. Gousha*

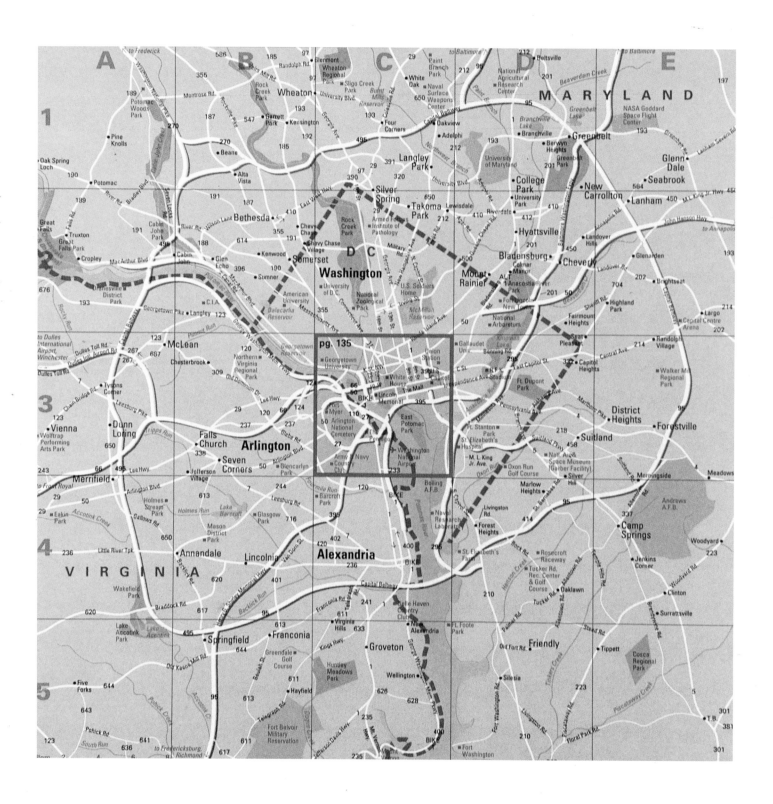

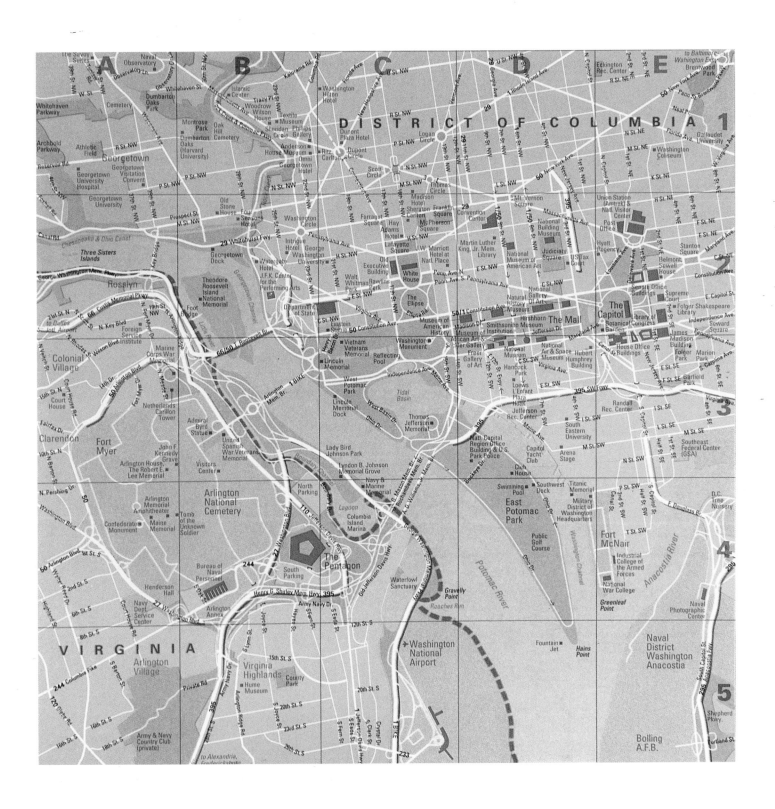

(THIS SPREAD) **RICHARD SAUL WURMAN** *ACCESS Press/H.M. Gousha*

Montgomery County

PA 9

I-276 PA Tpke

Exit 25

Chemical Rd

Germantown Pk

Ridge Pike

US 202

I-476

Philadelphia

Points of interest
1   Valley Forge National Historical Park
2   Philadelphia Zoo
3   Civic Center
4   Museum of Art
5   City Hall
6   Independence National Historical Park
7   Penn's Landing
8   Sports Complex
9   Airport

1

Exit 24   A

B

C   South Gulph Rd   D   E   F

I-76 Schuylkill Expwy

Lincoln Dr

Henry Ave

US 202

PA 320   Spring Mill Rd   PA 23   I-76 Schuylkill Expwy   G   Ridge Ave

US 1 Roosevelt Blvd

I-95

US 30 Lancaster Ave

PA 320   Conshohocken State Rd   H

Belmont Ave   US 1   I   US 1

Hunting Park Ave

Montgomery Ave   J

US 30 Lancaster Ave   Kelly Dr   K   Ridge Ave

PA 23   Monument Rd   PA 611 Broad St

US 1 City Ave   Belmont Ave   L

Ben Franklin Br

The Parkway   M   I-676–US 30–Vine St   4

Girard Ave   2   N   Arch St   NJ 38

Spring Garden St   39th St   O   5   Market St   6   7   I-676

Market St   22nd St   18th St   P   I-95

Spruce St   Q   PA 291 Broad St

Civic Center Blvd   3   R   South St

S

Schuylkill River   TU   V   W   X

I-76 Schuylkill Expwy   8   West Whitman St

9

Delaware River

I-95

**JOEL KATZ DESIGN ASSOCIATES** *Pennsylvania Department of Transportation*

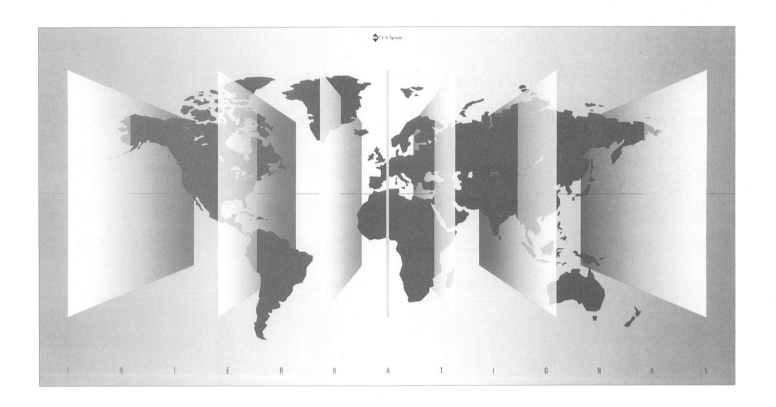

**MARK ANDERSON DESIGN** *US Sprint Communications Corporation*

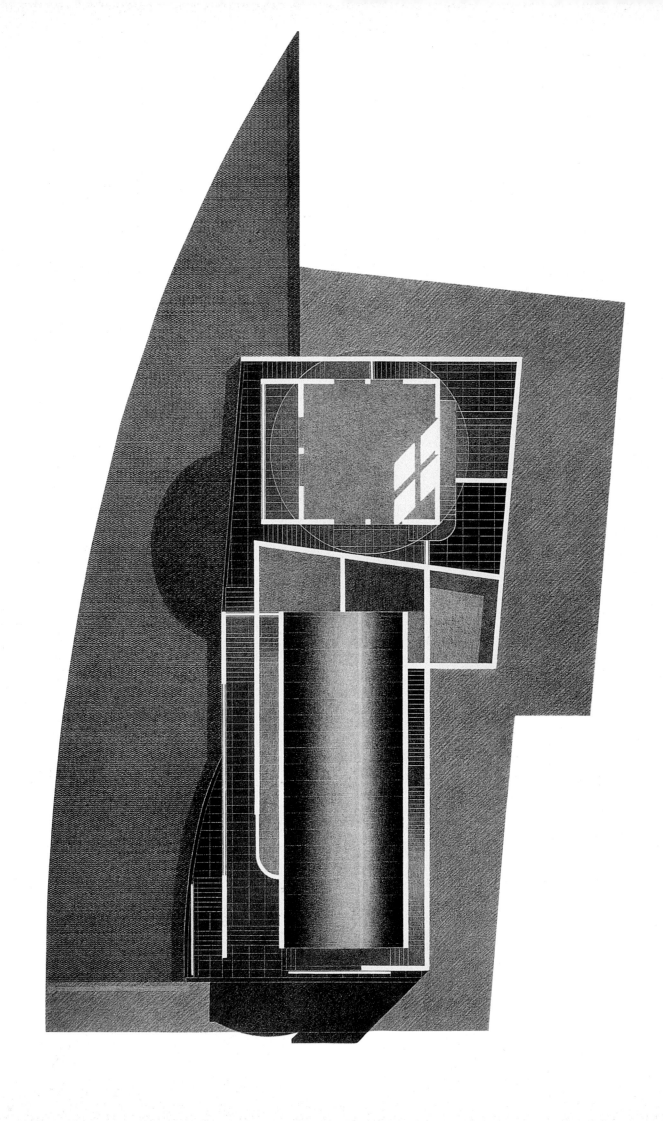

ARCHITECTURAL

ARCHITEKTUR

ARCHITECTURE

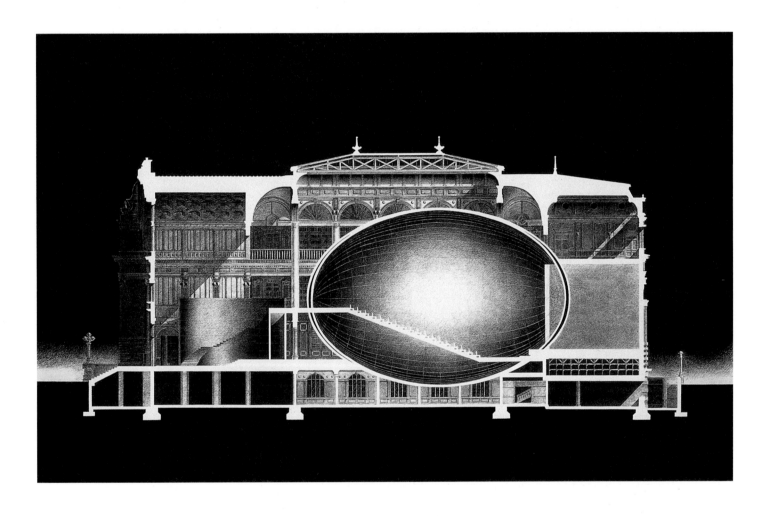

*(Preceding Spread and This Spread)* **IKKO TANAKA DESIGN STUDIO** *Toto Ltd.*

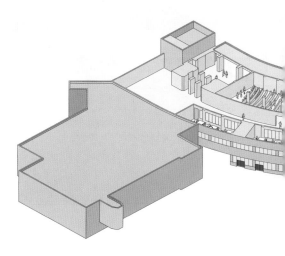

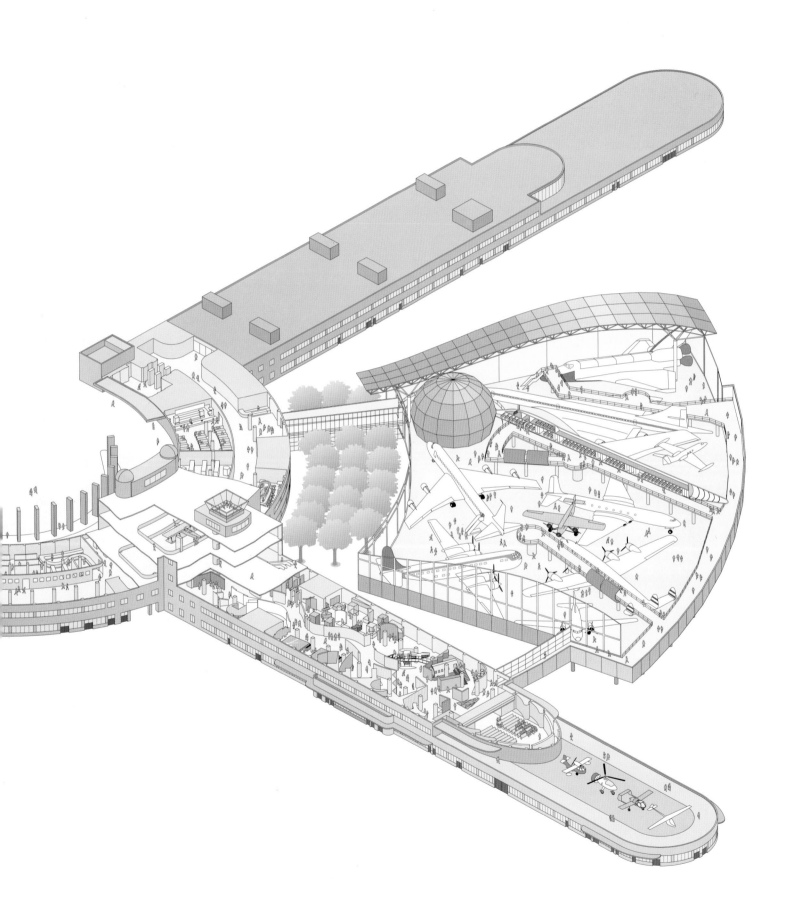

**AGNEW MOYER SMITH INC.** *Commissioners of Allegheny County*

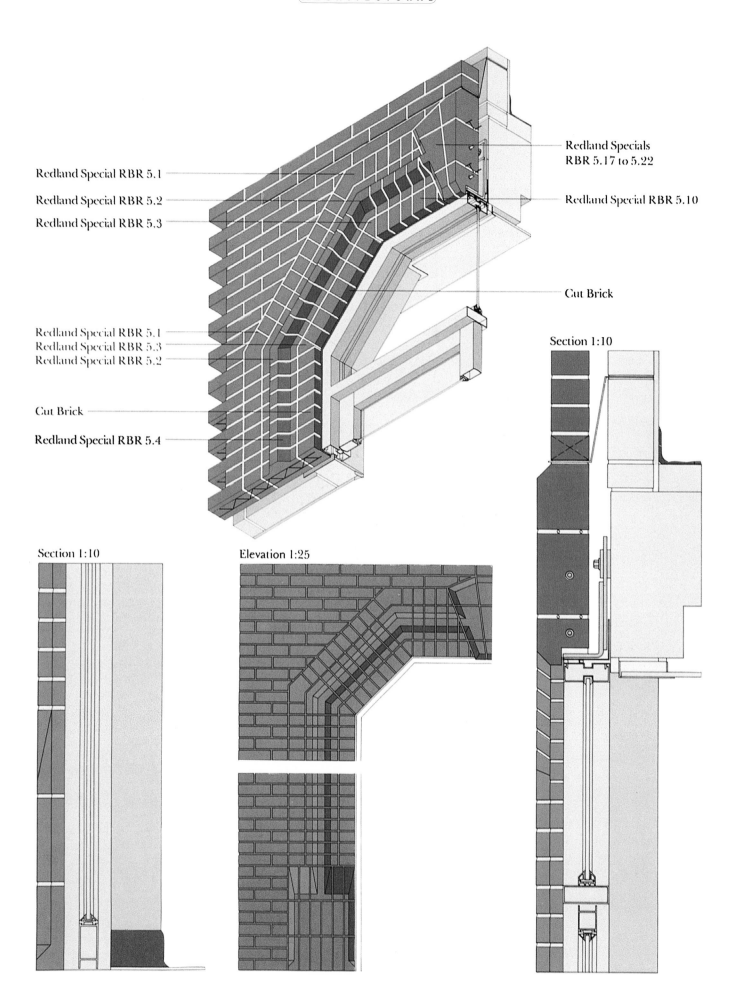

Redland Special RBR 5.1

Redland Special RBR 5.2

Redland Special RBR 5.3

Redland Special RBR 5.1
Redland Special RBR 5.3
Redland Special RBR 5.2

Cut Brick

Redland Special RBR 5.4

Redland Specials
RBR 5.17 to 5.22

Redland Special RBR 5.10

Cut Brick

Section 1:10

Section 1:10

Elevation 1:25

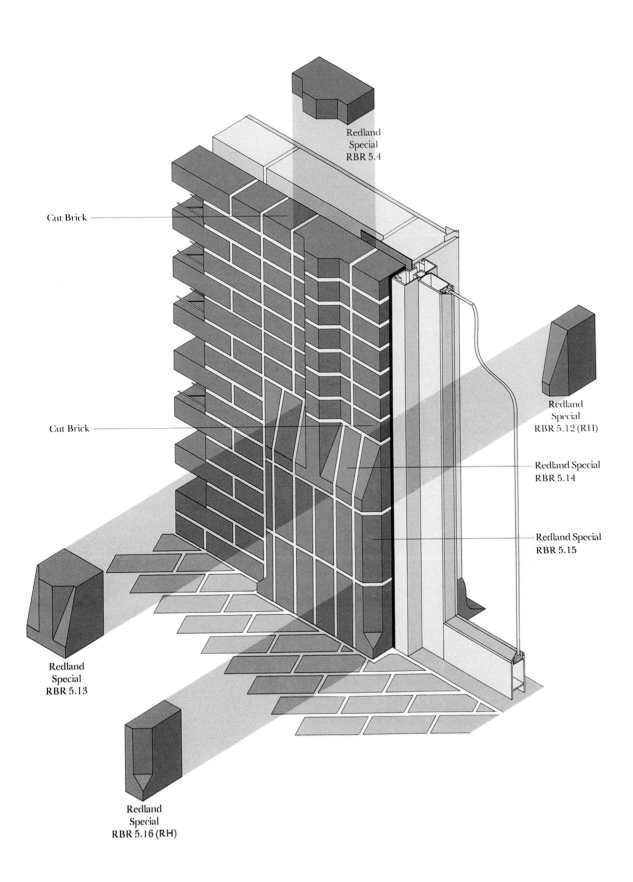

Redland
Special
RBR 5.4

Cut Brick

Cut Brick

Redland
Special
RBR 5.12 (RH)

Redland Special
RBR 5.14

Redland Special
RBR 5.15

Redland
Special
RBR 5.13

Redland
Special
RBR 5.16 (RH)

**WINGS DESIGN CONSULTANTS** *Redland Bricks*

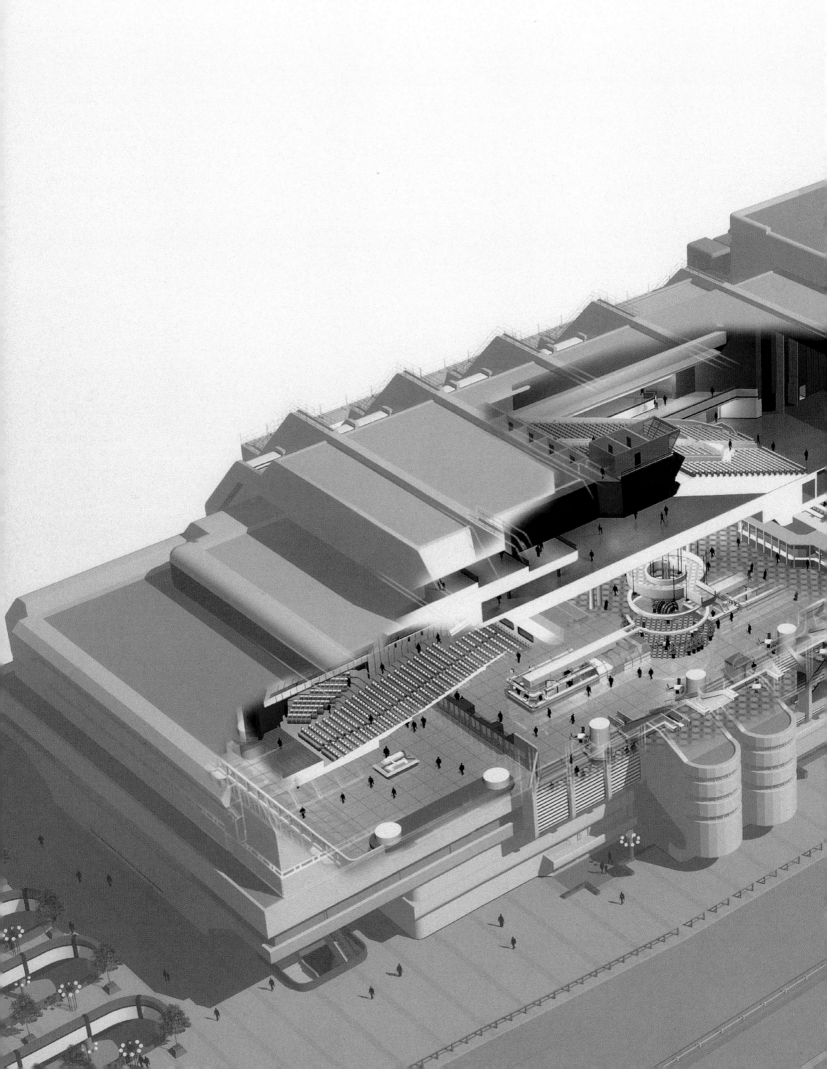

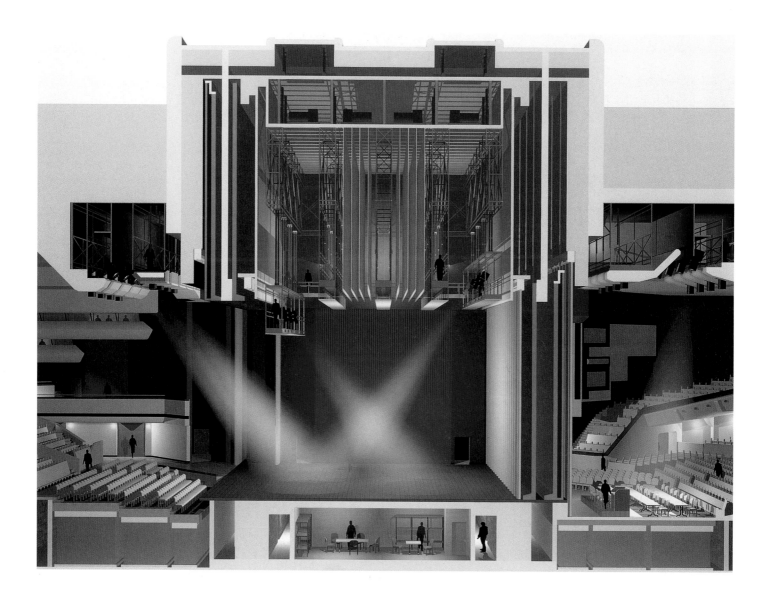

*(PRECEDING SPREAD AND THIS SPREAD)* **SCHRAMMS, GRAPHIK-DESIGN & DIGITAL MEDIA ART** *Messe Berlin GmbH*

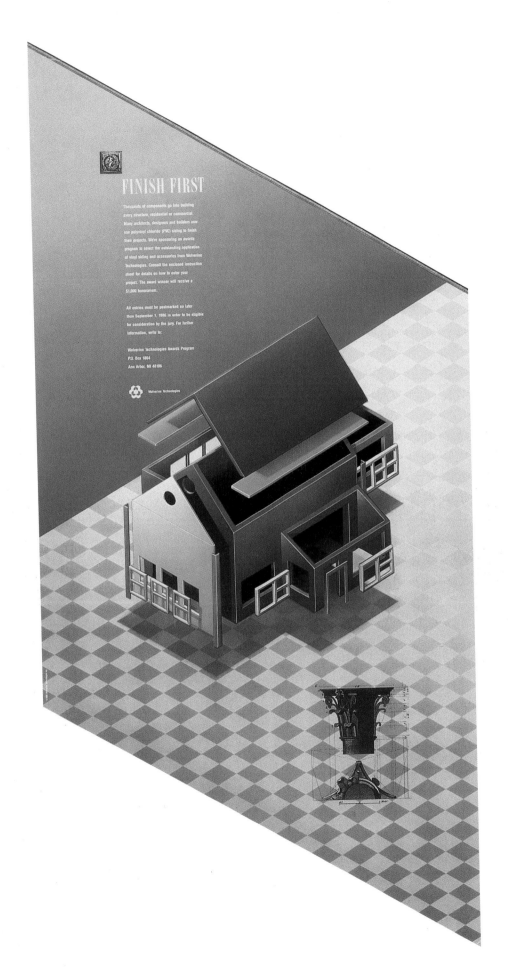

**GROUP 243, INC.** *Wolverine Technologies*

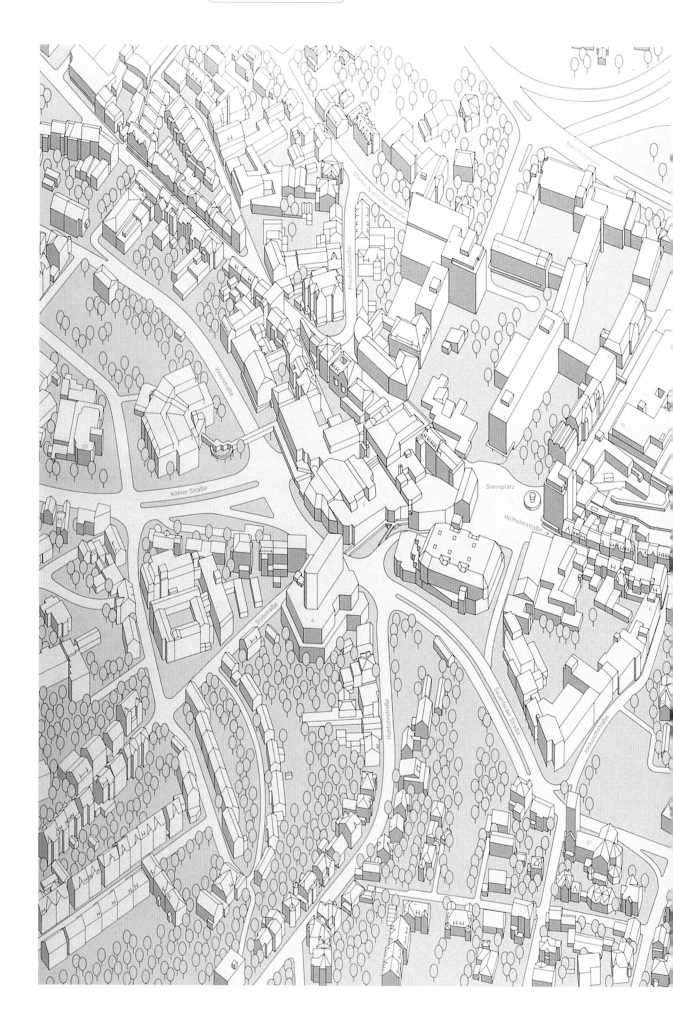

**ROTIS BÜROS** *Druckhaus Maack*

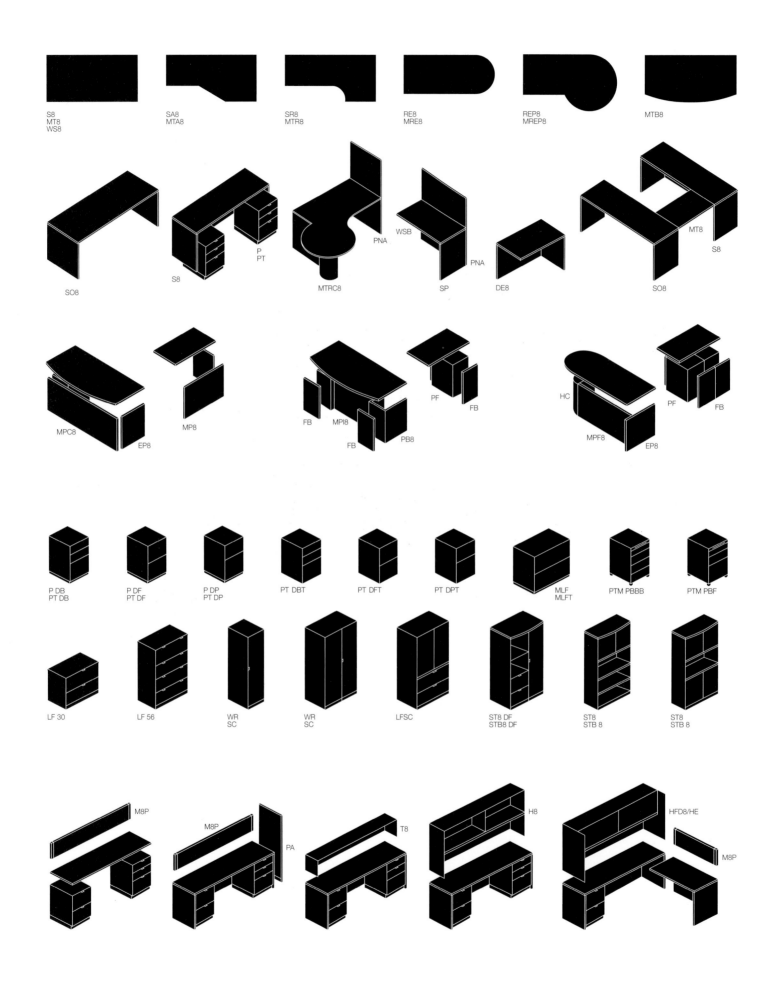

S8
MT8
WS8

SA8
MTA8

SR8
MTR8

RE8
MRE8

REP8
MREP8

MTB8

SO8

S8

P
PT

PNA

MTRC8

WSB

SP

PNA

DE8

MT8

S8

SO8

MPC8

EP8

MP8

FB

MPI8

FB

PB8

PF

FB

HC

MPF8

EP8

PF

FB

P DB
PT DB

P DF
PT DF

P DP
PT DP

PT DBT

PT DFT

PT DPT

MLF
MLFT

PTM PBBB

PTM PBF

LF 30

LF 56

WR
SC

WR
SC

LFSC

ST8 DF
STB8 DF

ST8
STB 8

ST8
STB 8

M8P

M8P

PA

T8

H8

HFD8/HE

M8P

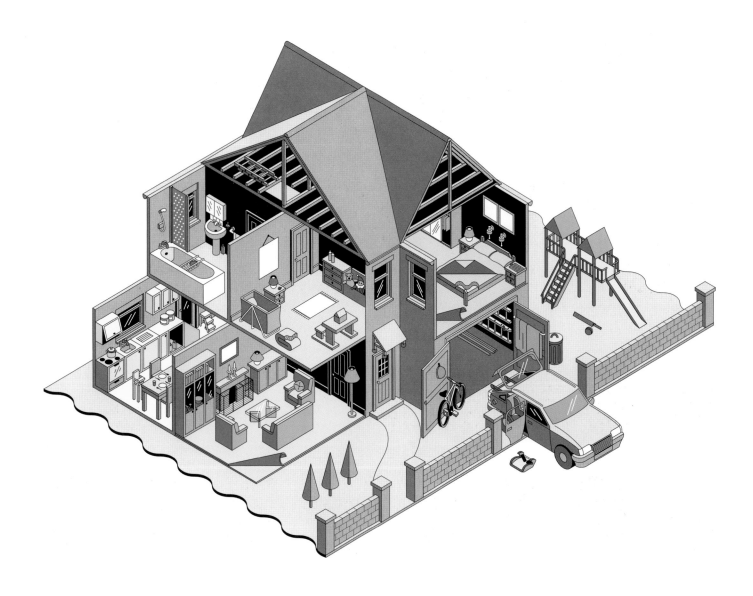

**GRUNDY & NORTHEDGE / UFFINDELL AND WEST** *British Standards Institution*

**Annapolis Mall**

In addition to gaining environmental and land use approvals, L&B lawyers **defeated court challenges** that sought to block Nordstrom's from becoming an anchor tenant in the expanded mall.

**Piney Glen Village**

L&B structured the development partnership and represented it in obtaining **federal and state wetlands permits,** addressing mitigation requirements, preserving open space, negotiating sales and development contracts and establishing a community association in this environmentally sensitive community in Potomac, Md.

**Leisure World**

For the developers of Maryland's largest retirement community, L&B obtained **Master Plan and zoning amendments,** created multiple condominium associations and negotiated shopping center leases.

**Kentlands**

To preserve the neo-tradit concept that drives this cu edge residential developme in Gaithersburg, Md., L&B lawyers created **unique co nity association documen** will enable the governance the community to evolve a the needs of its owners and residents change.

**King Farm**

L&B lawyers represent Helios/Towle, L.L.C. in **annexing this prominent site into the City of Rockville, Md.** Plans call for a new town of 3,200 dwelling units, 3.1 million sq ft of offices and retail space adjacent to the Shady Grove Metro station.

**American Center for Physics**

L&B obtained **land use approvals and permits** for development and construction of the architecturally significant headquarters of three prominent scientific and academic organizations in College Park, Md.

**Seventh-Day Adventists World Headquarters**

To obtain land use and adequacy-of-infrastructure approvals, L&B lawyers helped develop a computer-based **employee trip reduction program** that alleviates traffic congestion in Silver Spring, Md., and has become a model for the region.

**Hughes Medical Institute**

This landmark medical research campus blends into a residential Chevy Chase, Md., community where L&B lawyers cooperated with residents to resolve **traffic, zoning and land use issues.** L&B also assisted in gaining tax-exempt financing for the project.

**Avenel**

Featuring a PGA golf course that is Kemper Open, th use project was th project to incorpe **development righ**

**Kaiser Permanente**

L&B has helped the nation's oldest HMO purchase and develop buildings throughout the mid-Atlantic region, including this **250,000 sq ft headquarters** in Rockville, Md.

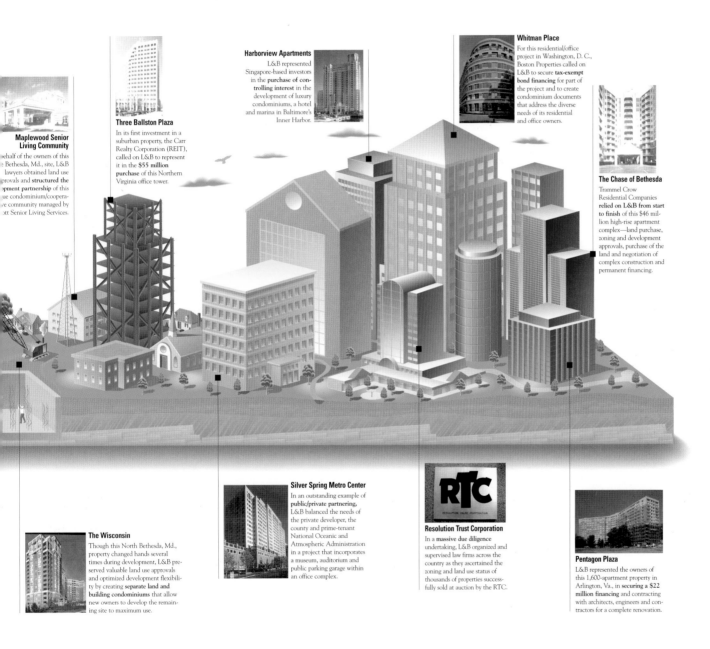

**Maplewood Senior
Living Community**

...ehalf of the owners of this
... Bethesda, Md., site, L&B
... lawyers obtained land use
...provals and **structured the
...pment partnership** of this
...ue condominium/coopera-
...ve community managed by
...ott Senior Living Services.

**Three Ballston Plaza**

In its first investment in a
suburban property, the Carr
Realty Corporation (REIT),
called on L&B to represent
it in the **$55 million
purchase** of this Northern
Virginia office tower.

**Harborview Apartments**

L&B represented
Singapore-based investors
in the **purchase of con-
trolling interest** in the
development of luxury
condominiums, a hotel
and marina in Baltimore's
Inner Harbor.

**Whitman Place**

For this residential/office
project in Washington, D. C.,
Boston Properties called on
L&B to secure **tax-exempt
bond financing** for part of
the project and to create
condominium documents
that address the diverse
needs of its residential
and office owners.

**The Chase of Bethesda**

Trammell Crow
Residential Companies
**relied on L&B from start
to finish** of this $46 mil-
lion high-rise apartment
complex—land purchase,
zoning and development
approvals, purchase of the
land and negotiation of
complex construction and
permanent financing.

**The Wisconsin**

Though this North Bethesda, Md.,
property changed hands several
times during development, L&B pre-
served valuable land use approvals
and optimized development flexibility by creating **separate land and
building condominiums** that allow
new owners to develop the remain-
ing site to maximum use.

**Silver Spring Metro Center**

In an outstanding example of
**public/private partnering,**
L&B balanced the needs of
the private developer, the
county and prime-tenant
National Oceanic and
Atmospheric Administration
in a project that incorporates
a museum, auditorium and
public parking garage within
an office complex.

**Resolution Trust Corporation**

In a **massive due diligence**
undertaking, L&B organized and
supervised law firms across the
country as they ascertained the
zoning and land use status of
thousands of properties success-
fully sold at auction by the RTC.

**Pentagon Plaza**

L&B represented the owners of
this 1,600-apartment property in
Arlington, Va., in **securing a $22
million financing** and contracting
with architects, engineers and con-
tractors for a complete renovation.

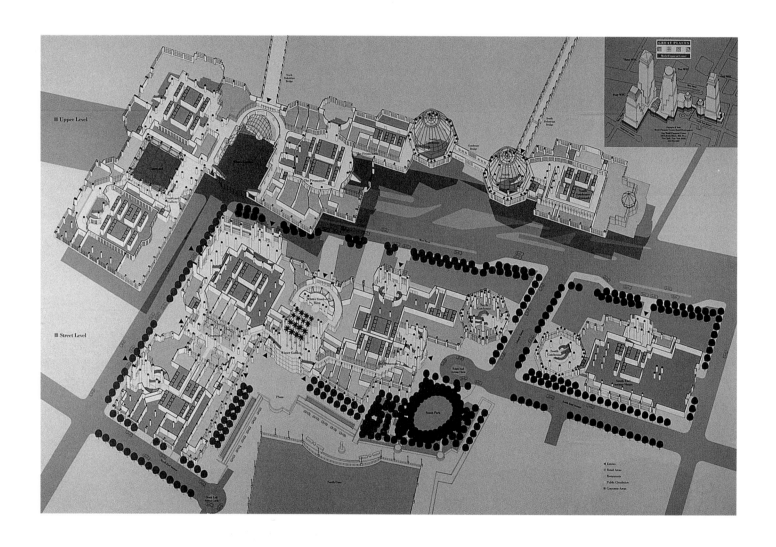

**DONOVAN & GREEN** *Olympia & York World Financial Center Retail Leasing*

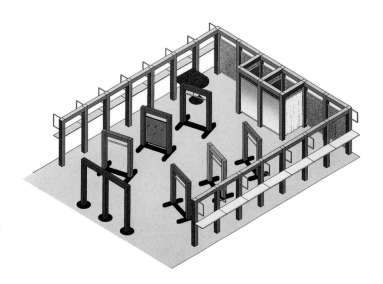

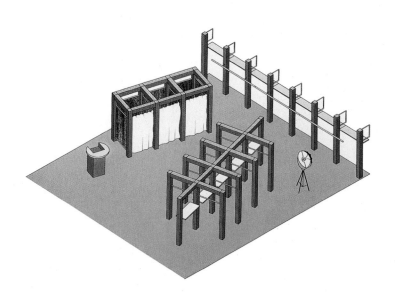

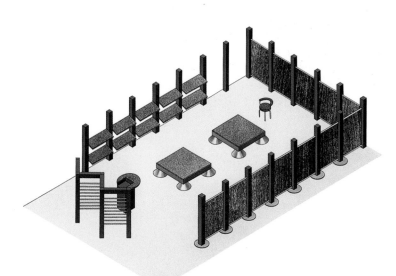

**GIORGIO GALLI DESIGN SAS** *Vitrashop*

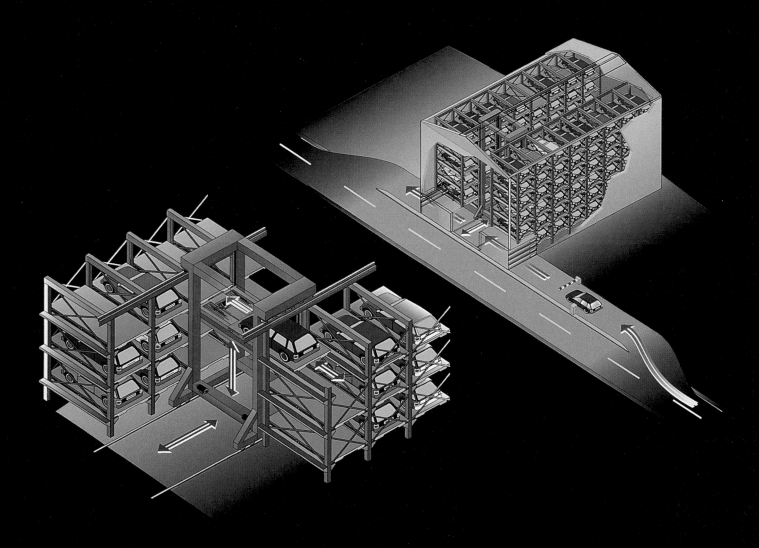

**ARTBEAT DESIGN GMBH** *Schiess de Fries*

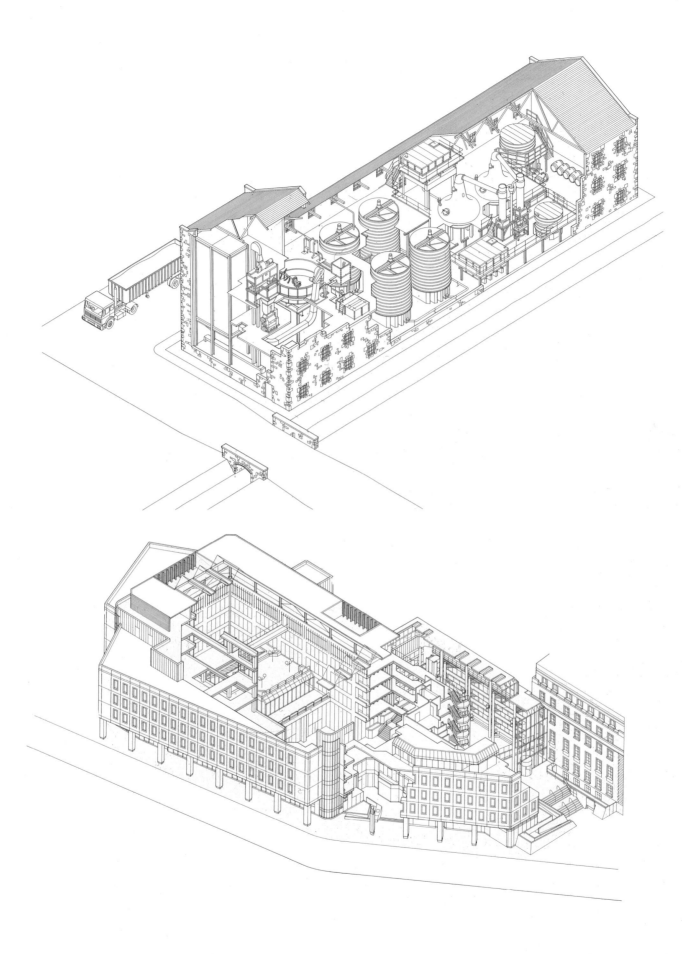

(TOP) **JAYBURN DESIGN GROUP** *United Distillers* ■ (BOTTOM) **SILK PEARCE** *Essex County Council*

**CHRISTOPH GOLDIN, CHRISTOPH FREY** *Schule für Gestaltung Zürich*

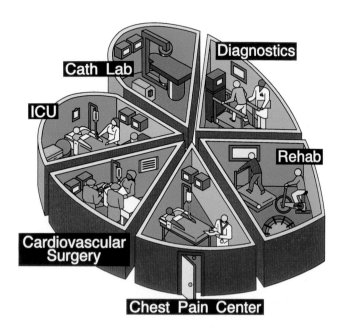

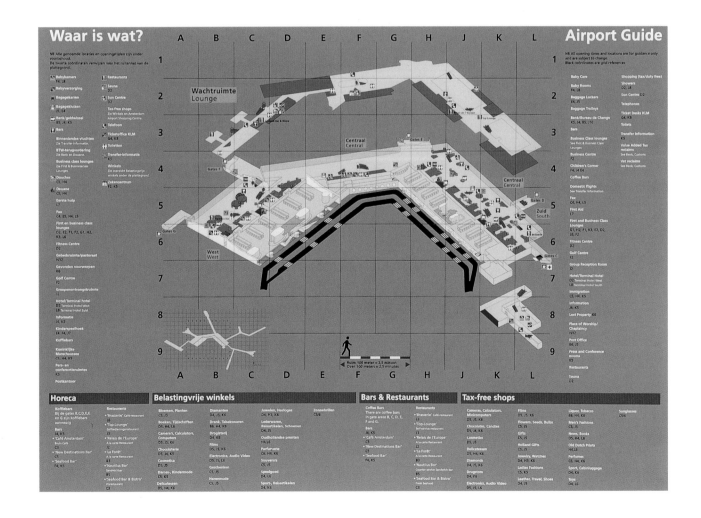

(TOP) **SABIN DESIGN GROUP** *Grossmont Hospital* ■ (BOTTOM) **BUREAU MIJKSENAAR** *Amsterdam Airport Schiphol*

**AITKEN BLAKELEY** *The Queen Elizabeth II Conference Centre*

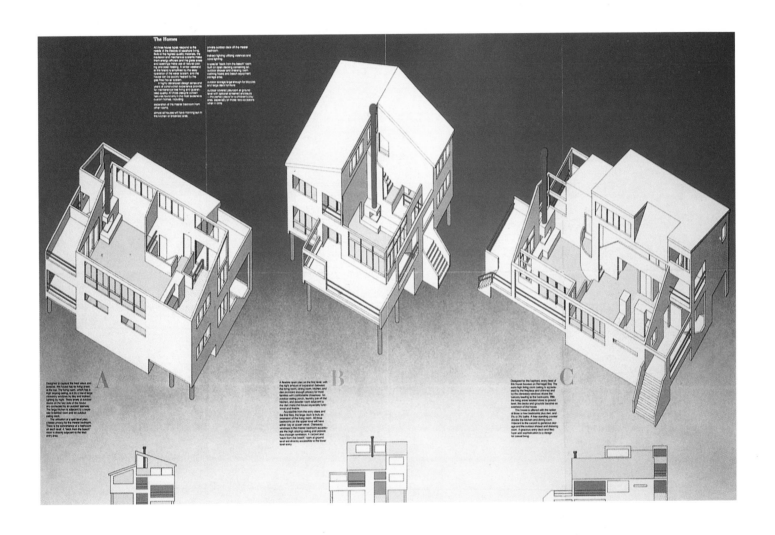

**GUSTAVO PEDROZA** *Techint*

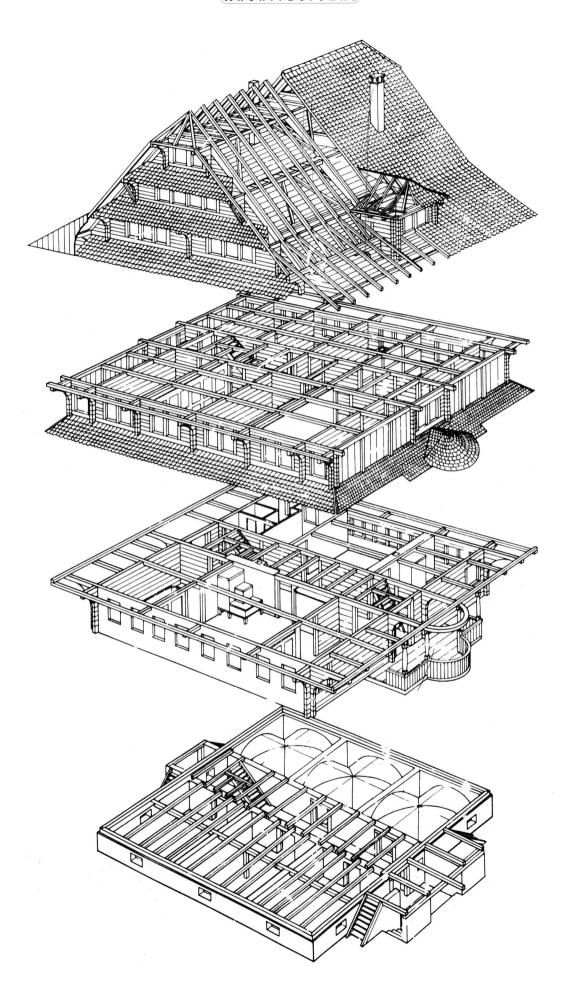

**JONAS BALTENSWEILER** *Denkmalpflege des Kantons Luzern*

SCIENTIFIC AND MEDICAL

WISSENSCHAFT

SCIENCES ET MÉDECINE

192

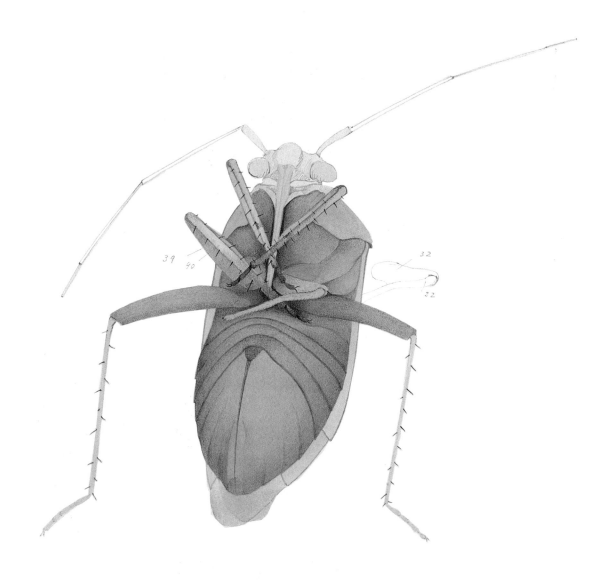

(PRECEDING SPREAD AND THIS SPREAD) **CORNELIA HESSE-HONEGGER** *Lars Müller/Swiss Federal Office of Culture*

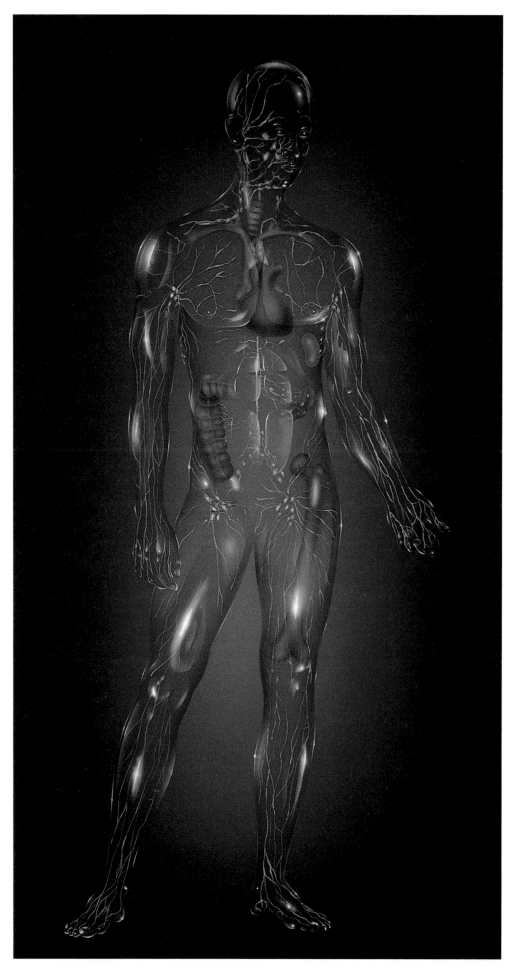

**NATIONAL GEOGRAPHIC SOCIETY** *in-house*

## HEART BYPASS
### DIRECT REVASCULARIZATION OF THE HEART

| 100,000 | 4½-5 hrs | | | | |
|---|---|---|---|---|---|
| Frequency in 1982 | Duration of Operation | recovery room 1-3 hrs | EKG in 12 hrs / telemetry for 48 hrs | | resume nonstrenuous exercise 6 wks |

### Nature of problem.

To continue pumping efficiently, your heart needs a continuous, plentiful supply of blood and oxygen, which is delivered from the lungs by the arteries. If these arteries become narrowed or clogged due to *atherosclerosis* (fatty deposits clinging to the artery lining), the heart muscle, deprived of essential nutrients, dies and is replaced by scar tissue. This process is called *myocardial infarction*. To prevent damage to the heart muscle, doctors can take a length of vein from your leg or abdomen and use it to *bypass* or detour around the clogged or narrowed section of the affected artery or arteries. Bypass surgery is considered an elective procedure, but it often has to be done on an emergency basis.

**Frequency.** Approximately 4 out of 5 bypass patients were men. Just over two-thirds of all patients were between the ages of 45 and 64.

### Surgical preparation.

In arriving at the decision to operate, your physician will have ordered several from among the following tests to help determine the condition of your heart, whether it can be helped by surgery, and whether you are strong enough to withstand the surgery. The tests include: **Chest x-ray, EKG, Echocardiogram, Stress EKG, Cardiac scan, Cardiac enzymes** and **Cardiac catheterization (with angioplasty).**

In conjunction with your actual admission to the hospital, the following routine tests will probably be performed: Complete blood count, SMA, Urinalysis, Chest x-ray, EKG and Blood clotting tests. Your blood will be typed and cross-matched in case a transfusion is necessary.

About an hour before your surgery, you will receive a sedative by injection. You will put on a surgical cap, gown and socks. An IV needle will be inserted in your hand or forearm, which will be connected to an intravenous line in the operating room.

**Anesthetic.** You will receive a general anesthetic.

### Procedure.

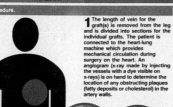

**1** The length of vein for the graft(s) is removed from the leg and is divided into sections for the individual grafts. The patient is connected to the heart-lung machine which provides mechanical circulation during surgery on the heart. An *angiogram* (x-ray made by injecting the vessels with a dye visible on x-rays) is on hand to determine the location of any obstructing plaques (fatty deposits or cholesterol) in the artery walls.

leg / vein for graft / sections of vein

**2** The chest wall is then opened and the heart exposed. An injected potassium solution produces temporary paralysis of the heart.

**3** The affected arteries are freed up enough to permit the surgeon to make an opening below each clogged section. The vein graft is stitched to this opening, serving as a bridge between unclogged segments of the artery system. Occasionally the graft joins 2 points in the same clogged artery, circumventing the blockage. In a multiple bypass operation, 1 length of vein can be used to make several connections, or several lengths can make single connections.

aorta / vein graft / coronary artery / clogged artery / heart / multiple vein graft / clogged artery / heart / clogged artery / heart / multiple vein graft

**4** When the grafts are completed, the heart's normal pumping is restarted and the patient is taken off the heart-lung machine.

### Stages of recovery.

Following surgery, you will remain in the ICU 2 days. Your heart action will be monitored by *telemetry* for the first 48 hours after your surgery. An EKG will be performed within the first 12 hours after the operation.

**Limitations.** You will probably be out of bed and walking within 2 to 3 days. You will be advised to take it easy for 6 weeks and then slowly progress into an exercise program. Most people can eventually return to their full normal activity within reason.

**Drugs.** You will be given oral medication for relief of postoperative pain, which you will experience both in the chest and in the leg from which the vein was removed.

**Complications.** Complications after bypass surgery include **temporary disturbances of cardiac rhythm** that can be controlled with medication, and **wound infection,** requiring that the surgical wound be cultured and an antibiotic administered.

**Scar.** The incision produces a long scar running down from the sternum to a point between the ribs. You will also have a scar on your leg where the vein was removed.

### Heart Glossary

**aneurysm** the wall of an artery or vein becomes weak and bulges out, forming a sac, caused by disease, injury or birth defect.

**angina pectoris** pain or tightness in the chest that may spread to the left arm and shoulder caused by an insufficient supply of blood to the heart.

**arteriosclerosis** commonly known as hardening of the arteries, refers to several diseases that cause the artery walls to become thick and lose their elasticity.

**atherosclerosis** a form of arteriosclerosis where the inner lining of the artery becomes thick due to the build up of fatty deposits (plaque). The artery channel becomes thinner, reducing the flow of blood.

**cardiac arrest** the heart stops beating and circulation stops.

**cerebral thrombosis** the formation of a blood clot in a blood vessel supplying or within the brain; 1 form of stroke.

**CVA** another term for stroke. It may be caused by a clot or hemorrhage that disrupts blood flow to or inside the brain.

**congestive heart failure** when a weakened heart muscle can not pump sufficient blood and fluid builds up in the lung and the veins leading to the heart putting an even greater strain on the system.

**coronary thrombosis** a blood clot in one of the arteries leading to the heart muscle, restricting blood supply. Also called **coronary occlusion.**

**heart attack** in most cases, when people talk about heart attack they are talking about myocardial infarction.

**myocardial infarction** this is what is commonly called a *heart attack.* When a coronary artery is blocked, blood supply to an area of heart muscle is cut off and that area is damaged or dies. If the affected area is large enough to interfere with the cells that give the heart the signal to beat, the heart may stop beating altogether.

**stroke** insufficient supply of blood to the brain causing loss of muscle control, usually on 1 side of the body, blurred vision, inability to speak, dizziness, or if severe, death.

**Coronary Angioplasty** *is a possible alternative to a bypass operation. A narrow tube or catheter is threaded into the diseased artery until it reaches the clogged area. At that point, a tiny balloon at the tip of the catheter is inflated several times. As the balloon expands it flattens out the deposits of plaque flatty tissue in the artery against the artery wall, thus widening the channel. The balloon is deflated and the tube is removed. This is most effective for patients with only 1 blocked artery, where the deposit is accessible and not too thick or hard to be compressed.*

### Warning Signs: Heart Attack

1. Uncomfortable pressure or squeezing in the center of the chest causing severe or mild pain that lasts 2 minutes or more.
2. Pain spreading to your shoulders, neck, arms, upper abdomen, jaw or back.
3. Dizziness, fainting, sweating, nausea or shortness of breath.
4. Unconsciousness.
5. Moist, cool, bluish skin.
6. No pulse detectable.
7. No breathing detectable.
8. Dilated pupils.

If you experience any of these symptoms or notice them in someone else, respond by taking the person to the nearest 24-hour ER with cardiac care, call an ambulance or administer CPR if you have been trained. People tend to deny that these symptoms are anything important. If you have any doubts about their cause, take the time to get medical attention.

70

71

**RICHARD SAUL WURMAN** *ACCESS Press*

**MICHELE CONSTANTINI** *ENPA (Italian Association for the Protection of Animals)*

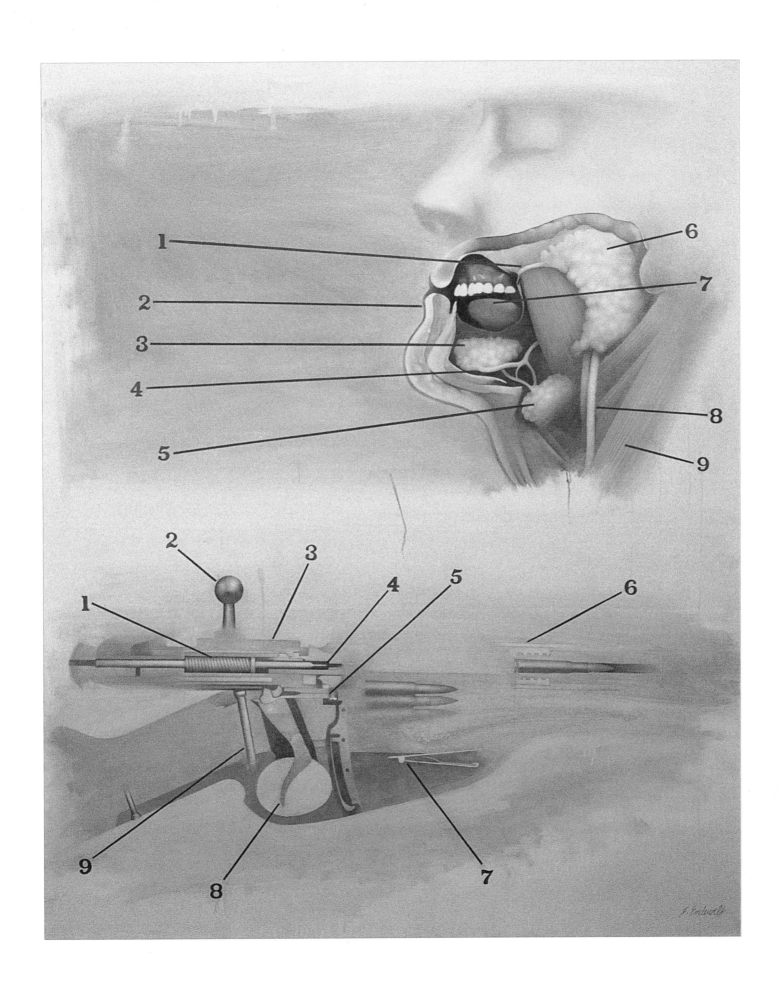

**JACK ENDEWELT** *self-promotion*

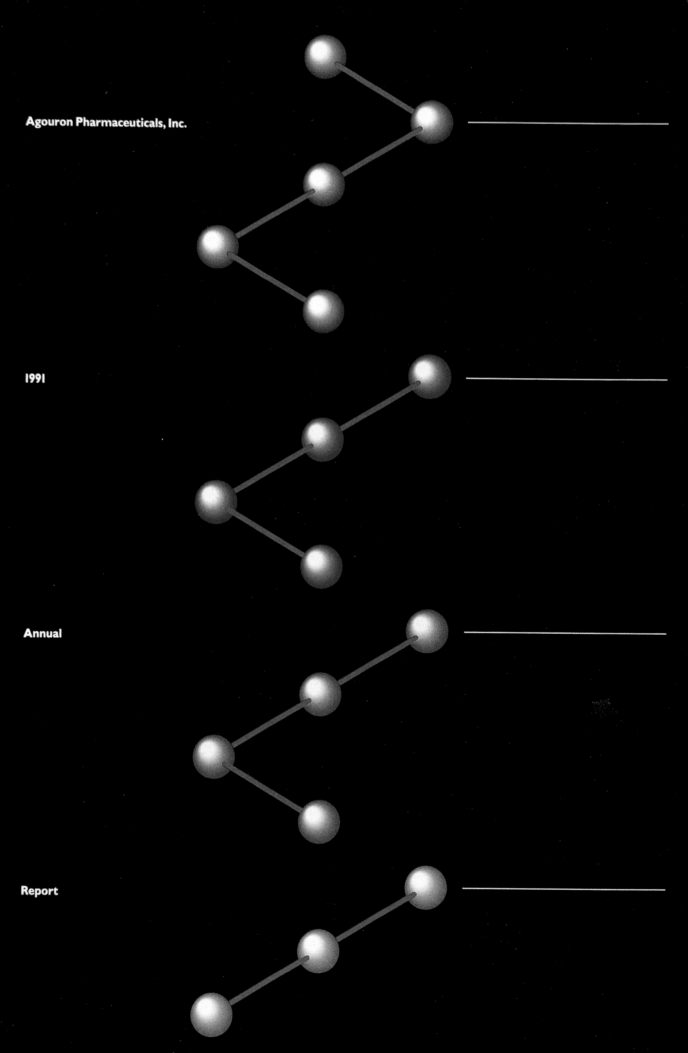

Agouron Pharmaceuticals, Inc.

1991

Annual

Report

Biochemists measure the affinity of candidate drugs for their molecular target.

Recent achievements: Evaluated 174 compounds against four different target proteins.

The pharmacology group tests the drug candidates for activity in cultured cells.

Evaluated 120 TS inhibitors in three tumor cell lines; identified 52 potent inhibitors of tumor cell growth *in vitro*.

Pharmacologists test drug candidates in rodent models to determine whether drug delivery to target tissues occurs in therapeutic doses.

Demonstrated *in vivo* antitumor activity in three new classes of TS inhibitors.

Scientists study the molecular pharmacology of promising drug candidates to determine their mechanism of action.

Tested TS inhibitors against multiple drug-resistant tumor cells to identify compounds with potentially different spectra of anti-tumor activity.

*(THIS SPREAD)* **BESSER JOSEPH PARTNERS** *Agouron Pharmaceuticals, Inc.*

# THE HEAD.

**THE HEAD.** You can think of your body as a space capsule with your head as the command module and your trunk as the service module.

Your head controls your life. You look, listen, smell and taste with it. You eat with it and breathe through it. You talk, sing, smile and frown with it. You remember, calculate and dream with it. You are recognised by it.

Your head contains your brain, the computer which guides and controls the human space mission. Millions of cables called nerves carry coded messages from the eyes, ears, nose, tongue and skin to the brain. By storing this information in its memory, the brain allows you to remember the past so that you can compare it with the present and make decisions about the future. It can turn these decisions into actions by sending messages along the cables to the muscles which work the joints of the skeleton. The brain also has control centres which govern the machinery in the service module. They automatically regulate the rate and rhythm of your heart and your breathing and tell you when to drink and when to eat. As you can see, the computer in your head controls your life.

**The skull** (1) is a rigid box in which the brain is supported by fluid-filled shock absorbers. It is mounted on a flexible column of seven bony hinges (2) so that the eyes and ears can be swivelled and tilted. The tooth-bearing jaws (3) have two hinges (4), one on each side, next to the entrance to the ear.

**The eye** (5) is a tiny balloon which has grown out of the front of the brain. The cells at the back are tuned to be sensitive to light enabling us to see the world around us. The eye is so delicate that it has to be protected by a bony socket and eyelids to cover the window, and a flow of tears to keep the window clean.

**The eye muscles** (6) attach the elastic ball of the eye to the back of the socket. There is a set of six muscles in each socket. The two sets work in harmony so that both eyes look at the same thing—otherwise you would get double vision.

**The ear** (7) has a shell-like funnel on the outside which catches and focuses vibrations in the air. These are turned into electrical impulses which we experience as sound.

**The nose** (8) is the main air entrance. It is lined with ripples and hairs over which the incoming air is warmed, moistened and cleaned before going down into the lungs. Special cells in the lining of the nose respond to molecules breathed in from the air. These cells give us our sense of smell.

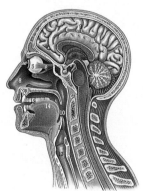

**The brain** (9) is divided into two halves. The left side controls and receives information from the right side of the body and the right side controls and receives information from the left side of the body. A bridge of cables links the two halves so that the right hand knows what the left hand is doing.

The brain has many control centres. The video tapes which store visual information are at the back of the brain. Sounds are recorded at the sides. Speech is co-ordinated near the front. Hunger and thirst, breathing, heartbeat and temperature are controlled in the base of the brain.

More complex activities such as memory and judgment take place at the front of the brain.

**The throat** (10) is the passage for the air we breathe and the food we eat. The food and air pass one another at the epiglottis (11). This is a flap at the back of the throat which closes the windpipe when food passes over it. This prevents the food from going down the wrong way. Coughing is an extra safeguard. It automatically blows food out of the windpipe should it touch the top of the larynx.

**The larynx** (12) guards the entrance to the lungs and allows you to use your breath for speaking. When you talk, the vocal cords inside the larynx vibrate with the movement of air to give you the noises which your tongue and lips can turn into speech.

**Our teeth** (13) are not all the same shape. The front ones are like chisels to cut the food into bits. Those at the back are flat-topped for grinding the food so that it can be mixed with saliva and softened for swallowing. Altogether we have thirty-two teeth.

**The tongue** (14) shapes words on the way out and tastes food on the way in. Its surface is covered with millions of sense organs which tell the difference between sweet and sour, salt and bitter. Sweet and salt are felt at the tip of the tongue, sour at the sides, and bitter at the back.

**The facial muscles** (15), apart from opening and closing the eyes and mouth, change the features of the face so that we can express our feelings.

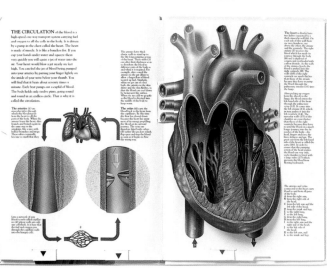

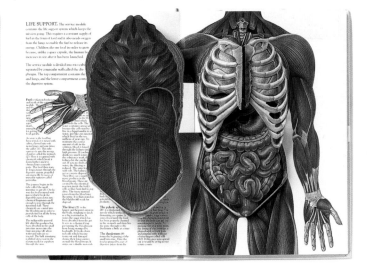

**DAVID PELHAM, HARRY WILLOCK** *Jonathan Cape Ltd.*

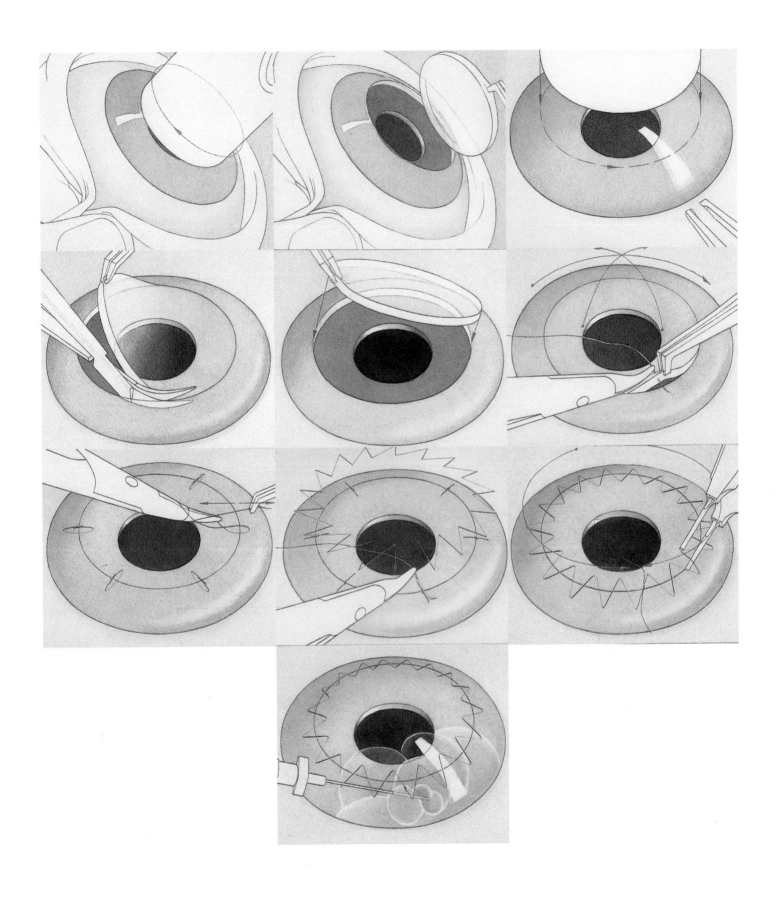

(THIS PAGE) **CHRISTOPH GÖLDLIN, THERES BIEDERMANN** *Schule für Gestaltung Zürich* ■ (NEXT PAGE) **PETER KRÄMER** *Deutsche Lufthansa AG*

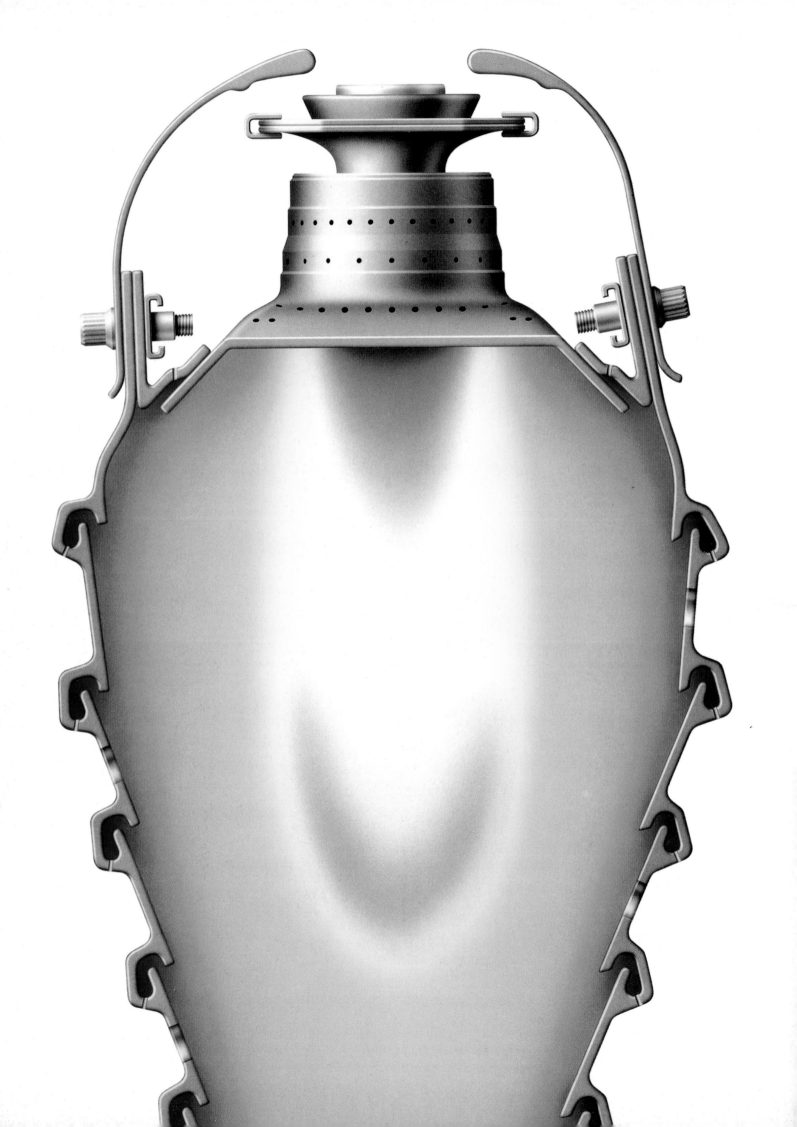

CAPTIONS AND CREDITS


LEGENDEN UND KÜNSTLERANGABEN


LÉGENDES ET ARTISTES

COVER ART DIRECTOR: *Carl Magnusson* ILLUSTRATOR: *Peter Krämer* INDUSTRIAL DESIGN: *Emanuela Frattini* CLIENT: *The Knoll Group* COUNTRY: *USA* ■ *Diagram of the "Propellor" table leg designed for wire management.* ● *Illustration eines Tischbeins mit verdeckter Kabelführung für Büroeinrichtungen.* ▲ *Illustration d'un pied de table spécialement conçu pour dissimuler des câbles.*

PAGE 2 ART DIRECTOR: *Peter Breul* ILLUSTRATOR: *Peter Krämer* PUBLISHER: *Frankfurter Allgemeine GmbH* COUNTRY: *Germany* ■ *Digital illustration created as part of a special magazine issue on watches and jewelry.* ● *Diese digitale Illustration stammt aus einer Ausgabe des FAZ MAGAZINS, in der es um Uhren und Schmuck geht.* ▲ *Cette illustration a paru dans un numéro de FAZ MAGAZIN consacré à l'horlogerie et à la bijouterie.*

PAGE 4 ART DIRECTOR/ILLUSTRATOR: *Wolfgang Franke* AGENCY: *Franke Techn. Grafik* CLIENT: *SIG* YEAR PUBLISHED: *1986* COUNTRY: *Switzerland*

PAGE 6 ART DIRECTOR/DESIGNER/ILLUSTRATOR: *Marty Smith* AGENCY/CLIENT: *Marty Smith Technical Illustration* COUNTRY: *USA* ■ *Promotional piece of a spectrometer.* ● *Ein Spektrometer als Promotion für einen technischen Zeichner.* ▲ *Spectromètre promotionnel pour un dessinateur technique.*

PAGE 20 ART DIRECTOR/DESIGNER: *Ronnie Peters* AGENCY: *Infogram* CLIENT: *Siemens Nixdorf* COUNTRY: *Germany*

PAGES 36, 38-41 ART DIRECTOR/DESIGNER/ILLUSTRATOR/AGENCY: *Walter Pepperle* CLIENT: *DG HYP* COUNTRY: *Germany*

PAGES 42-45 ART DIRECTOR: *Steve Tolleson* DESIGNERS: *Steve Tolleson, Jennifer Sterling* COPYWRITER: *Lindsey Beaman* AGENCY: *Tolleson Design* CLIENT: *Fox River Paper* YEAR PUBLISHED: *1994* PRINTER: *Lithographix* COUNTRY: *USA* ■ *Diagrams charting performance in relation to industry performance, and emphasizing how the measurements relate to the design industry.* ● *Darstellung der Leistung eines Papierherstellers im Rahmen der Unternehmensgruppe und im Vergleich zur gesamten Branche, wobei besonders auf die Design-Branche Bezug genommen wird.* ▲ *Représentations graphiques des résultats d'un fabricant de papier par rapport au groupe et à la branche, plus spécifiquement à l'industrie du design.*

PAGE 46 ART DIRECTOR: *Philip Gips* DESIGNER: *David Suh* AGENCY: *Gips + Balkind + Associates/The GBA Group* CLIENT: *HBO/Cinema Plus* YEAR PUBLISHED: *circa 1985* ■ *Graphs created for a prospectus to attract investors for selected films. They plot growth in the motion picture industry, and in the video rental and sales division.* ● *Diagramme für einen Prospekt, mit dem Investoren für ausgewählte Filme gewonnen werden sollten. Sie zeigen das Wachstum im Film- sowie im Videoverleih- und Verkaufsbereich.* ▲ *Diagrammes d'un prospectus visant à attirer des investisseurs pour des films. Ils illustrent la croissance enregistrée dans la distribution et la vente de films et de vidéos.*

PAGE 47 DESIGNERS: *James Koval, Steve Ryan* PHOTOGRAPHER: *Howard Bjornsen* AGENCY: *VSA Partners, Inc.* CLIENT: *Smithfield Foods, Inc.* COUNTRY: *USA* ■ *Variation of the traditional pie chart created for an annual report for Smithfield Foods, a company that specializes in pork products.* ● *Variation des traditionellen Tortendiagramms für einen Jahresbericht von Smithfield Foods, eine Firma, die auf Produkte aus Schweinefleisch spezialisiert ist.* ▲ *Variation du traditionnel camembert pour un rapport annuel de Smithfield Foods, société spécialisée dans les produits porcins.*

PAGE 48 ART DIRECTOR: *Bill Cahan* DESIGNER: *Craig Clark* AGENCY: *Bill Cahan & Associates* COPYWRITER: *Tim Peters* CLIENT: *Oak Technology* YEAR PUBLISHED: *1995* TYPEFACE: *Univers Condensed* PRINTER: *Watt/Peterson* COUNTRY: *USA* ■ *Yearly and quarterly financial data illustrated for a multimedia company's annual report. Since sound is an important component of multimedia, the agency chose to create a diagram which resembles a stereo decibel meter.* ● *Die Finanzdaten eines Vierteljahres und gesamten Jahres für den Jahresbericht einer Multimedia-Firma. Da Ton eine bedeutende Komponente des Multimediabereiches ist, wurde ein Diagramm erstellt, das einem Stereo-Decibelmeter gleicht.* ▲ *Extrait du rapport annuel d'une société multimédia: résultats financiers trimestriels et annuels présentés sous la forme des indicateurs de niveau (vumètres) d'une chaîne stéréo.*

PAGE 49 ART DIRECTOR/DESIGNER: *Kevin Bailey* AGENCY: *Savage Design Group, Inc.* CLIENT: *Plains Resources, Inc.* YEAR PUBLISHED: *1995* TYPEFACE: *Franklin Gothic Heavy, Matrix X13* PRINTER: *Champagne Fine Printing* COUNTRY: *USA* ■ *Diagram demonstrating selected financial information for a three-year period for an energy resources company.* ● *Darstellung ausgewählter Finanzdaten eines Energieversorgungsbetriebs über eine Dreijahresperiode.* ▲ *Diagramme illustrant les résultats financiers d'une entreprise d'électricité sur une période de trois ans.*

PAGE 50 ART DIRECTOR/DESIGNER/ILLUSTRATOR: *Randall Jones* AGENCY: *McAdams, Richman and Ong* CLIENT: *National Media Corporation* COUNTRY: *USA* ■ *Graphs from an annual report for the world's largest producer of infomercials reflecting an "exponential" theme and enhancing visualization of growth.* ● *Diagramme aus dem Jahresbericht des weltweit grössten Produzenten von TV-Spots mit redaktionellem Anstrich, wobei das Schwergewicht auf der Darstellung des Wachstums liegt.* ▲ *Diagrammes extraits du rapport annuel du plus grand producteur mondial d'infomercials mettant l'accent sur la croissance de la société.*

PAGE 51 ART DIRECTOR: *Lowell Williams* DESIGNERS: *Bill Carson, Jeff Williams* AGENCY: *Pentagram Design Austin* PHOTOGRAPHER: *Pat Haverfield* COPYWRITER: *Kate Irvin* CLIENT: *The Coca-Cola Company* YEAR PUBLISHED: *1995* TYPEFACE: *Bodoni* PRINTER: *GAC–Graphic Arts Center* COUNTRY: *USA* ■ *Diagram illustrating the growth of the Coca-Cola Company's stock over a period of ten years.* ● *Der Anstieg des Aktienkapitals der Firma Coca-Cola über eine Zehnjahresperiode ist Gegenstand dieses Diagrams.* ▲ *Diagramme illustrant l'évolution du capital-actions de Coca-Cola sur une période de dix ans.*

PAGE 52 ART DIRECTOR: *Tor Pettersen* DESIGNERS: *Tor Pettersen, Nicholas Kendal* PHOTOGRAPHER: *Paul Bradforth* ILLUSTRATOR: *Alex Robertson* AGENCY: *Tor Pettersen & Partners Ltd.* CLIENT: *RMC Group Services Ltd.* COUNTRY: *England* ■ *Chart created for a security company showing the increase in burglary over ten years. The header reads "An Alarming Potential for Growth."* ● *Diagramm für einen Sicherheitsdienst, das den Anstieg von Einbrüchen darstellt: «Ein alarmierendes Wachstumspotential.»* ▲ *«Un potentiel de croissance alarmant». Diagramme pour une société de surveillance illustrant l'augmentation des cambriolages.*

PAGE 53 ART DIRECTOR/DESIGNER: *Christian Preuschl-Haldenburg* PHOTOGRAPHY: *Photographic Services, National Library of Australia* ILLUSTRATOR: *Christian Preuschl-Haldenburg* CLIENT: *National Library of Australia* COUNTRY: *Australia* ■ *Diagram showing the increase in production and export of major minerals in Australia over a period of years.* ● *Darstellung des Anstiegs von Produktion und Export wichtiger Mineralien Australiens über eine Zeitspanne von mehreren Jahren.* ▲ *Représentation de l'augmentation de la production et des exportations des principales ressources minières d'Australie sur une période de plusieurs années.*

PAGES 54, 55 ART DIRECTOR: *Earl Gee* DESIGNERS: *Earl Gee, Fani Chung* PHOTOGRAPHER: *Geoffrey Nelson* COPYWRITER: *Edelman Public Relations Worldwide* AGENCY: *Gee + Chung Design* CLIENT: *Collagen Corporation* YEAR PUBLISHED: *1992* TYPEFACE: *Garamond #3* PRINTER: *Anderson Lithograph* COUNTRY: *USA* ■ *Ten-year historical data of a manufacturer of injectable implants and biomedical devices to repair aged or damaged tissue. For this project, the agency wanted to create a clean, scientific, and memorable comparison of data in a manner appropriate to the client. In order to "humanize" the abstract financial information, the scale of common scientific measuring devices was used.* ● *Die Entwicklung eines Herstellers injizierbarer Implantate und biomedizinischer Geräte für die Wiederherstellung gealterten oder zerstörten Hautgewebes, dargestellt über einen Zeitraum von zehn Jahren. Dem Bereich des Auftraggebers entsprechend, entschied sich die Agentur für einen klaren, wissenschaftlichen und einprägsamen Datenvergleich. Für die Darstellung der Finanzdaten wählte sie ein medizinisches Messgerät, um sie optisch attraktiver zu machen.* ▲ *Evolution sur une période de dix ans d'un fabricant d'implants injectables et d'appareils biomédicaux destinés à revitaliser les tissus de la peau abîmés ou soumis au vieillissement. L'agence a opté pour une comparaison claire et scientifique. Pour présenter les résultats financiers de manière plus séduisante, elle a choisi un instrument de mesure médical.*

PAGES 56, 57 ART DIRECTOR/DESIGNER: *Donna Bonavita* ILLUSTRATOR: *Guy Billout* COPYWRITER: *Jackie Rose* AGENCY: *KPMG National Marketing Design Group* CLIENT: *KPMG* YEAR PUBLISHED: *1994* TYPEFACE: *Times Roman, Univers 45, Univers 65* PRINTER: *Virginia Lithograph* COUNTRY: *USA* ■ *Diagrams depicting growth of total yearly financial support, the individual groups of funds for the fiscal year, and the amount of money the client matched in donations. Gothic columns represent the Foundation and the sprouting leaf represents growth. To show divisions of funds ac-*

*cording to segments, an overseer continues his job by dropping the last coin onto a pile. To demonstrate the amount of matching funds contributed, flags painted on a mountain range mark each year's financial standing. A non-marked flag is painted in a cloud in anticipation of the next year's climb. ● Darstellungen des Wachstums der gesamten jährlichen finanziellen Zuwendungen an eine Stiftung desAuftraggebers, der einzelnen Fonds im Finanzjahr und des Geldbetrages, den die Firma selbst an Spenden einbrachte. Gothische Säulen dienen hier zur Darstellung der Stiftung. Das spriessende Blatt steht für Wachstum. Um die Aufteilung der Fonds in die verschiedenen Bereiche darzustellen, wird von der Aufsichtsperson die letzte Münze auf einen Haufen geworfen. Auf eine Bergkette gemalte Flaggen stehen für den Betrag, den der Auftraggeber selbst an Spenden einbringt. Eine nicht markierte Flagge in den Wolken steht für den erhofften Mehrbetrag im nächsten Jahr. ▲ Représentations de l'évolution des dons financiers annuels versés à la société, des différents fonds de l'exercice comptable et des dons reversés à des instituts. La fondation est représentée par des colonnes gothiques. Le bourgeon symbolise la croissance. La répartition des fonds est illustrée par un contrôleur jetant la dernière pièce sur un tas. Les drapeaux peints sur une chaîne de montagnes symbolisent le montant des dons faits par le client. Le drapeau vierge du nuage illustre l'augmentation des dons espérée pour l'année suivante.*

**PAGE 58** ART DIRECTOR: *John Hornall* DESIGNERS: *John Hornall, Julia LaPine, Mary Hermes, Brian O'Neill* COPYWRITER: *Anne Bugge* AGENCY: *Hornall Anderson Design Works, Inc.* CLIENT: *Westmark International* YEAR PUBLISHED: *1992* PRINTER: *Watt/Peterson* COUNTRY: *USA* ■ *Financial growth charts for a company which specializes in medical diagnostic ultrasound and patient monitoring information systems. Since proprietary digital technology propelled the client to the forefront of its industry, the agency determined that a visual presentation featuring digital technology would be a dramatic means of underscoring its leadership position. ● Darstellung der finanziellen Wachstumsraten einer Firma, die auf medizinische Ultrasound-Geräte spezialisiert ist. Da der Auftraggeber durch seinen Vorsprung in digitaler Technologie führend in seiner Branche ist, entschied sich die Agentur für digitale Technologie, um die Daten eindrucksvoll darzustellen. ▲ Graphique sur la croissance financière d'une société spécialisée dans les appareils médicaux à ultrasons et le monitoring. Le client étant leader dans le domaine de la technologie numérique, l'agence a opté pour une représentation numérique des données.*

**PAGE 59** ART DIRECTOR: *John Hornall* DESIGNERS: *John Hornall, Heidi Favour, Julia LaPine, John Anicker* ILLUSTRATOR: *Lynn Tanaka* COPYWRITER: *John Sammons* AGENCY: *Hornall Anderson Design Works, Inc.* CLIENT: *Airborne Express* YEAR PUBLISHED: *1993* PRINTER: *Bradley Printing* COUNTRY: *USA* ■ *Charts for an annual report created to reflect the financial reports of an express delivery service company. The design challenge was to strongly position the company despite a less than ideal financial performance during the previous year. The bold use of color shows the company has nothing to hide and is in a good position even though its performance was unsatisfactory. ● Darstellung der Finanzdaten für den Jahresbericht einer Kurierfirma. Die Herausforderung bei der Erstellung des Diagramms waren die nicht gerade idealen finanziellen Ergebnisse des Auftraggebers. Die kräftigen Farben suggerieren, dass die Firma nichts zu verbergen hat und trotz der unbefriedigenden Ergebnisse des Vorjahres gut dasteht. ▲ Diagramme des résultats financiers d'une société de livraison expresse conçu pour un rapport annuel. Le défi consistait à asseoir la position de la société en dépit des résultats financiers peu satisfaisants de l'exercice écoulé. Les couleurs franches suggèrent que la société joue la transparence et reste dynamique malgré ce revers.*

**PAGE 59** ART DIRECTORS/DESIGNERS: *Jérôme Oudin, Jérôme Saint-Loubert Bié, Susanna Shannon* PHOTOGRAPHER: *Jérôme Saint-Loubert Bié* STUDIO: *design dept.* CLIENT/PUBLISHER: *Synthélabo/Alliage* COUNTRY: *France*

**PAGE 59** ART DIRECTOR: *Nakagawa Kenzo* DESIGNERS: *Nakagawa Kenzo, Nobuyama Hiroyasu, Morikami Satoshi* AGENCY: *Bolts & Nuts Studio* CLIENT: *Wacoal* YEAR PUBLISHED: *1992* COUNTRY: *Japan*

**PAGE 60** ART DIRECTOR/DESIGNER: *Emmett Morava* ILLUSTRATOR/PHOTOGRAPHER: *Jay Freis* COPYWRITER: *Larry Pearson* AGENCY: *Morava & Oliver Design Office* CLIENT: *First Nationwide Financial Corp.* COUNTRY: *USA*

**PAGE 61** ART DIRECTOR: *Ron Jefferies* DESIGNER/ILLUSTRATOR: *John Tom* COPYWRITER: *Jo Bandy* AGENCY: *The Jefferies Association* CLIENT: *Fidelity National Financial, Inc.* YEAR PUBLISHED: *1992* TYPEFACE: *Garamond #3, Futura* PRINTER: *George Rice & Sons* COUNTRY: *USA* ■ *Diagram describing the fiscal performance for a*

*financial corporation. To dynamically portray the client's success through graphs, the agency used bright colors, simple geometric shapes, and displayed the graphs on a full page. ● Darstellung der finanziellen Ergebnisse eines Finanzunternehmens. Um den Erfolg des Finanzunternehmens eindrucksvoll darzustellen, wählte die Agentur leuchtende Farben für die einzelnen Graphiken und einfache geometrische Formen, die eine ganze Seite füllen. ▲ Représentation des résultats d'une société financière. Pour illustrer le succès de l'entreprise de façon dynamique, l'agence a choisi des couleurs franches, des formes géométriques simples et a présenté les graphiques sur une pleine page.*

**PAGE 62** DESIGNER: *Ronnie Peters* CLIENT: *Student project for Rhode Island School of Design* COUNTRY: *USA* ■ *Diagram representing three variables: time, activity, and cost. The designer decided to portray time as fluid, winding over a 24 hour period from midnight down to mid-day and back to midnight, seven times for one week. Depth denotes cost, and color represents the particular activity. ● Diagramm mit drei Variablen: Zeit, Aktivität und Kosten. Die Zeit wird hier in einem Flussdiagramm dargestellt, das sich auf eine Zeitspanne von 24 Stunden von Mitternacht über Mittag bis zu Mitternacht erstreckt, und zwar für sieben Tage. Die Tiefe zeigt die Kosten, während Farbe die spezielle Aktivität angibt. ▲ Diagramme représentant trois variables: temps, activité et coûts. Le graphiste a représenté le temps qui s'écoule sur une durée de 24 heures, de minuit à midi et de midi à minuit et ce, sept fois pour une semaine. La profondeur indique les coûts, la couleur, l'activité de la société.*

**PAGE 62** ART DIRECTORS: *Tor Pettersen, Jeff Davis* DESIGNER: *Nicholas Kendal* ILLUSTRATOR: *David Hunter* AGENCY: *Tor Pettersen & Partners Ltd.* CLIENT: *Lucas Industries Plc.* COUNTRY: *England*

**PAGE 63** ART DIRECTOR/DESIGNER: *Ronnie Peters* AGENCY: *Infogram* CLIENT: *Self-promotion* YEAR PUBLISHED: *1996* COUNTRY: *USA* ■ *The designer needed a compelling way to visualize the US budget deficit, so he showed the increase in income versus the increase in spending and the years when income exceeded spending. ● Um das Haushaltdefizit der USA eindrucksvoll darzustellen, wird hier der Anstieg der Einnahmen dem Anstieg der Ausgaben gegenübergestellt und eine Statistik der Jahre gezeigt, in denen die Einnahmen die Ausgaben übertrafen. ▲ Graphique illustrant l'augmentation du déficit budgétaire des Etats-Unis, l'accroissement des dépenses et les années où les recettes excèdent les dépenses.*

**PAGE 64** ILLUSTRATOR: *Tilly Northedge* AGENCY: *Grundy & Northedge* CLIENT: *CAMPAIGN MAGAZINE, Haymarket Publishing* YEAR PUBLISHED: *1993* COUNTRY: *England* ■ *Diagram depicting the amount of money different countries spend on advertising and the media used. Because a variety of information had to be contained on a double-page spread in a strong manner, an eye was used as an overall holding device, with the colored areas representing the statistics and making up the iris. ● Diagramm der Werbeausgaben verschiedener Länder in den verschiedenen Medien. Da die Doppelseite eine Vielzahl von Informationen verdeutlichen musste, diente ein Auge als verbindendes Element, wobei die kolorierten Bereiche, die zur Iris werden, die statistischen Erhebungen enthalten. ▲ Diagramme représentant les dépenses publicitaires de différents pays et les supports utilisés. Vu le nombre d'informations devant être présentées avec un maximum d'impact sur la double page, l'œil se présente comme un élément conducteur tandis que les zones en couleur formant l'iris regroupent les données statistiques.*

**PAGE 65** ART DIRECTOR: *Roger Cook* ILLUSTRATOR: *Peter Krämer* AGENCY: *Cook + Shanosky Associates* CLIENT: *Black & Decker* COUNTRY: *USA* ■ *Diagrams and illustrations created for the Black & Decker annual report. ● Diagramme und Illustrationen für den Jahresbericht von Black & Decker. ▲ Diagrammes et illustrations pour le rapport annuel de Black & Decker.*

**PAGE 66 (TOP)** ART DIRECTOR/DESIGNER: *Enrico Sempi* AGENCY: *Tangram Strategic Design* CLIENT: *Banca Popolare di Novara* COUNTRY: *Italy*

**PAGE 66 (BOTTOM)** ART DIRECTOR/DESIGNER: *Antonella Trevisan* AGENCY: *Tangram Strategic Design* CLIENT: *Banca Popolare di Novara* COUNTRY: *Italy*

**PAGE 67** ART DIRECTOR: *Susan Hochbaum* DESIGNERS: *Susan Hochbaum, Kevin Lauterbach* AGENCY: *Pentagram Design* CLIENT: *Foamex* COUNTRY: *USA*

**PAGES 68, 69** ART DIRECTOR: *Steve Tolleson* DESIGNERS: *Steve Tolleson, Mark Winn* ILLUSTRATOR: *Mark Fox* AGENCY: *Tolleson Design* CLIENT: *Komag, Inc.* TYPEFACE:

*Geometric* PRINTER: *Lithographix* COUNTRY: *USA* ■ *Diagrams conveying the company's financial, technical, and performance information in means other than traditional copy.* ● *Diagramme anstelle des sonst üblichen Textes zur Erläuterung von Informationen über die finanzielle, technische und allgemeine Entwicklung einer Firma.* ▲ *Diagrammes sur les résultats financiers et techniques d'une société en lieu et place du traditionnel commentaire.*

**PAGE 70** ART DIRECTOR: *Kit Hinrichs* DESIGNERS: *Jeff West, Kit Hinrichs* ILLUSTRATOR: *Jeff West* COPYWRITER: *Delphine Hirasuna* AGENCY: *Pentagram Design, Inc.* CLIENT: *Simpson Paper Company* YEAR PUBLISHED: *1995* TYPEFACE: *Gill Sans* PRINTER: *George Rice* COUNTRY: *USA* ■ *Diagram depicting world population and its distribution by country. It was created to showcase the use of computer illustration on varieties of the client's paper.* ● *Darstellung der Weltbevölkerung und ihrer Verteilung auf die verschiedenen Länder. Das Diagramm diente zur Demonstration der Eignung von Papierqualitäten des Auftraggebers für Computerillustrationen.* ▲ *Représentation de la population mondiale et de sa répartition par pays. Il s'agissait de démontrer que les différents papiers du fabricant se prêtent à l'impression d'illustrations réalisées sur ordinateur.*

**PAGE 71** ART DIRECTOR/DESIGNER: *Jack Anderson* AGENCY/CLIENT: *Hornall Anderson Design Works, Inc.* YEAR PUBLISHED: *1992* COUNTRY: *USA* ■ *To depict the structure of the design firm in an innovative way, M&M candies were used in this chart to lend a more playful, creative manner in contrast to the usual technical chart.* ● *Bonbons verleihen dieser Darstellung der Mitarbeitertruktur einer Designfirma einen spielerischen Charakter.* ▲ *Organigramme d'une société de design auquel les bonbons confèrent un caractère ludique.*

**PAGES 72, 73** ART DIRECTOR: *Shigeaki Matsubara* DESIGNERS: *Noboru Kato, Kiyotake Ogawa* ILLUSTRATOR: *Kiyotake Ogawa* AGENCY: *Ryus Inc.* CLIENT: *Canon Sales Co., Ltd.* COUNTRY: *Japan* ■ *Diagrams created for a Canon company brochure.* ● *Diagramme für die Firmenbroschüre von Canon.* ▲ *Diagrammes pour une plaquette d'entreprise Canon.*

**PAGE 74** ART DIRECTOR: *Roger Cook* DESIGNERS: *Roger Cook, Michael Milligan* AGENCY: *Cook and Shanosky Associates, Inc.* CLIENT: *Medical Inter-Insurance Exchange* YEAR PUBLISHED: *1996* TYPEFACE: *Universe Light, Black* PRINTER: *CR Walden* COUNTRY: *USA*

**PAGE 75** ART DIRECTOR/DESIGNER: *Carl Seltzer* AGENCY: *Carl Seltzer Design Office* CLIENT: *Fremont General* YEAR PUBLISHED: *1993* TYPEFACE: *Futura Bold* PRINTER: *Anderson Litho* COUNTRY: *USA* ■ *Diagram showing the growth of Investors' Thrift (owned by the client) in assets. For easier reading and greater interest, the agency chose to show in a circular format with gradated color information that would normally be displayed in a bar chart.* ● *Darstellung des Wachstums einer Spar- und Darlehenskasse in Vermögenswerten. Um das Interesse des Betrachters zu wecken und das Verständnis zu fördern, wurde hier statt des üblichen Säulendiagrams ein Kreisdiagramm mit Farbabstufungen gewählt.* ▲ *Diagramme illustrant la croissance d'une caisse d'épargne en éléments d'actif. Pour une meilleure lisibilité et une présentation plus attrayante, l'agence a opté pour un cercle et un dégradé de couleurs en lieu et place des traditionnelles colonnes.*

**PAGES 76, 78, 79** ART DIRECTOR/DESIGNER: *William Haines* ILLUSTRATOR: *Joe Garnett* COPYWRITER: *Richard Berggren* AGENCY: *William Haines Graphic Design* CLIENT: *Earle M. Jorgensen Corp.* YEAR PUBLISHED: *1990* TYPEFACE: *Helvetica* PRINTER: *Anderson Litho* COUNTRY: *USA* ■ *Diagram developed to make the workings of an aluminum coil processor easily understandable.* ● *Hier ging es um das Verständnis des Funktionablaufs einer Maschine zur Herstellung von Aluminiumspulen.* ▲ *Représentation du processus de fabrication de bobines d'aluminium.*

**PAGES 80, 81 (BOTTOM)** ART DIRECTOR/DESIGNER/ILLUSTRATOR: *William Haines* COPYWRITER: *Lani Marshall* AGENCY: *William Haines Graphic Design* CLIENT: *Chevron USA Inc.* YEAR PUBLISHED: *1995* PRINTER: *Costello Brothers* COUNTRY: *USA* ■ *Map of an oil refinery and its operations.* ● *Darstellung einer Ölraffinerie und ihrer Arbeitsweise.* ▲ *Plan d'une raffinerie et de son fonctionnement.*

**PAGE 81 (TOP)** ART DIRECTOR: *Roger Cook* DESIGNERS: *Roger Cook, Cathryn Cook* ILLUSTRATOR: *Stacey Lewis* AGENCY: *Cook and Shanosky Associates, Inc.* CLIENT: *New Jersey Natural Gasses* YEAR PUBLISHED: *1993* TYPEFACE: *Memphis Light, Bold* PRINTER: *CR Waldman* COUNTRY: *USA*

**PAGES 82, 83** ART DIRECTOR/DESIGNER: *Hugh DeWitte* ILLUSTRATOR: *Robert Forsbach* COPYWRITER: *John Sealander* AGENCY: *EDS Marketing Communications* CLIENT: *EDS* YEAR PUBLISHED: *1994* TYPEFACE: *New Baskerville* PRINTER: *South Press* COUNTRY: *USA* ■ *Diagram showing the flow of information and connection between point of sale and other businesses. Rather than showing an engineering model, the agency chose to show a street scene in the virtual information community and how all the players connect with one another.* ● *Diagramm des Informationsflusses und der Verbindungen zwischen der Verkaufsstelle und anderen Geschäftsstellen. Die Agentur entschied sich für eine virtuelle Strassenszene, wobei gezeigt wird, wie die einzelnen Spieler miteinander verbunden sind.* ▲ *Diagramme illustrant le flux d'informations et les connexions entre le point de vente et d'autres entreprises. L'agence a choisi une scène de rue virtuelle pour montrer les liens entre les différents acteurs.*

**PAGES 84, 85** ART DIRECTOR: *Peter Harrison* DESIGNERS: *Peter Harrison, Christina Freyss* DESIGN FIRM: *Pentagram Design* CLIENT: *Cooper-Hewitt National Design Museum* YEAR PUBLISHED: *1992* PRINTER: *Applied Graphics* COUNTRY: *USA* ■ *Guide created for the "Power of Maps" exhibition at the Cooper-Hewitt Design Museum. The design was based on a fundamentally tactile and visual map reference–folding–allowing the content to surprise and engage the viewer.* ● *Die Bedeutung von Landkarten war Thema einer Ausstellung, für die dieses Diagramm entworfen wurde. Grundlage des Entwurfes war das taktile Erlebnis einer faltbaren Karte, die Überraschungen für den Betrachter in sich birgt und auf diese Weise sein Interesse weckt.* ▲ *Diagramme réalisé pour une exposition consacrée à la cartographie. L'idée était de proposer une expérience tactile grâce à une carte pliable au contenu surprenant et séduisant.*

**PAGE 86 (TOP)** ART DIRECTOR: *Ian Lanksbury* ILLUSTRATOR: *Tilly Northedge* AGENCIES: *Grundy & Northedge, Addison Design Group* CLIENT: *Northwest Water* YEAR PUBLISHED: *1985* TYPEFACE: *Frutiger, Helvetica Black* COUNTRY: *England* ■ *Diagram of water cycle: collection, cleaning, delivery to customer, treatment of waste water. The agency wanted to make a complex industrial process attractive and interesting. A combination of cross-sections and symbols were used to show the process in a modern style.* ● *Darstellung des gesamten Zyklus der Wasserversorgung: Sammlung, Reinigung, Lieferung an die Verbraucher und Behandlung des Abwassers. Um diesen komplexen industriellen Prozess attraktiv und interessant zu machen, setzte die Agentur eine modern wirkende Kombination von Querschnitten und Symbolen ein.* ▲ *Représentation du cycle complet de l'approvisionnement en eau: collectage, épuration, distribution aux consommateurs et traitement des eaux d'égout. Pour illustrer ce processus industriel complexe, l'agence a combiné coupes transversales et symboles dans un style moderne et séduisant.*

**PAGE 86 (BOTTOM)** ART DIRECTOR/DESIGNER: *John Nowland* ILLUSTRATOR: *Kelly Burton* AGENCY: *John Nowland Design* CLIENT: *Consolidated Graphics Corporation* YEAR PUBLISHED: *1990* COUNTRY: *Australia* ■ *Diagram detailing the complete production process of a full-color booklet.* ● *Darstellung des gesamten Ablaufs der Herstellung einer farbigen Broschüre.* ▲ *Illustration du processus de fabrication d'une brochure en couleur.*

**PAGE 87** ART DIRECTOR: *CJ Thompson* DESIGNER/ILLUSTRATOR: *Jeff West* COPYWRITER: *Chip Morgan* AGENCY: *Gordon Bailey & Associates, Inc.* CLIENT: *Penneco Packaging Specialty Products* YEAR PUBLISHED: *1995* TYPEFACE: *Gill Sans* PRINTER: *Daly Graphics* COUNTRY: *USA* ■ *"Top off" axiometric view of an imaginary restaurant showing the many uses of plastic waste disposal bags in a food service environment.* ● *Aufriss-Diagramm eines fiktiven Restaurants, das die verschiedenen Einsatzmöglichkeiten von Plastikabfallsäcken zeigt.* ▲ *Diagramme éclaté d'un restaurant fictif illustrant les différentes utilisations de sacs poubelle en plastique.*

**PAGES 88, 89** ART DIRECTOR/DESIGNER/ILLUSTRATOR: *Paula Scher* AGENCY: *Pentagram Design* CLIENT: *Champion International Corporation* COUNTRY: *USA*

**PAGE 90** ART DIRECTOR/ILLUSTRATOR: *Guido Kruesselsberg* AGENCY: *artbeat Design GmbH* CLIENT: *Lentjes Umwelttechnik* YEAR PUBLISHED: *1992* COUNTRY: *Germany* ■ *Technical sketch for recovery of produced steam.* ● *Die Verwertung von erzeugtem Dampf ist Gegenstand dieser technischen Zeichnung.* ▲ *Dessin technique sur la récupération de la vapeur.*

**PAGE 91** DESIGNER/ILLUSTRATOR: *Frank Bayer* AGENCY: *Atelier Frank Bayer* CLIENT: *Westfalia Becorit* COUNTRY: *Germany*

**PAGES 92, 93** ART DIRECTOR: *Bill Krarup* ILLUSTRATOR: *Tilly Northedge* AGENCIES: *Grundy & Northedge, Addison Design Group* CLIENT: *S.R. Gent* YEAR PUBLISHED: *1994* COUNTRY: *England* ■ *Diagrams explaining the details of the delivery and manufacturing methods used by a garment manufacturer. The client described speed as the critical factor in all four processes of their delivery and manufacturing methods. The agency decided to use watches as the device for explaining the methods.* ● *Darstellung der Liefer- und Herstellungsabläufe einer Bekleidungsfabrik, bei denen Schnelligkeit eine wesentliche Rolle spielt. Die Agentur entschied sich deshalb für Uhren, um die Abläufe zu erläutern.* ▲ *Représentation graphique du processus de fabrication et des méthodes de livraison d'une entreprise textile. La vitesse étant un facteur-clé, l'agence a choisi des montres pour illustrer le travail du client.*

**PAGES 94, 95** ART DIRECTOR: *Al Gluth* DESIGNER/ILLUSTRATOR: *Jeff West* COPYWRITER: *Lester Van Dyke* AGENCY: *Gluth Weaver Design* CLIENT: *Battle Mountain Gold* YEAR PUBLISHED: *1995* TYPEFACE: *Gill Sans* PRINTER: *Graphic Arts Center* COUNTRY: *USA* ■ *Diagrams depicting development costs and refining processes of gold mining operations. The illustrations allowed for a conceptual and engaging overview of a technical process to fit in the space of a spread.* ● *Darstellung der Entwicklungskosten und des Raffinerieprozesses von Gold. Die Illustrationen ermöglichten im Rahmen einer Doppelseite die eindrucksvolle Darstellung des technischen Prozesses.* ▲ *Représentation graphique de l'évolution des coûts et du processus de raffinage de l'or. Les illustrations du processus technique sont présentées avec un maximum d'impact sur une double page.*

**PAGE 96 (TOP)** ART DIRECTOR/ILLUSTRATOR: *Guido Kruesselsberg* AGENCY: *artbeat Design GmbH* CLIENT: *Schiess de Fries* YEAR PUBLISHED: *1992/1993* COUNTRY: *Germany* ■ *Illustrated model of a dry dock.* ● *Illustriertes Modell eines Trockendocks.* ▲ *Plan d'une cale sèche.*

**PAGE 96 (BOTTOM)** ART DIRECTOR/ILLUSTRATOR/AGENCY: *Kurt Heinemann* CLIENT: *ICPR Intern (Commission for the Protection of the Rhine)* YEAR PUBLISHED: *1994* PRINTER: *E. Kurz & Co.* COUNTRY: *Germany* ■ *Diagram illustrating how plant protection products travel into the Rhine river in Germany.* ● *Hier wird gezeigt, wie Pflanzenschutzmittel in den deutschen Teil des Rheins gelangen.* ▲ *Diagramme montrant comment les insecticides se répandent dans le Rhin en Allemagne.*

**PAGE 97** ART DIRECTOR: *David Hillman* DESIGNER: *Wolf Spoerl* AGENCY: *Pentagram Design, London* CLIENT: *Ericsson Information Systems* COUNTRY: *Sweden* ■ *Flow chart from* INFORMATION RESOURCE MANAGEMENT, HUMAN FACTORS & INFORMATION SYSTEMS, *a publication issued by the client. Shown is the conversion of the existing international telecommunications system to a digital system. This was planned to be implemented in phases over a period of twenty years.* ● *Ablaufdiagramm aus* INFORMATION RESOURCE MANAGEMENT, HUMAN FACTORS & INFORMATION SYSTEMS, *eine Publikation von Ericsson Information Systems. Dargestellt ist die in einem Zeitraum von 20 Jahren (1980-2000) geplante schrittweise Umstellung des bestehenden internationalen Telekommunikationssystems auf ein Digitalsystem.* ▲ *Organigramme publié dans* INFORMATION RESOURCE MANAGEMENT, HUMAN FACTORS & INFORMATION SYSTEMS, *un périodique d'Ericsson Information Systems. On y présente la reconversion prévue du système international de télécommunications tel que nous le connaissons, pour passer en l'espace de 20 ans (1980-2000) à un système numérique.*

**PAGE 98** ART DIRECTOR: *Nancy Essex* ILLUSTRATOR: *Peter Krämer* AGENCY: *SX2 Essex Two Incorporated* CLIENT: *The Marmon Group, Inc.*

**PAGES 100, 101** ART DIRECTOR: *Tor Pettersen* DESIGNER: *Nicholas Kendal* ILLUSTRATOR: *David Keen* AGENCY: *Tor Pettersen & Partners Ltd.* CLIENT: *Stolt-Nielsen S.A.* COUNTRY: *England* ■ *Diagram showing the client's fleet by class, name, and weight.* ● *Die Flotte einer Reederei, dargestellt nach Art, Namen und Bruttoregistertonnen der Schiffe.* ▲ *Diagramme de la flotte d'une compagnie de navigation présentée selon le type, le nom et le tonnage des bateaux.*

**PAGES 102, 103** ART DIRECTOR: *James Cross* COPYWRITER: *Jane Arnold* COPYWRITER: *Maxwell Arnold* AGENCY: *Cross Associates* CLIENT: *Simpson Paper Company* ■ *Diagram showing capabilities of various paper types designed as part of a promotional piece.* ● *Darstellung der Eigenschaften verschiedener Papierqualitäten für eine Werbebroschüre.* ▲ *Représentation des qualités de différents papiers réalisée pour une brochure publicitaire.*

**PAGE 104** ART DIRECTOR/DESIGNER/ILLUSTRATOR: *Vittorio Del Basso* CLIENT: *ABB Transportation Systems Ltd./SLM Swiss Locomotive and Machine Works* COUNTRY: *Switzerland* ■ *Diagrams of high-speed, multi-purpose, mainline locomotives of the Swiss Federal Railways.* ● *Technische Darstellung der Hochgeschwindigkeits-Mehrzweck-Streckenlokomotiven Re 460 der Schweizerischen Bundesbahnen.* ▲ *Locomotives grande vitesse Re 460 des Chemins de fer suisses.*

**PAGE 105** ART DIRECTOR/DESIGNER/ILLUSTRATOR: *Vittorio Del Basso* CLIENT: *ABB Stal Support* COUNTRY: *International* ■ *(Top) The gas turbine within a 35MW combined cycle plant K-10-1 with air-cooled condenser. (Bottom) Rendering of a 25MW gas turbine GR 10.* ● *(Oben) 35 MW kombinierten Anlage mit luftgekühltem Kondensator. (Unten) Darstellung einer 25MW Gasturbine sowie.* ▲ *(En haut) D'une installation combinée 35 MW dotée d'un condensateur refroidi par air. (En bas) Représentation d'une turbine à gaz 25 MW*

**PAGES 106, 107** ART DIRECTOR: *Allen Carroll* ILLUSTRATOR: *David Kimble* AGENCY: *National Geographic Society in-house* PUBLISHER: *National Geographic Society* COUNTRY: *USA* ■ *"Ford perfects mass production." Illustration of the Ford assembly line. The cutaway view provides a detailed look at the layout of this early factory.* ● *«Ford perfektioniert die Massenproduktion.» Illustration einer Montagestrasse bei Ford. Der Aufriss bietet detaillierten Einblick in die Anlage dieser Fabrik aus frühen Jahren.* ▲ *«Ford perfectionne la production de masse.» Représentation d'une chaîne de montage des usines Ford. L'éclaté présente une vue détaillée de cette ancienne usine.*

**PAGES 108, 109** ART DIRECTOR: *Allen Carroll* DESIGNER: *Robert E. Pratt* ILLUSTRATOR: *Rick Bullington (supervisor, computer staff)* COPYWRITER: *Dr. Bradford A. Smith* AGENCY: *National Geographic Society in-house* PUBLISHER: *National Geographic Society* COUNTRY: *USA* ■ *Poster supplement to* NATIONAL GEOGRAPHIC MAGAZINE *presenting 3-D and electronic imagery of planets and moons. The planets were created using images taken from spacecraft, with colors processed for a more realistic appearance.* ● *Plakatbeilage vom* NATIONAL GEOGRAPHIC MAGAZINE *mit dreidimensional wirkenden, elektronischen Bildern von Planeten und Monden. Die von einem Raumschiff aus gemachten Aufnahmen von den Planeten wurden farblich verändert, um ihnen ein realistischeres Aussehen zu verleihen.* ▲ *Poster encarté dans un numéro du* NATIONAL GEOGRAPHIC MAGAZINE: *images électroniques et 3D de planètes et de lunes.*

**PAGES 110, 111** ART DIRECTOR/DESIGNER: *Rudolf Zündel* CLIENT: *Vorarlberger Nachrichten* PRINTER: *Vorarlberger Medienhaus* COUNTRY: *Austria* ■ *Renderings for a newspaper illustrating the following situations: a) the Lauberhorn ski routes b) a traffic accident; c) a planned street through the city of Bregenz and planned buildings on the site of a former railway station. All diagrams were produced on Macintosh with Freehand software.* ● *Verschiedene Darstellungen für eine Zeitung: a) die Lauberhornskipisten, b) Ablauf eines Verkehrsunfalls; c) eine geplante Stadtstrasse und die neu zu erstellenden Gebäudekomplexe auf dem ehemaligen Bahnhofsgelände der Stadt Bregenz.* ▲ *Diagrammes pour un journal réalisés sur Macintosh/Freehand: a) les pistes de ski du Lauberhorn; c) accident de la route; b) projet d'une route traversant la ville de Bregenz et d'immeubles sur le site d'une ancienne gare.*

**PAGES 112, 113** ART DIRECTOR: *Roger Cook* AGENCY: *Cook + Shanosky Associates* CLIENT: *Black & Decker* COUNTRY: *USA* ■ *Diagrams and illustrations created for the Black & Decker annual report.* ● *Diagramme und Illustrationen aus dem Jahresbericht von Black & Decker.* ▲ *Diagrammes et illustrations extraits du rapport annuel de Black & Decker.*

**PAGES 114, 115** ART DIRECTORS: *Tim McClure, Rex Peteet* DESIGNERS: *Rex Peteet, Derek Welch* DESIGN FIRM: *Sibley/Peteet Design* ADVERTISING AGENCY: *GSD + M* ILLUSTRATOR: *Mick Wiggins* CLIENT: *Southwest Airlines* YEAR PUBLISHED: *1995* PRINTER: *Williamson Printing* COUNTRY: *USA* ■ *Diagrams created for the 1994 Southwest Airlines annual report introducing the idea of a "blueprint" for how the client airline has become a successful low-cost airline. The agency strived to arrive at the most logical common denominator and symbol for each of the points needing to be emphasized throughout the report. Each symbol then had an expanded story to tell which was supported with additional icons and call-outs to complete the picture.* ● *Diagramme für den Jahresbericht 1994 der Southwest Airlines, die aufzeigen, wie die Firma zu einer erfolgreichen Niedrigpreislinie wurde. Die Agentur versuchte, für all die Punkte, die im Jahresbericht hervorgehoben werden sollten, einen logischen gemeinsamen Nenner zu finden. Jedes Symbol leitet einen ausführlicheren Bericht ein, unterstützt von zusätzlichen Ikonen.* ▲ *Diagrammes pour le rapport annuel 1994 de Southwest Airlines illustrant comment la* compagnie s'est imposée avec succès grâce à ses vols bon marché. L'agence a cherché un dénominateur commun pour tous les points marquants. Chaque symbole donne lieu à un commentaire détaillé, renforcé par des icônes supplémentaires.

PAGE 116 ART DIRECTOR/DESIGNER/ILLUSTRATOR: *Jack Endewelt* COUNTRY: *USA* ∎ *(Top) "Two Views of Colt Revolver." This diagram examines the properties of the colt revolver in some detail. To make an informative picture function as art, the illustrator utilized personal expression, detail, and placement to take the subject out of context. (Middle) "Winchester Rifle." This diagram examines and explains the workings of the rifle, indicating type of ammunition used, etc. The illustrator presented the object from different points of view, and utilized texture, placement, ancillary objects, typography, and painting to create contextual divergence. (Bottom) "Faucet, Open and Closed." This diagram displays the properties and operation of a faucet. The illustrator presented two views of the faucet. Color, texture, placement, tonal variance and painting were used to create contextual distinction.* ● *(Oben) «Zwei Ansichten eines Revolvers.» Detaillierte Darstellung eines Colts, wobei sich der Illustrator um ein malerisches Bild bemühte. (Mitte) «Winchester». Dargestellt ist die Funktions des Gewehrs, die passende Munition, etc. Die Illustration zeigt die Winchester aus verschiedenen Blickwinkeln, wobei Plazierung, Beiwerk, Typographie und Malerei für eine ungewöhnliche Wirkung sorgen. (Unten) «Abzug, gespannt und gesichert.» Das Diagramm zeigt die Eigenschaften und Funktionsweise eines Abzugs. Hier werden zwei Ansichten auf malerische Art dargestellt.* ▲ *(En haut) Vues d'un colt. Représentation picturale et détaillée d'un colt. (Au milieu) «Winchester Rifle»: diagramme illustrant le fonctionnement de l'arme, le type de munitions utilisées, etc. L'illustration la montre sous différents angles, position, accessoires, textures, typographie et peinture créant un effet original. (En bas) «Détente»: diagramme et illustrations expliquent le mécanisme de la détente.*

PAGE 117 ART DIRECTOR/DESIGNER/ILLUSTRATOR: *Jack Endewelt* COUNTRY: *USA* ∎ *"Faucets." This diagram examines the properties and the operation of various faucets. To make an informative picture function as art, the illustrator presented a variety of related subject matter from different viewpoints, and employed typography and paint to create contextual variance.* ● *«Abzüge.» Hier werden die Eigenschaften und die Funktionsweise verschiedener Abzüge untersucht. Die eingesetzten Bildmittel dienen zur Verfremdung des Diagrammcharakters.* ▲ *«Détentes»: comparaison des mécanismes de différents types de détentes. Typographie et peinture confèrent un caractère artistique aux informations techniques.*

PAGE 118 ART DIRECTOR: *Chris Devito* ILLUSTRATOR: *Peter Krämer* AGENCY: *Bates USA* CLIENT: *Texaco* YEAR PUBLISHED: *1995* COUNTRY: *USA* ∎ *This illustration representing a modern, universal type of American car engine was part of a multiple-picture ad for the client's oil.* ● *Diese Illustration eines modernen, amerikanischen Standardmotors gehört zu einer Anzeige für Texaco-Öl.* ▲ *Illustration d'un moteur américain sophistiqué pour une publicité Texaco.*

PAGE 119 (TOP) ART DIRECTOR: *Alberto Gracia Izquierdo* ILLUSTRATOR: *Peter Krämer* CLIENT: *Deutsche Lufthansa AG* YEAR PUBLISHED: *1994* TYPEFACE: *Lufthansa-Helvetica* PRINTER: *Mohndruck* COUNTRY: *Germany* ∎ *This diagram is part of a series entitled "Checklist" published in the* LUFTHANSA BORDBUCH *inflight magazine. The series informs passengers about modern aircraft technology. Because normal gangways are relatively large and illustrated details would end up very small, the illustrator chose to use a diagram to depict the built-in stairway of a Fokker 50 plane.* ● *Diese Illustration gehört zur "Checklist"-Serie des* LUFTHANSA BORDBUCHS. *Diese Serie informiert die Fluggäste über moderne Luftfahrttechnik. Dargestellt ist die eingebaute Gangway einer Fokker 50.* ▲ *Diagramme extrait de la série «Checklist» du magazine de la Lufthansa, consacrée à l'aéronautique de pointe. L'illustration montre l'escalier intégré d'un Fokker 50.*

PAGE 119 (BOTTOM) ART DIRECTORS: *Jeff Davis, Tor Pettersen* DESIGNER: *Jeff Davis* ILLUSTRATOR: *David Hunter* COPYWRITER: *Tor Pettersen* AGENCY: *Tor Pettersen & Partners Ltd.* CLIENT: *Lucas Industries Plc.* YEAR PUBLISHED: *1994* TYPEFACE: *Futura Italic, Concord* PRINTER: *CTD Printers* COUNTRY: *United Kingdom* ∎ *Diagram representing the client's vision of a large airliner of the future and a totally integrated aircraft management system.* ● *Die Vision eines grossen Flugzeugs der Zukunft mit integriertem Flugsystem.* ▲ *Représentation d'un avion futuriste doté d'un système de vol intégré.*

PAGES 120, 121 ART DIRECTOR/DESIGNER: *Ronnie Peters* CLIENT: *IBM* COUNTRY: *USA* ∎ *Diagrams illustrating the IBM Thinkpad setup process, created to accompany user*

manuals. *Two colors were used for these diagrams to show action, motion, or for indication. The hands are made to look generic, neither male or female.* ● *Diagramme für das Anwenderhandbuch von IBMs Thinkpad-Laptop. Die zweite Farbe dient zur Verdeutlichung von einzelnen Vorgängen und Informationen. Die Hände sind so dargestellt, dass sie weder spezifisch weiblich noch männlich wirken.* ▲ *Diagrammes extraits d'un manuel sur le Thinkpad, un laptop d'IBM. Utilisation de deux couleurs, dont l'une pour l'action, le mouvement et les informations. Les mains, neutres, sont «unisexes».*

PAGE 122 ART DIRECTOR/ILLUSTRATOR: *Wolfgang Franke* AGENCY: *Franke Techn. Grafik* CLIENT: *CTC Wärme AG* YEAR PUBLISHED: *1993* COUNTRY: *Switzerland* ∎ *Cross-section of the 360 LRN heating tank.* ● *Schnittzeichnungen eines 360 LRN-Heizkessels.* ▲ *Coupe transversale d'une chaudière.*

PAGE 123 ART DIRECTOR/ILLUSTRATOR: *Wolfgang Franke* AGENCY: *Franke Techn. Grafik* CLIENT: *CTC Wärme AG* YEAR PUBLISHED: *1993* COUNTRY: *Switzerland* ∎ *Cross-section of the 323N heating tank. The drawing was rendered by hand using pencil, ink, and airbrush.* ● *Querschnitt des 323N Heizkessels. Die Zeichnung wurde von Hand nach Konstruktionszeichnungen erstellt (Bleistift, Tusche, Airbrush).* ▲ *Coupe transversale d'une chaudière. Dessin à la main d'après des plans de construction (crayon, encre, airbrush).*

PAGE 124 (TOP) ILLUSTRATOR: *Tom Liddell* AGENCY: *Studio Liddell* CLIENT: *Rank Zerox* YEAR PUBLISHED: *1989* COUNTRY: *England* ∎ *Diagram illustrating the workings of a photocopier.* ● *Funktionsdarstellung eines Photokopierers.* ▲ *Illustration du fonctionnement d'une photocopieuse.*

PAGE 124 (BOTTOM) ART DIRECTOR: *Peter Harrison* DESIGNER: *Ivette Montes De Oca* ILLUSTRATOR: *Jared Schneidman* AGENCY: *Pentagram Design* CLIENT: *Texaco Inc.* YEAR PUBLISHED: *1995* PRINTER: *Davis-Delaney-Arron, Inc.* COUNTRY: *USA* ∎ *The diagram depicts the various levels of Texaco's oil development project in the North Sea: above-surface, underwater, and in the sea bed. Numbered captions describe the development process and enlarged details show technological innovations.* ● *Das Diagramm zeigt die verschiedenen Ebenen des Aufbaus einer Texaco-Ölbohrinsel in der Nordsee: über dem Meeresspiegel, unter Wasser und im Meeresgrund. Numerierte Legenden informieren über den Entwicklungsprozess und vergrösserte Details verdeutlichen technologische Innovationen.* ▲ *Diagramme représentant les différents stades de la construction d'une plateforme de forage Texaco dans la mer du Nord: au-dessus de l'eau, sous l'eau et au fond de la mer. Les légendes numérotées donnent des informations sur l'évolution de la construction, et les détails, agrandis, montrent les innovations technologiques.*

PAGE 125 ART DIRECTOR: *Guido Kruesselsberg* ILLUSTRATOR: *Verena Zwaetz* AGENCY: *artbeat Design GmbH* CLIENT: *MAB Lentjes* YEAR PUBLISHED: *1992* COUNTRY: *Germany* ∎ *Diagram of a sludge incineration plant.* ● *Darstellung einer Klärschlammverbrennungsanlage.* ▲ *Diagramme d'une station d'incinération des boues de curage.*

PAGE 126 ILLUSTRATOR: *Chuck Carter* AGENCY: *National Geographic Society in-house* PUBLISHER: *National Geographic Society* YEAR PUBLISHED: *1995* COUNTRY: *USA* ∎ *Diagrams created to illustrate the architectural features of the pyramids and to demonstrate how they drove Egypt's economy.* ● *Diagramme zur Erläuterung der Architektur der Pyramiden und des positiven Einflusses der Pyramiden auf die ägyptische Wirtschaft.* ▲ *Diagrammes illustrant l'architecture des pyramides et leur influence positive sur l'économie égyptienne.*

PAGE 127 ART DIRECTOR: *Earl Gee* DESIGNERS: *Earl Gee, Fani Chung* ILLUSTRATOR: *Greg Wenzel* COPYWRITER: *Julie Gibbs* AGENCY: *Gee + Chung Design* CLIENT: *Oracle Corporation* YEAR PUBLISHED: *1995* TYPEFACE: *Univers 75* PRINTER: *Anderson Lithographic* COUNTRY: *USA* ∎ *This diagram utilizes an e-mail exchange as a demonstration of an educational usage of the information highway. The client, a database management software company, sought to graphically depict the impact of technology in creating the "Global Electronic Classroom." An illustration from the movie "Jurassic Park" is used as a backdrop.* ● *Hier wird anhand einer E-mail Korrespondenz aufgezeigt, wie der Information Highway für Lehrzwecke genutzt werden kann. Der Auftraggeber, eine Datenbank-Software Firma, wollte eine graphische Darstellung der Bedeutung von Technologie für das «globale elektronische Klassenzimmer». Als Hintergrund dient ein Bild aus dem Film «Jurassic Park».* ▲ *Diagramme montrant comment les autoroutes de l'information peuvent être utilisées à des fins éducatives à l'exemple du courrier électronique. Le client, une société de services et de conseil en infor-*

*matique spécialisée dans les systèmes de gestion de bases de données, souhaitait illustrer l'impact de la technologie au moyen d'une «Salle de classe entièrement électronique». En toile de fond, une scène du film «Jurassic Parc».*

**PAGES 128, 129** ART DIRECTOR: *Karl Gude* DESIGNERS/ILLUSTRATORS: *M. Carrasco, M. Doelling, R. Dominguez, J. Goertzen, K. Gude, M. Hernandez, A. Lucas, J. Nunoz, G. Sampedro, D. Sanchez, M. Tascon, R. Toro, J. Velasco* AGENCY: *The Associated Press, El Periodico, El Mundo* COPYWRITERS: *D.W. Gude, D. Desilets, M. Stevenson* YEAR PUBLISHED: *1992* TYPEFACE: *Times, Helvetica* ■ *Diagrams created for the 1992 Olympics in Barcelona.* ● *Für die Olympiade geschaffene Diagramme.* ▲ *Diagrammes créés pour les Jeux olympiques.*

**PAGES 130, 131** ART DIRECTOR/DESIGNER: *Michael Benes* ARTIST: *Dave Hannum* AGENCY: *Polaroid in-house* CLIENT: *Polaroid Corporation* COUNTRY: *USA* ■ *Technical illustrations of the Polaroid Spectra/Image system, from a Polaroid annual report. (a) Section of the electronics (b) 21-part detector camera (c) production line with seven robots engaged on the Spectra (d-f) views of camera closed, opened, and as a cutaway to elucidate on the lighting system and the aperture.* ● *Technische Darstellungen des Polaroid-Spectra/Image-Systems, aus dem Jahresbericht von Polaroid. (a) Ein Teil der Elektronik; (b) 21-teilige Sucherkamera; (c) eine mit sieben Robotern arbeitende Produktionslinie für die Image-Kamera; (d-f) Darstellungen der Kamera, hier zur Erläuterung des Belichtungssystems und der Blende geschlossen, geöffnet und aufgeschnitten gezeigt.* ▲ *Diagrammes techniques relatifs au système Polaroïd Spectra/Image, dans le rapport annuel de Polaroïd. (a) Vue partielle de l'électronique; (b) le viseur composé de 21 éléments; (c) chaîne de production du système Image équipée de sept robots; (d-f) vues de l'appareil fermé, ouvert et éclaté, illustrant les raffinements du système optique et de sa lentille frontale asphérique.*

**PAGE 132** ART DIRECTOR: *Jack Anderson* DESIGNERS: *Jack Anderson, Denise Weir, Lian Ng* ILLUSTRATORS: *Todd Connor, Bruce Morser, Dean Williams* COPYWRITER: *Joan Brown* AGENCY: *Hornall Anderson Design Works, Inc.* CLIENT: *Windstar Cruises* YEAR PUBLISHED: *1992* PRINTER: *George Rice & Sons* COUNTRY: *USA* ■ *Diagram illustrating the route followed by one of the client's cruise ships. The agency decided to use softly illustrated maps to create an elegant and sophisticated feel.* ● *Darstellung einer Schiffsroute für eine Reederei. Die Agentur entschied sich für den Einsatz zart illustrierter Karten, um einen eleganten, anspruchsvollen Eindruck zu erwecken.* ▲ *Diagramme du routing d'une compagnie de navigation. L'agence a porté son choix sur des cartes illustrées avec finesse pour un résultat élégant et sophistiqué.*

**PAGES 134, 135** ART DIRECTOR: *Clifford Selbert* DESIGNER: *Linda Kondo* ILLUSTRATOR: *Daniel Craig* AGENCY: *Clifford Selbert Design, Inc.* CLIENT: *New York Botanical Gardens* YEAR PUBLISHED: *1990* COUNTRY: *USA* ■ *Map created to guide visitors around the New York Botanical Gardens. Bold floral images were the main graphic focus of these maps.* ● *Plan für die Besucher des Botanischen Gartens von New York. Die floralen Motive sind die wichtigsten graphischen Elemente dieser Pläne.* ▲ *Plan destiné aux visiteurs du jardin botanique de New York. Les motifs floraux constituent le principal élément graphique.*

**PAGES 136, 137** ART DIRECTOR: *Patrick Seymour* DESIGNER: *Catarina Tsang* ILLUSTRATOR: *Martin Haggland* AGENCY: *Tsang Seymour Design* CLIENT: *Joseph Hilton Associates Inc.* YEAR PUBLISHED: *1995* TYPEFACE: *Monotype, New Baskerville, Franklin Gothic* PRINTER: *Tanagraphics, NY* COUNTRY: *USA* ■ *Midtown and downtown Manhattan commercial real estate map. The map was designed as a reference and promotional tool which could be used as both a portable map and a framed piece. Issues of scale, ease of use, and legibility were of primary concern. Once scale and size were determined, the principal communicating device became color. Distinct colors queued to a defined area made the separate figures of each district visible at a glance. Conventional colors were used for grass and water as a means of contextual reference. The manner of folding was based on architectural blueprints for ease of access on the street.* ● *Karte der Liegenschaften im Zentrum und im südlichen Teil von Manhattan. Bei dieser Karte zum Mitnehmen oder Aufhängen ging es in erster Linie um leichte Handhabung und Lesbarkeit. Nachdem Massstab und Grösse festgelegt waren, wurde Farbe zum wichtigsten Kommunikationsinstrument. Ausgeprägte Farben wurden jeweils einem bestimmten Bereich zugeordnet, so dass die separaten Zahlen für jeden Distrikt auf den ersten Blick erkennbar sind. Konventionelle Farben wurden für Grünflächen und Wasser eingesetzt. Das Faltkonzept, das eine leichte Handhabung auf der Strasse erlaubt, entspricht dem von Bauplänen.* ▲ *Plan des immeubles du centre et du sud de Manhattan. Carte promotionnelle fonctionnelle et décorative. Le côté pratique et la lisibilité constituaient les critères-clés. Au-delà de l'échelle et du*

*format, les couleurs sont un élément de communication prépondérant. Des couleurs distinctes ont été attribuées à chaque secteur afin que les chiffres des différents arrondissements ressortent clairement. Pour représenter les espaces verts et l'eau, des couleurs conventionnelles ont été utilisées. Inspiré des plans d'architecture, le système de pliage se distingue par son côté pratique.*

**PAGES 138, 139** ART DIRECTOR: *Jack Anderson* DESIGNERS: *Jack Anderson, Denise Weir, Lian Ng* ILLUSTRATORS: *Todd Connor, Bruce Morser, Dean Williams* COPYWRITER: *Joan Brown* AGENCY: *Hornall Anderson Design Works, Inc.* CLIENT: *Windstar Cruises* YEAR PUBLISHED: *1992* PRINTER: *George Rice & Sons* COUNTRY: *USA* ■ *Diagram illustrating the routes followed by the client's cruise ships. The agency decided to use softly illustrated maps to create an elegant and sophisticated feel.* ● *Die Routen der Kreuzfahrtschiffe einer Reederei. Die sanft illustrierten Karten sorgen für einen eleganten, anspruchsvollen Eindruck.* ▲ *Diagramme du routing d'une compagnie de navigation. L'agence a porté son choix sur des cartes illustrées avec finesse pour un résultat élégant et sophistiqué.*

**PAGE 140** DESIGNER/AUTHOR/PUBLISHER: *Richard Saul Wurman* CARTOGRAPHER: *John Grimwade* CLIENT:: *The Initial Press Syndicate* COUNTRY: *USA* ■ *Map of Newport, Rhode Island.* ● *Karte von Newport, Rhode Island.* ▲ *Carte de Newport, Rhode Island.*

**PAGE 141** ART DIRECTOR: *Nakagawa Kenzo* DESIGNERS: *Nakagawa Kenzo, Nobuyama Hiroyasu, Morikami Satoshi, Inda Hiroyuki* COPYWRITER: *Tanaka Azusa* AGENCY: *NDC Graphics Inc.* CLIENT: *Tower Shop* YEAR PRODUCED: *1994* COUNTRY: *Japan* ■ *Map of choice sites for viewing cherry blossoms in Yokohama, Japan.* ● *Plan der schönsten Orte zur Kirschblütenzeit in Yokohama, Japan.* ▲ *Plan des plus beaux endroits de Yokohama au Japon lorsque les cerisiers sont en fleur.*

**PAGES 142, 143** ART DIRECTORS/DESIGNERS: *Jack Reineck, Gay Reineck* ILLUSTRATION/AGENCY: *Reineck & Reineck* CLIENT: *Rufus Graphics* COUNTRY: *USA* ■ *Map and guide to Fisherman's Wharf in San Francisco.* ● *Karte und Führer von Fisherman's Wharf in San Francisco.* ▲ *Plan et guide du Fisherman's Wharf à San Francisco.*

**PAGE 144** ART DIRECTOR: *Michael Cronan* DESIGNER: *Anthony Yell* AGENCY: *Cronan Design* CLIENT: *Robert Lamb Hart* YEAR PUBLISHED: *1995* TYPEFACE: *A Garamond* PRINTER: *Diversified Graphics, Inc.* COUNTRY: *USA* ■ *Map from a Santa Lucia Preserve entitlement book relating size and location of development in relation to the surrounding region.* ● *Plan aus einer Broschüre, aus dem Grösse und Lage einer Überbauung im Verhältnis zur umliegenden Region hervorgeht.* ▲ *Plan extrait d'une brochure, illustrant l'envergure et la situation d'un projet de construction par rapport à l'environnement.*

**PAGE 145 (TOP)** ART DIRECTORS/DESIGNERS: *Jack Reineck, Gay Reineck* ILLUSTRATION: *Reineck & Reineck* COPYWRITER: *Karen Taylor* AGENCY: *Reineck & Reineck* CLIENT: *Rufus Graphics* COUNTRY: *USA* ■ *Bird's-eye view of the Grand Canyon delineating its natural features, trails, and points of interest.* ● *Der Grand Canyon aus der Vogelperspektive, wobei neben den geographischen Gegebenheiten Wege und Sehenswürdigkeiten eingezeichnet sind.* ▲ *Vue d'oiseau du Grand Canyon indiquant les caractéristiques géographiques, les chemins et les principales curiosités.*

**PAGE 145 (BOTTOM)** ART DIRECTORS/DESIGNERS: *Jack Reineck, Gay Reineck* ILLUSTRATION/AGENCY: *Reineck & Reineck* CLIENT: *Rufus Graphics* COUNTRY: *USA* ■ *This diagram, viewed from the south rim, gives the visitor an accurate and detailed overview of the natural features, roads, trails, and points of interest of the Yosemite valley.* ● *Der Plan des Yosemite Valley, vom Süden her aus der Vogelperspektive gesehen, vermittelt dem Betrachter einen detaillierten Überblick der landschaftlichen Gegebenheiten der Strassen, Pfade und Sehenswürdigkeiten.* ▲ *Vue d'oiseau de la Yosemite Valley indiquant de manière détaillée les caractéristiques géographiques, les routes, les chemins et les principales curiosités.*

**PAGES 146, 147** ART DIRECTOR/DESIGNER: *Beau Gardner* ILLUSTRATOR: *Allyn Bacher* COPYWRITER: *Tom Bisky* AGENCY: *Beau Gardner Associates* CLIENT: *Con Edison* YEAR PUBLISHED: *1992* TYPEFACE: *Helvetica Black Condensed, Helvetica Light Condensed* COUNTRY: *USA* ■ *Map of Consolidated Edison's service area in New York City as well as transportation lines and areas of special interest. To accommodate changing information for reuse of the map, the agency designed it in layers for flexibility.* ● *Karte der vom Elektrizitätswerk Consolidated Edison versorgten Gebiete in Manhattan mit*

*Verkehrslinien und Sehenswürdigkeiten. Das spezielle Design der Karte macht es möglich, sie problemlos auf den neusten Informationsstand zu bringen.* ▲ *Plan des quartiers de New York City alimentés par la centrale électrique Consolidated Edison avec indication des lignes des transports urbains et des curiosités. Le concept de la carte permet de la réactualiser aisément.*

**PAGES 148-153** ART DIRECTOR: *Michael Gericke* DESIGNERS: *Michael Gericke, Donna Ching, Sharon Harel* ILLUSTRATOR: *Hammond Incorporated* AGENCY: *Pentagram Design* CLIENT: *Hammond Incorporated* COUNTRY: *USA*

**PAGE 154** DESIGNER: *Russ Brami* AGENCY: *Brami Design* CLIENT: *New England Chapter, Society of Office and Industrial Realtors* YEAR PUBLISHED: *1994* TYPEFACE: *Palatino* PRINTER: *Graphic Litho* COUNTRY: *USA* ■ *Map of downtown Boston highlighting significant buildings by "footprint" and category. Since downtown Boston is an ideal area for foot travel, the agency wanted to make the structure and organization of its irregular patterns clear through the articulation of pavement streets and green spaces. A serene palette and a silkscreen-like application without traplines were used to produce a crisp image that is enhanced by a hierarchy of text sizes in a single type family.* ● *Karte der City von Boston, wobei wichtige Gebäude nach Kategorien aufgeteilt sind und Fussabdrücke die Fusswege kennzeichnen. Hier sollte die Struktur und Anlage des Gewirrs der Fusswege durch Betonung der gepflasterten Strassen und Grünflächen verdeutlicht werden. Die Frische und der flächige Auftrag der Farben sorgen für ein freundliches Bild, unterstützt vom Einsatz der Typographie, d.h. einer Schrift in verschiedenen Grössen.* ▲ *Plan de Boston indiquant les principaux bâtiments par catégorie, les empreintes de pas signalant les itinéraires à suivre. La mise en relief des rues pavées et des espaces verts reflète la complexité de l'organisation urbaine. Les couleurs des à-plats confèrent fraîcheur et dynamisme, rehaussés par la typo utilisant un caractère en divers points.*

**PAGE 155** ART DIRECTOR: *Wilhelm Malkemus* DESIGNER: *Hans-Günter Sünbold* CONCEPT: *Architekturbüro Christel + Bruchhäuser* CLIENT: *Stadt Frankfurt am Main* COUNTRY: *Germany* ■ *This map was created for the 1200-year anniversary of the city of Frankfurt on the Main, Germany. It details the highrise buildings which earned the city the name of "Mainhattan."* ● *Dieses Faltblatt mit Stadtplan und einer Darstellung der Hochhäuser wurde von der Stadt Frankfurt am Main anlässlich der 1200-Jahresfeier in Auftrag gegeben.* ▲ *«Mainhattan». Dépliant comprenant un plan et les gratte-ciel de Francfort-sur-le-Main, réalisé à l'occasion de l'anniversaire de la ville qui fêtait ses 1200 ans.*

**PAGES 156-159** DESIGNER/AUTHOR/CO-PUBLISHER: *Richard Saul Wurman* PROJECT DIRECTORS: *Maria Giudice, Michael Everitt, Bonnie Scranton* CLIENT: *ACCESS Press/H.M. Gousha* PRINTER: *Graphic Arts Center* ■ *Maps from Richard Saul Wurman's US Atlas* ● *Karten aus einem Atlas der USA.* ▲ *Carte extraite d'un atlas américain.*

**PAGE 160** ART DIRECTOR/DESIGNER: *Joel Katz* DESIGN OFFICE: *Joel Katz Design Associates* COPYWRITER: *Lois Morasco* CLIENT: *Pennsylvania Department of Transportation* YEAR PUBLISHED: *1985* TYPEFACE: *Times, Univers* ■ *View of Philadelphia's highway network and alternative routes necessary during highway building. From a folding tourist prospectus issued by the Pennsylvania Department of Transportation.* ● *Übersicht des Strassennetzes und der durch Strassenbau erforderlichen Ausweichmöglichkeiten in der Umgebung von Philadelphia. Aus einem Faltprospekt des Pennsylvania Department of Transportation.* ▲ *Plan du réseau routier et des voies de déviation permettant de contourner les chantiers routiers dans les environs de Philadelphie. Dépliant du Pennsylvania Department of Transportation destiné aux touristes.*

**PAGE 161** ART DIRECTORS: *Tony Milner, Mark Anderson* DESIGNER/ARTIST: *Earl Gee* AGENCY: *Mark Anderson Design* CLIENT: *US Sprint Communications Corporation* COUNTRY: *USA* ■ *Poster for the US Sprint Communications Corporation with information about geographic areas for which various satellites are responsible.* ● *Plakat für die US Sprint Communications Corp. Hier wird verdeutlicht, für welche Gebiete der Erde die verschiedenen Satelliten zuständig sind.* ▲ *Affiche pour la US Sprint Communications Corp. On y voit la répartition des zones géographiques en fonction des divers satellites en orbite autour du globe.*

**PAGES 162, 164, 165** ART DIRECTOR: *Ikko Tanaka* DESIGNERS: *Ikko Tankaka, Kan Akita* AGENCY: *Ikko Tanaka Design Studio* CLIENT: *Toto Ltd.* COUNTRY: *Japan*

**PAGES 166, 167** ART DIRECTOR: *Reed Agnew* DESIGNER: *Norm Goldberg* ILLUSTRATORS: *Kurt Hess, Rick Henkel* AGENCY: *Agnew Moyer Smith Inc.* CLIENT: *Commissioners of Allegheny County* YEAR PUBLISHED: *1993* TYPEFACE: *New Baskerville* PRINTER: *Westinghouse Printing Division* COUNTRY: *USA* ■ *Map and detail of the Pittsburgh Air and Space Museum located in Pennsylvania. The agency used a detailed cutaway isometric drawing to show context.* ● *Karte und Detail des Luft- und Raumfahrtmuseums in Pittsburgh, Pennsylvania. Aufriss mit isometrischer Perspektive, um den Kontext der der Ausstellungsstücke zu zeigen.* ▲ *Carte et détail du Musée de l'aéronautique de Pittsburgh, en Pennsylvanie. Représentation isométrique éclatée illustrant l'environnement des objets exposés.*

**PAGES 168, 169** ART DIRECTOR: *Malcolm Park* DESIGNERS: *Malcolm Park, Ian Bray* ILLUSTRATORS/PHOTOGRAPHERS: *Colin Knox, James Jackson* COPYWRITERS: *Simon Hancock, Robin Hood-Leeder* AGENCY: *Wings Design Consultants* CLIENT: *Redland Bricks* COUNTRY: *USA* ■ *Door threshold and jamb construction detail for a corporate product brochure.* ● *Die Konstruktion von Türschwelle und Türpfosten sowie ein Detail, dargestellt für eine Firmenbroschüre.* ▲ *Plan du seuil et du montant d'une porte et détail d'une brochure publicitaire.*

**PAGES 170, 171** ART DIRECTOR: *Uwe Schramm* ILLUSTRATORS: *Uwe Schramm, Josef Risling, Torsten Krökel, Jackie Helgert* AGENCY: *Schramms, Graphik-Design & Digital Media Art* CLIENT: *Messe Berlin GmbH* COUNTRY: *Germany* ■ *This guide system was created for the biggest convention center in Europe. The presentation shows the different levels through four single levels and a complete overview by showing the the relation of the view from the outside.* ● *Dieses Leitsystem wurde für eines der grössten Tagungszentren in Europa entwickelt. Die Darstellung zeigt die verschiedenen Ebenen und gibt einen Gesamtüberblick durch Erläuterung der Relation zur Aussenansicht.* ▲ *Signalétique conçue pour le plus grand centre de conférences en Europe. La présentation montre les différents niveaux et donne une vue d'ensemble de l'extérieur.*

**PAGE 172** ART DIRECTOR: *Uwe Schramm* ILLUSTRATORS: *Uwe Schramm, Josef Risling, Torsten Krökel, Jackie Helgert* AGENCY: *Schramms, Graphik-Design & Digital Media Art* CLIENT: *Messe Berlin GmbH* COUNTRY: *Germany* ■ *Sectional of a stage at a Berlin convention center.* ● *Längsschnitt durch die Bühnenanlage und den Schnürboden der Messe Berlin.* ▲ *Coupe longitudinale de la scène et du cintre d'un centre de congrès à Berlin.*

**PAGE 173** DESIGNER: *Carol Mooradian* PHOTOGRAPHER/ILLUSTRATOR: *Tom Masters & McNamara Assoc.* AGENCY: *Group 243, Inc.* CLIENT: *Wolverine Technologies* COUNTRY: *USA* ■ *Diagram created for a call for entry for a vinyl siding application contest.* ● *Darstellung für die Einladung zur Teilnahme an einem Wettbewerb des Baugewerbes.* ▲ *Diagramme réalisé pour un concours de l'industrie du bâtiment.*

**PAGES 174, 175** ART DIRECTOR/DESIGNER: *Otl Aicher* PHOTOGRAPHER/ILLUSTRATOR: *Reinfriede Bettrich* AGENCY: *Rotis Büros* CLIENT: *Druckhaus Maack* ● *Poster demonstrating the capabilities of a printer.* ■ *Plakat zur Darstellung der Möglichkeiten und Qualitätsarbeit einer Druckerei.* ▲ *Affiche illustrant les services d'une imprimerie.*

**PAGE 176** DESIGNERS: *Pat Hansen, Kip Henrie* ILLUSTRATORS: *Domonic Dunbar, Kip Henrie* AGENCY: *Hansen Design Company* CLIENT: *MagnaDesign* YEAR PUBLISHED: *1995* TYPEFACE: *Helvetica Light* PRINTER: *Grossberg Tyler Lithographers* COUNTRY: *USA* ■ *These illustrations of the various components which constitute the client's integrated modular furniture systems were created for a sales piece used by facilities planners. Simple line drawings were used to present the products in a clear understandable fashion.* ● *Diese Illustrationen der verschiedenen Teile eines Möbelelementsystems stammen aus einem Prospekt, der von Innenarchitekten benutzt wird. Einfache Zeichnungen dienen zur leicht verständlichen Erläuterung.* ▲ *Illustrations des éléments d'un système de meubles modulaire extraites d'une brochure destinée aux architectes d'intérieur. Des dessins simples présentent les produits de manière claire.*

**PAGE 177** ART DIRECTOR: *Erika Uffindell* DESIGNER: *Gary Black* ILLUSTRATOR: *Tilly Northedge* AGENCIES: *Grundy & Northedge, Uffindell and West* CLIENT: *British Standards Institution* YEAR PUBLISHED: *1995* COUNTRY: *England* ■ *Home setting presenting a variety of items which have undergone testing and been awarded certification by the British Standards Institution. To make all items visible in a home setting, the agency utilized "cut-away" walls and an isometric angle. The illustration was colored informationally rather than realistically to place visual emphasis on the products.* ● *Verschiedene Gegenstände, die vom British Standards*

*Institute getestet und ausgezeichnet wurden, dargestellt im häuslichen Umfeld. Um die Gegenstände sichtbar zu machen, entschied sich die die Agentur für Aufrisse und eine isometrische Sichtweise. Bei der Kolorierung der Illustration ging es nicht um realistische sondern um informative Gesichtspunkte zugunsten der Produkte.* ▲ *Objets testés et agréés par le British Standards Institute, présentés dans un environnement domestique. Pour faire ressortir les objets, l'agence a utilisé une perspective isométrique.*

**PAGES 178, 179** ART DIRECTOR: *Burkey Belser* DESIGNER: *Chris Leonard* ILLUSTRATOR: *Dale Glasgow* COPYWRITER: *George Kell* AGENCY: *Greenfield/Belser Ltd.* CLIENT: *Linowes and Blocher* YEAR PUBLISHED: *1996* PRINTER: *S + S Graphics* COUNTRY: *USA* ■ *Diagram defining the full range of the firm's services and confirming through case studies the importance of its client base. Because developers and businesses want to manage new ventures with a greater certainty that costs will stay under control and that projects will be successful, the agency had to create a diagram that would confirm the client is a logical choice for land use issues in Maryland, Washington DC, and Northern Virginia.* ● *Darstellung des gesamten Umfangs der Dienstleistungen einer Firma, wobei Fallbeispiele auf die Erfahrung der Firma und Bedeutung ihrer bisherigen Auftraggeber hinweisen. Da Bauunternehmen und Firmen bei der Erstellung neuer Überbauungen hinsichtlich der Kosten und des Erfolgs ihrer Projekte sicher gehen wollen, sollte mit diesem Diagramm verdeutlicht werden, dass der Auftraggeber die einzig richtige Wahl ist, wenn es um die Nutzung von Land in Maryland, Washington DC und Northern Virginia geht.* ▲ *Diagramme présentant la gamme de prestations d'une société. Les cas de figure illustrés soulignent l'expérience de l'entreprise et l'étendue de sa clientèle. Les entreprises de construction et les sociétés mandataires exigeant plus de garanties quant au contrôle des coûts et au succès des projets de construction, l'agence a créé un diagramme montrant que son client est le bon partenaire lorsqu'il s'agit d'exploiter des terrains dans le Maryland, à Washington DC et en Virginie du Nord.*

**PAGE 180** ART DIRECTOR: *Nancye Green* DESIGNER: *Jenny Barry* ILLUSTRATOR: *Carlos Diniz* COPYWRITER/AGENCY: *Donovan & Green* CLIENT: *Olympia & York World Financial Center Retail Leasing* YEAR PUBLISHED: *1986* COUNTRY: *USA* ■ *Diagram created to interest prospective tenants in the two-level, dispersed retail spaces within the World Financial Center in New York. The agency had to create a visually compelling and clear diagram of a complex series of disconnected spaces within a large-scale urban development. They developed a two-level, exploded diagram and used color coding to indicate the types of spaces and location keys.* ● *Hier geht es darum, das Interesse potentieller Mieter an zweistöckigen Verkaufsflächen im World Financial Center in New York zu wecken. Verlangt war ein eindrucksvolles, klares Diagramm einer ganzen Reihe nicht zusammenhängender Räumlichkeiten in einem riesigen Gebäudekomplex. Das Ergebnis ist eine axonometrische Darstellung, die mit zwei Ebenen und Farbkodierung arbeitet, um die verschiedenen Arten der Räumlichkeiten und ihre Lage zu veranschaulichen.* ▲ *Diagramme promotionnel pour la location d'espaces de vente sur deux étages situés dans le World Financial Center à New York. L'objectif était de réaliser un diagramme clair et attractif représentant toute une série d'espaces distincts réunis au sein d'un gigantesque complexe. Le résultat: un graphique axonométrique éclaté à deux niveaux. Le code couleurs sert à identifier les différents espaces et leur situation.*

**PAGE 181** ART DIRECTOR/DESIGNER: *Giorgio Galli* AGENCY: *Giorgio Galli Design SAS* CLIENT: *Vitrashop* YEAR PUBLISHED: *1990* COUNTRY: *Switzerland* ■ *Diagrams of furniture systems for a Vitrashop catalog.* ● *Darstellungen von Möbelsystemen für einen Vitrashop-Katalog.* ▲ *Diagrammes pour des systèmes de meubles réalisés pour un catalogue Vitrashop.*

**PAGE 182** ART DIRECTOR/ILLUSTRATOR: *Guido Kruesselsberg* AGENCY: *artbeat Design GmbH* CLIENT: *Schiess de Fries* YEAR PUBLISHED: *1992* COUNTRY: *Germany* ■ *Technical sketch of a multistory parking lot.* ● *Technische Zeichnung eines mehrstöckigen Parkhauses.* ▲ *Dessin technique d'un parking à plusieurs niveaux.*

**PAGE 183 (TOP)** DESIGNER: *Mick Dean* ILLUSTRATOR: *Stephen Gyapay* AGENCY: *Jayburn Design Group* CLIENT: *United Distillers* ■ *Diagram illustrating the making of Scotch whiskey.* ● *Illustration der Herstellung von Scotch Whiskey.* ▲ *Illustration de la fabrication d'un scotch.*

**PAGE 183 (BOTTOM)** DESIGNER: *Jack Pearce* ILLUSTRATOR: *Stephen Gyapay* AGENCY: *Silk Pearce* CLIENT: *Essex County Council* COUNTRY: *England* ■ *Diagram of Chelmsford County Hall in England.* ● *Plan der Chelmsford County Hall in England.* ▲ *Plan du Chelmsford County Hall en Angleterre.*

**PAGE 184** ART DIRECTOR: *Christoph Göldlin* ARTIST: *Christoph Frey* AGENCY: *Schule für Gestaltung Zürich* COUNTRY: *Switzerland* ■ *Reconstruction of the construction phases of a farmhouse in Zürich from the fifteenth to the twentieth century.* ● *Rekonstruktion der verschiedenen Bauphasen eines Bauernhauses in Zürich vom 15. bis zum 20.Jahrhundert.* ▲ *Reconstruction des différentes étapes de construction d'une ferme à Zurich du XVᵉ au XXᵉ siècle. Dessin à la plume.*

**PAGE 185 (TOP)** ART DIRECTOR: *Monique Martineau* DESIGNER/ILLUSTRATOR: *Tracy Sabin* AGENCY: *Sabin Design* CLIENT: *Grossmont Hospital* COUNTRY: *USA* ■ *To create a visual representation of the different functions performed at the chest pain center of a regional hospital, each function was portrayed as an activity occurring in its own separate room. The rooms as a whole form a heart shape, referring to the focus of the chest pain center being the evaluation and treatment of cardiovascular problems.* ● *Um die verschiedenen Funktionen des Kardiologie-Zentrums in einem regionalen Krankenhaus zu verdeutlichen, wurde jede Funktion als einzelner Vorgang in einem separaten Raum dargestellt. Zusammen ergeben die Räume eine Herzform.* ▲ *Pour illustrer les interventions pratiquées dans le centre de cardiologie d'un hôpital régional, chacune d'entre elles est représentée dans une salle distincte. Réunies, les salles forment un cœur.*

**PAGE 185 (BOTTOM)** PHOTOGRAPHER: *Fridjof Versnel* AGENCY: *Bureau Mijksenaar* CLIENT: *Amsterdam Airport Schiphol*

**PAGE 186** ART DIRECTOR/DESIGNER: *Gary Blakeley* ILLUSTRATOR: *Mulkern Rutherford* AGENCY: *Aitken Blakeley* CLIENT: *The Queen Elizabeth II Conference Centre* COUNTRY: *Great Britain* ■ *Plans from a brochure about the Queen Elizabeth II Conference Centre in London. The diagram illustrates roof construction and one of the floors.* ● *Pläne aus einer Broschüre über das Queen-Elizabeth-II-Konferenzzentrum in London. Gezeigt sind die für den Umschlag verwendeten Darstellungen der Dachkonstruktion und eines Stockwerkes.* ▲ *Plans tirés d'une brochure descriptive du Centre de conférences Queen Elizabeth II à Londres. Vues de la construction du toit et d'un étage pour la page de couverture.*

**PAGE 187** ART DIRECTOR: *Joel Katz* DESIGNER: *Jerome Cloud* ARTIST: *Laurinda Stockwell* AGENCY: *Katz Wheeler Design* CLIENT: *LBI Associates* COUNTRY: *USA* ■ *Graphics from a sales brochure for beach houses.* ● *Darstellungen aus einem Verkaufsprospekt für Strandhäuser.* ▲ *Représentations graphiques extraites d'un prospectus pour des maisons de plage.*

**PAGE 188** ART DIRECTOR/DESIGNER/ARTIST/AGENCY: *Gustavo Pedroza* CLIENT: *Techint* COUNTRY: *Argentina* ■ *Technical drawing of the Brazo Largo Bridge in Argentina.* ● *Technische Zeichnung der Brazo-Largo-Brücke in Argentinien.* ▲ *Dessin technique représentant le pont du Brazo Largo en Argentine.*

**PAGE 189** DESIGNER/ILLUSTRATOR: *Jonas Baltensweiler* CLIENT: *Denkmalpflege des Kantons Luzern* COUNTRY: *Switzerland* ■ *This three-dimensional rendering of the farmhouse Buttenberg (1770) in Schötz, Luzern shows the findings concerning the condition of the building.* ● *Dreidimensionale Darstellung der Befunde hinsichtlich des baulichen Zustands des Bauernhauses Buttenberg (1770) in Schötz, Luzern.* ▲ *Représentation tridimensionnelle de la ferme Buttenberg (1770) à Schötz, Lucerne, illustrant les découvertes faites sur l'état du bâtiment.*

**PAGES 190, 192, 193** ARTIST: *Cornelia Hesse-Honegger* PUBLISHER: *Lars Müller* PUBLISHER: *Swiss Federal Office of Culture* YEAR PUBLISHED: *1992* COUNTRY: *Switzerland* ■ *Illustrations for a study on misshapen leaf bugs near nuclear power plants. (Page 190) "Aristapedia." Laboratory mutated housefly. Parts of the legs of these flies grow out of the feelers, and the wings are bent and no longer transparent. The eyes and body are yellow, and the chitin armor is more brittle than that of wild flies. (Page 192) Soft bug from Pripjat, Ukraine. The middle leg is short, wavy, and without a foot, but with toes at the end of its leg. (Page 193) Fire bug from Bernau, Switzerland. The two legs on the left side are light and bent. The chitin armor is soft instead of hard and firm.* ● *Die Illustrationen gehören zu einer Studie über Missbildungen an Blattkäfern in der Nähe von Atomkraftwerken. (190) Die Stubenfliege wurde durch Bestrahlung mutiert und im Labor gezüchtet. Es wachsen ihr Beinteile aus den Fühlern, die Flügel sind verbogen und nicht mehr transparent, die Augen und der Körper sind gelb. Ausserdem ist der Chininpanzer viel spröder als bei der wildlebenden Fliege. (192) Weichwanze aus Pripjat, Ukraine: Das mittlere Bein ist gewellt, kurz und ohne Fuss, nur mit Zehen am Ende des Beines. (193) Feuerwanze aus Bernau, Schweiz: Zwei Beine auf der linken Seite sind hell und verbogen. Der Chininpanzer, Aussenskelett der*

*Insekten, ist hier weich anstatt hart und stabil. ▲ Insectes mutants suite à une exposition à un rayonnement. (190) Mouche domestique de laboratoire: des bouts de pattes croissent de ses antennes, ses ailes, pliées, ne sont plus transparentes; les yeux et le corps sont jaunes. Par ailleurs, la chitine est beaucoup plus fragile que celle de la mouche sauvage. (192) Punaise molle de Pripjat, Ukraine: le segment central de la patte est ondulé, trop court. L'extrémité de la patte présente des «orteils». (193) Punaise de feu du Bernau, Suisse: deux pattes sont pliées, le squelette extérieur de l'insecte est mou au lieu d'être rigide.*

**PAGE 194** ART DIRECTOR/DESIGNER: *David M. Seager* STUDIO: *National Geographic Society in-house* PUBLISHER: *National Geographic Society* COUNTRY: *USA* ■ *Illustration of the immune system. The lymph nodes and lymphatic vessels connect the disparate organs that make up the immune system.* ● *Darstellung des Immunsystems. Die Lymphknoten und -gefässe verbinden die verschiedenen Organe, die das Immunsystem ausmachen.* ▲ *Représentation du système immunitaire. Les ganglions et les vaisseaux lymphatiques relient les différents organes du système immunitaire.*

**PAGE 195** DESIGNER/AUTHOR/PUBLISHER: *Richard Saul Wurman* PROJECT DIRECTORS: *Michael Everitt, Peter Bradford* CLIENT: *ACCESS Press* ■ *Spread from an illustrated medical guide.* ● *Darstellung für einen illustrierten medizinischen Führer.* ▲ *Représentation extraite d'un guide médical illustré.*

**PAGE 196** ART DIRECTOR/ILLUSTRATOR: *Michele Constantini* CLIENT: *ENPA (Italian Association for the Protection of Animals)* YEAR PUBLISHED: *1992* TYPEFACE: *Fauna* PRINTER: *Grafiche Nord Milano* COUNTRY: *Italy* ■ *Illustration for an article done in pencil and white gouache on colored paper.* ● *Illustration für einen Artikel. Bleistift und Gouache in Weiss auf farbigem Papier.* ▲ *Illustration d'un article. Crayon et gouache blanche sur papier couleur.*

**PAGE 197** ART DIRECTOR/DESIGNER/ILLUSTRATOR: *Jack Endewelt* COUNTRY: *USA* ■ *"Combination Head and Rifle." This diagram examines the properties of both objects in some detail. The illustrator emphasizes the vulnerability of living things vis-à-vis objects which kill. The illustrator felt that showing both from this viewpoint emphasized the negative relationship.* ● *«Kombination Kopf und Gewehr.» Hier geht es um die Eigenschaften beider Bildgegenstände, wobei der Illustrator die Verletzlichkeit von Lebewesen Dingen, die töten, gegenüberstellt.* ▲ *«Combinaison tête et carabine»: diagramme mettant en évidence les propriétés des objets représentés. L'illustrateur entendait souligner la vulnérabilité des êtres vivants face aux armes qui tuent.*

**PAGES 198, 199** ART DIRECTORS: *Rik Besser, Douglas Joseph* DESIGNER/ILLUSTRATOR: *Rik Besser* ILLUSTRATOR: *Koji Takei* COPYWRITER: *Agouron Pharmaceuticals, Inc.* AGENCY: *Besser Joseph Partners* CLIENT: *Agouron Pharmaceuticals, Inc.* YEAR PUBLISHED: *1991* TYPEFACE: *Garamond #3, Gill Sans* PRINTER: *Grossberg Tyler* COUNTRY: *USA* ■ *Diagrams demonstrating the four stages of drug development and the four stages of biological evaluation.* ● *Die vier Stufen der Herstellung von Tabletten und die vier Stufen der biologischen Auswertung.* ▲ *Diagrammes montrant les quatre phases de fabrication de comprimés et de leur évaluation biologique.*

**PAGE 200** ART DIRECTOR/DESIGNER: *David Pelham* ARTIST: *Harry Willock* PUBLISHER: *Jonathan Cape Ltd.* COUNTRY: *England* ■ *Double spreads showing the three-dimensional moveable illustrations from the pop-up book* THE HUMAN BODY. *Subjects shown are the head, circulation (arteries and heart) and the process of nourishment as life support from the stage of consumption to digestion.* ● *Doppelseiten mit dreidimensionalen, beweglichen Darstellungen aus dem Buch* THE HUMAN BODY. *Gezeigt sind der Kopf, die Blutzirkulation (Arterien und Herz) und die lebenserhaltende Nahrungsaufnahme bis hin zur Verdauung.* ▲ *Doubles pages du livre* THE HUMAN BODY *comportant des représentations tridimensionnelles mobiles, soit une tête, l'appareil circulatoire (artères et cœur) et l'alimentation, de l'ingestion à la digestion.*

**PAGE 201** ART DIRECTOR: *Christoph Göldlin* ARTIST: *Theres Biedermann* AGENCY: *Schule für Gestaltung Zürich* COUNTRY: *Switzerland* ■ *Sequences during a cornea transplant in the eye. The donor eye is shown in green, the recipient eye is shown in blue.* ● *Ablauf einer Hornhaut-Transplantation am Auge. Das Spenderauge ist grün, das Empfängerauge blau dargestellt.* ▲ *Représentation séquentielle d'une transplantation de cornée. L'œil du donneur est en vert, celui du receveur en bleu.*

**PAGE 202** ART DIRECTOR: *Alberto Gracia Izquierdo* ILLUSTRATOR: *Peter Krämer* CLIENT: *Deutsche Lufthansa AG* PRINTER: *Mohndruck* COUNTRY: *Germany*

**PAGE 224** ARTIST: *Cornelia Hesse-Honegger* PUBLISHER: *Lars Müller* PUBLISHER: *Swiss Federal Office of Culture* YEAR PUBLISHED: *1992* COUNTRY: *Switzerland* ■ *Lady bug from Three Mile Island. A black growth rises from a depression, which reshapes the wing.* ● *Marienkäfer aus der Nähe von Three Mile Island: Ein schwarzer Auswuchs erhebt sich über der Delle, die den Flügel verunstaltet.* ▲ *Coccinelle de la région de Three Miles Island: une excroissance noire surgit de la bosse et défigure l'aile.*

INDICES

VERZEICHNISSE

INDEX

. . . . . . . . . . . . . . . . . . . . . . . . . . . . . . . . . . . . . . . . . . . . . . . . . . . . . . . . . . . . . . . . . . . . . . . . . . . . . . . . . .

C R E A T I V E   D I R E C T O R S · A R T   D I R E C T O R S · D E S I G N E R S

. . . . . . . . . . . . . . . . . . . . . . . . . . . . . . . . . . . . . . . . . . . . . . . . . . . . . . . . . . . . . . . . . . . . . . . . . . . . . . . . . .

. . . . . . . . . . . . . . . . . . . . . . . . . . . . . . . . . . . . . . . . . . . . . . . . . . . . . . . . . . . . . . . . . . . . . . . . . . . . . . . . . .

I L L U S T R A T O R S · P H O T O G R A P H E R S · C O P Y W R I T E R S

. . . . . . . . . . . . . . . . . . . . . . . . . . . . . . . . . . . . . . . . . . . . . . . . . . . . . . . . . . . . . . . . . . . . . . . . . . . . . . . . . .

GRAPHIS PUBLICATIONS


GRAPHIS PUBLIKATIONEN


PUBLICATIONS GRAPHIS

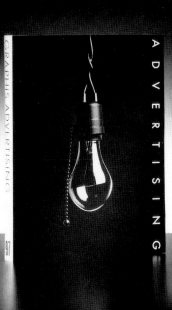

ADVERTISING

GRAPHIS ADVERTISING

97

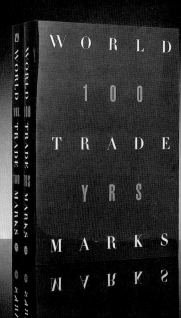

DESIGN

GRAPHIS DESIGN

97

LOGO

GRAPHIS LOGO
GRAPHIS LOGO
GRAPHIS LOGO

1 2 3

WORLD
100
TRADE
YRS
MARKS

WORLD 100 YRS TRADE MARKS

GRAPHIS NEW MEDIA 1

**NEW MEDIA 1**

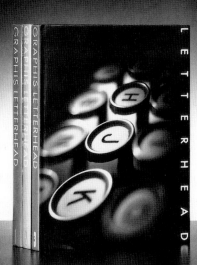

LETTERHEAD

GRAPHIS LETTERHEAD
GRAPHIS LETTERHEAD
GRAPHIS LETTERHEAD

3

GRAPHIS BROCHURES

BROCHURES

2

ANNUAL

GRAPHIS ANNUAL REPORTS
GRAPHIS ANNUAL REPORTS
GRAPHIS ANNUAL REPORTS
GRAPHIS ANNUAL REPORTS
GRAPHIS ANNUAL REPORTS

1 2 3 4 5

REPORT

# GRAPHIS BOOKS

Graphis 303

Graphis 304

Graphis 305

Makela Lewis Moberly Sagmeister Nowland Fallon McElligott Berlin Haase & Knels

Schwab Illustrators Demarchelier Koolhaas Kosolapov Stolichnaya Troxler

Johnson Conran IKEA Mead Show Grundy & Northedge Slover Tachibana

# G R A P H I S   M A G A Z I N E